THEATER IN THE AMERICAS

A Series from Southern Illinois University Press

SCOTT MAGELSSEN

Series Editor

ADAPTURGY

THE DRAMATURG'S ART AND THEATRICAL ADAPTATION

JANE BARNETTE

Southern Illinois University Press
Carbondale

Southern Illinois University Press
www.siupress.com

Printed in the United States of America

21 20 19 18 4 3 2 1

Cover illustration: Briana Brock as "The Whiteness of the Whale," from *Moby-Dick* by Herman Melville, adapted for the stage by John Gentile. Costume design by Jamie Bullins. Kennesaw State University, 2008. *Photograph by Robert Pack, Widescreen Video Productions.*

Library of Congress Cataloging-in-Publication Data
Names: Barnette, Jane, author.
Title: Adapturgy : the dramaturg's art and theatrical adaptation / Jane Barnette.
Description: Carbondale : Southern Illinois University Press, [2018] | Series: Theater in the Americas. | Includes bibliographical references and index.
Identifiers: LCCN 2017013487 | ISBN 9780809336272 (paperback) | ISBN 9780809336289 (ebook)
Subjects: LCSH: Theater—Production and direction. | Dramaturges. | BISAC: PERFORMING ARTS / Theater / General. | PERFORMING ARTS / Theater / Direction & Production. | PERFORMING ARTS / Theater / History & Criticism.
Classification: LCC PN2053 .B312 2018 | DDC 792.02/3—dc23 LC record available at https://lccn.loc.gov/2017013487

Printed on recycled paper. ♲

To my parents, Doug and Linda Jane Barnette

CONTENTS

FIGURES

ACKNOWLEDGMENTS

The ideas and research for this book began in collaboration with my colleagues at Kennesaw State University (KSU), where I had the privilege of being the resident dramaturg of the Department of Theatre and Performance Studies from 2006 to 2014. It was working with John Gentile as a mentor that first inspired me to delve deeper into adaptation dramaturgy. My friendships with Karen Robinson, Harrison Long, Dean Adams, Margaret Baldwin, Ivan Pulinkala, Hannah Harvey, Patrick Sutton, and Henry Scott (as directors) and Ming Chen, Jamie Bullins, and Rebecca Makus (as designers) encouraged my dramaturgical thinking, especially for adaptations. Several student dramaturgs, designers, and actors at KSU were also influential: Paula Bowen, Briana Brock, Paul Castañeda, Tracey Cordle, Mershawn Foley, Robert Hadaway, Melissa Harvey, Phillip Justman, Marium Khalid, James Maloof, Kathleen Saracen, John Stewart, Michael Williams, John Tucker, and Erik Teague. An incentive grant from KSU's Center for Excellence in Teaching and Learning provided support for the development of *Red Badge of Courage*, a project I undertook alongside and could not have completed without the extraordinary vision and cooperation of Michael Haverty. I am especially thankful for the vibrant community of colleagues who supported me during my years at KSU, including: Laura Davis, Michele DiPietro, LeeAnn Lands, Natasha Lovelace-Habers, Cherie Miller, Patricia Poulter, and Linda Stewart.

No project this size is completed in a vacuum—this one benefited from the unwavering support of my colleagues at the University of Kansas (KU), especially from Mechele Leon and Nicole Hodges Persley, my mentors, but also Leslie Bennett, Jason Bohon, Dennis Christilles, John Gronbeck-Tedesco, Michelle Heffner Hayes, Iris Smith Fischer, Jeanne Klein, Paul Meier, James

Moreno, Kathy Pryor, Rebecca Rovit, and Peter Zazzali. The university supported my research in numerous ways, including a start-up grant, the New Faculty General Research Fund, and the General Research Fund, for which I am grateful. Among the several research trips these funds enabled was a crucial one: a guest artist residency at Auburn University in 2015. I thank my collaborators there, with special recognition to Scott Phillips and Fereshteh Rostampour, for inviting me to campus and trusting me with their newest facilities and their talented students.

In the field at large, I am fortunate to rely on an intellectual community made up of many scholar-artists—for this project I am especially indebted to Gwendolyn Alker, Freddie Ashley, Chase Bringardner, Jen Buckley, Debra Caplan, Zachary Dorsey, Christin Essin, Ernie Capello, Sydney Cheek O'Donnell, Gibson Cima, Sara Freeman, Martine Kei Green-Rogers, Kyle Gillette, Kristin Haverty, D. J. Hopkins, Amy Hughes, Katja Krebs, Erin Moodie, Joe Murray, Jules Odendahl-James, Rachel Perlmeter, Peter Petralia, Geoff Proehl, Kara Reilly, Megan Monaghan Rivas, Tlaloc Rivas, Magda Romanska, Susanne Shawyer, Dan Smith, Joanne Tompkins, Adam Versényi, Bethany Wood, and Chris Woodworth. The support of two colleagues was central to this project: Andrew Sofer, who led an outstanding book proposal workshop at the Mellon School for Theater and Performance Research in 2013, and Michael Chemers, who introduced me to the editors at Southern Illinois University (SIU) Press.

I am privileged to have Scott Magelssen's sage editorial feedback, alongside the guidance of Kristine Priddy, the stellar copyediting of Wayne Larsen and production by Linda Buhman, and the wisdom of the anonymous readers who helped shape this book's development. While any errors within this volume are mine alone, I am certain that the work is stronger because of SIU Press's critical generosity. Portions of this book were published in the *Journal of Adaptation in Film and Performance* (vol. 9, no. 2, 2016; Bristol: Intellect) and *Contemporary Approaches to Adaptation*, edited by Kara Reilly (Palgrave, 2017). I thank these publishers for their permission to include this text here.

I extend my gratitude to the generous theatre practitioners who shared insight about adaptation processes during my research: John Collins, Ben Williams, Kate Scelsa, Keneza Schaal, and Vin Knight, of Elevator Repair Service; David Catlin, Richard Garner, Matt Kizer, Bryan Mercer, Gregg Murray, Nick Pappas, Tanner Slick, and Blair Thomas. Equally vital to my research are my students in adaptation dramaturgy at both KSU and KU, with a spotlight on my Authors and Adaptation coteacher extraordinaire, Darren Canady.

To Paul Edwards, who introduced me to the art of literary adaptation for the stage: thank you for lighting the path. To Oscar Brockett and Laura Worthen, who first encouraged me to try my hand at dramaturgy: thank you for leading the way.

Most crucially, to my family, which has come to mean something different from what it did when this project began. Christine, Anna, and Emily Bial, thank you for your encouragement and your extraordinary patience with me these last few years. Sara, Kelsey, and Mason Cooper, your confidence in my work has always been contagious and uplifting. Jan and Ed Kadletz, I am forever grateful for the conversations we shared about literature, history, and love. Izzy, my fierce feline friend, my shadow: thank you for choosing me. To my partner, Henry Bial, who saw the value of my scholarship when I was unable to, and whose buoyancy and love sustained me during the writing and research process. Finally, I thank my steadfast supporters, my parents Doug and Linda Jane Barnette, to whom this book is dedicated.

ADAPTURGY

INTRODUCTION

The history of theatre is a history of adaptation—in the West, the Ancient Greeks based their drama on history and mythology, the Romans adapted from them and every other culture they encountered, the medieval Christian theatre consisted of adaptations of the Bible, and of course William Shakespeare was influenced by all of the above. In the United States, theatrical adaptation is also a vital contributor to the history of popular culture. From *Uncle Tom's Cabin* to *Ben-Hur* to *The Wonderful Wizard of Oz*, many of our most well-known stories have been retold for the stage. In 2016 alone, Broadway had several adaptations running, the range of which demonstrates how elastic the approach to adapting for the stage has become. There were adaptations of novels (*Misery*), films (*An American in Paris*), graphic novels (*Fun Home*), and biographies (*Hamilton*). Some of these adaptations were previously adapted in other media (*Misery* was a film before it became a play), and others show promise for future adaptations into other formats—perhaps the most supple of all thus far in its ability to morph anew was Lin-Mañuel Miranda's blockbuster hit musical *Hamilton*. The fact that this particular musical—a hip-hop remix of Rob Chernow's biography of Alexander Hamilton—leads the curve with adaptation potential comes as no surprise to fans and scholars of hip-hop music, itself a genre of borrowing, pastiche, and adaptation.[1]

The adaptation trend is not limited to Broadway. In university and regional theatre seasons alike, the tendency to include adaptations shows no sign of slowing down. Many regional theatres, for example, include *A Christmas Carol* in their regular holiday rotation, based on Charles Dickens's novel (adapted by one of several different writers for the stage, usually as a musical but also as a play). Frequently, these adapted scripts are based on texts in the public domain (to ensure both financial and creative freedom), including world premieres written by local playwrights as well as theatre practitioners who specialize in adaptation. With regard to theatre for young audiences, the adapted script has become the standard rather than new or established plays (except those that are established adaptations), because the titles are both recognizable to family audiences and connectable to lesson plans for teachers and the educational standards to which they are held accountable.

This book is designed as a resource for those who seek to understand and participate in the process of adaptation for the stage. The examples we will attend to are primarily adaptations of literature for the nonmusical stage, but the techniques and approaches covered within apply to all theatrical adaptations. Specifically, this is a book about adaptation dramaturgy, or what I call *adapturgy*—the cultivation of a reflective, textured research milieu within which adapted works for the stage will thrive.

Adapturgy has three parts: "Defining Practice," "Theorizing Practice," and "Practicing Theory." The order matters here (although readers can read chapters and sections in isolation as well), insofar as the middle section is meant to be bookended by explorations of dramaturgical practice. The first part tackles the two creative fields of adaptation and dramaturgy, before exploring the ways that combining them heightens the relevance and understanding of both. Here, we begin to see how the artistic and intellectual power of both concepts grows exponentially when we link them together, as adapturgy. Adaptation and dramaturgy each signal both a noun and a verb, or a product and a process. Consequently, this book is both a "theory book" about creative practice as well as a "practical book" about theory. This approach guides the organization of the two remaining sections: "Theorizing Practice" (part 2) and "Practicing Theory" (part 3).

The second part explores three different methods for analyzing theatrical adaptations, each of which is grounded in a dramaturgically detailed case study. These methods build upon contemporary and emerging adaptation theories, aligning them with concerns and questions crucial to practitioners of live performance. We begin our discussion of adaptation dramaturgy theory by taking up one of the most memorable phrases used to describe the appeal of adaptation—that of "palimpsestuous pleasures," generally credited to literary theorist Linda Hutcheon.[2] The palimpsest has offered rich fruit for adaptation, translation, and intertextual analysis for decades in various contexts. For our purposes, the notion of palimpsestuousness will be applied to the embodied and aurally complex approach to adaptation taken up by the ensemble Elevator Repair Service, in their production of *The Sound and the Fury* at the Public Theatre in 2015. As an example of a company that does exquisite adapturgy without an official dramaturg per se, this section also provides insight into the ways that the dramaturgical sensibility proves inescapable in the process of adapting for the stage.[3]

Following chapter 4, and located strategically in the very center of this volume, is my introduction of the Janus effect into adaptation theory. This captivating Roman god, best known for being "two-faced," offers several layers of meaning for the adaptation dramaturg. I explore both the generative potential as well as the derogatory connotation of Janus, recognizing that both understandings matter when considering the role of dramaturgy within adaptations. Chapter 5 is also where readers have an opportunity to consider how depictions of theatrical adaptation might be embedded within an offshoot of film adaptation, through my use of Alejandro G. Iñárritu's award-winning 2014 film *Birdman or (the Unexpected Virtue of Ignorance).* The theatrical adaptation of Raymond Carver's short story "What We Think about When We Think about Love," a central part of the film's plot, provides insight into how such star-driven Broadway vehicles are often viewed by fidelity-based critics. Appropriately enough for a chapter about Janus, I argue that the film demonstrates both extremes of adaptation: the kind without the benefit of dramaturgical insight and the kind that is only possible with the nuanced complexity of adapturgy.

The final chapter in part 2, "Geographies of Adaptation," addresses the importance of space/place theory for dramaturgs. On the heels of a chapter that discussed a threshold god, it is fitting to devote the following chapter to a fuller examination of how space (both practical and theoretical) influences adaptations. Using various iterations of *Moby-Dick* as it was adapted for several different spaces, chapter 6 engages with one of the most vexing questions for adaptation theory: how artists manage the transformation of imaginary space into embodied, three-dimensional performance. This chapter also addresses the impact of site-specific and immersive theatre on how we understand the process and product of adaptation, as well as how such interactive performances engage differently with dramaturgy itself.

The third and final part of the book offers concrete examples drawn from my experience in adaptation dramaturgy over the past decade, focusing on dramaturgy for the adapted script, the production dramaturgy of stage adaptations, and the role of the dramaturg in the postmortem stage of production. This last chapter also applies the philosophy of the postmortem to the book itself, thereby serving as a kind of metacognitive (thinking about thinking) exercise. Readers will have another opportunity to consider approaches to staging the space and language of imagination with the first chapter in the final section, "Practicing Theory." Chapter 7, "Working with the Script," showcases the process of creating a nonnarrative adaptation of *The Red Badge of Courage* (*Red Badge*). As a production inextricably integrated with technical and design elements such as puppetry, animation, and original music, this script is unusual for the multiple opportunities it provides for creative and dramaturgical interpretation of the source into multiple languages for the stage. The role of the puppet, combined with the animation in *Red Badge* allows us to see how adapters might tackle the narrative voice with spectacle rather than spoken words.

In the eighth chapter, "Working with the Production," we move from dramaturgical tasks more closely aligned with new play dramaturgy to those typically reserved for production dramaturgs and the creative team tasked with mounting a show. In several different arenas but with an emphasis on casting, this chapter reveals the dramaturgical instincts behind the production of adapted scripts. As such, the examples used to illustrate the wide range of possibilities are drawn from three of the case studies explained in earlier chapters, as well as several other adaptations for which I served as dramaturg.

To conclude, I discuss the impact and challenges of the postmortem for adapturgy in particular, reflecting on changes that were made to the script and production for each of the case studies surveyed in this volume. Fully embracing the dual nature established herein—that this is a theory book about practice and a practical book about theory—in chapter 9, "Postmortem Adapturgy," I turn the tactics of the postmortem on the book as a whole, as if it were a production for the stage that had just closed. It is my hope that this sort of metacognitive contemplation will inspire the continued development of adapturgy as an emerging field, just as the same kind of self-evaluative process ideally functions within the postmortem conducted for theatre productions.

Stage adaptations require contemplative dramaturgy. As award-winning dramaturg Geoff Proehl reminds us, "To know (and know how little we know) yet still go on is a central feature of what it means to take upon us the role of dramaturg at any moment in any process."[4] Such recognition of the dramaturgical landscape—of the road not traveled, as well as the navigation leading to this particular adaptation for this particular production—becomes absolutely vital for the adaptation dramaturg.

As readers will soon discover, the values and strengths of adaptation—as well as the reasons it has historically been so controversial—have telling intersections with the art and science of dramaturgy. The exponential rise in scholarship about and practice in both adaptation and dramaturgy in the last two decades is not a coincidence, and it is my hope that this book encourages educators as well as practitioners of theatre to embrace the challenges and skills of these two fields combined.

PART ONE

DEFINING PRACTICE

1. ADAPTATION FOR THE STAGE: A DRAMATURGICAL INTERVENTION

The word *adaptation* can mean several different things, all related to some kind of alteration or change. An extraordinarily flexible word, adaptation is commonly understood as a product, but can also refer to the *process* by which something is adapted. In biology, the *Oxford English Dictionary* tells us, it refers to "a process of change or modification by which an organism or species becomes better suited to its environment or ecological niche, or a part of an organism to its biological function, either through phenotypic change in an individual or (esp.) through an evolutionary process effecting change through successive generations."[1] The notion of adaptation in the scientific vein has been taken up within the humanities for those who study cultural theory and, following Pierre Bourdieu's concept of cultural production, we might imagine the mechanics of adaptation as an ecosystem of sorts.[2] To take this analogy further, some critics and theorists of adaptation have embraced the evolutionary part of the word's definition, perhaps encouraged by the suggestion of Charles Darwin within Spike Jonze and Charlie Kaufman's oft-cited film *Adaptation*.[3]

In her influential book *A Theory of Adaptation*, comparative literature scholar Linda Hutcheon embraces this biological approach to defining adaptation, making the observation that "Adaptation, like evolution, is a transgenerational phenomenon."[4] Continuing this analogy, she considers the way that the adaptation of stories over generations can be considered in much the same way as Richard Dawkins defined memes.[5] Theorized as a viral unit that transmits practice, ideas, or symbols through cultures and over time, a meme is thought to behave according to evolutionary principles. Ultimately, Hutcheon concludes that (like memes) "adaptation is how stories evolve and mutate to fit new times and different places."[6] Given the proliferation of information shared via the Internet and the speed with which ideas can spread digitally, the consideration of adaptation (especially within digital media) as meme is compelling.

On the basic level, the definition of adaptation that best applies to the subject of this volume is: "an altered or amended version of a text, musical composition, etc., (now *esp.*) one adapted for filming, broadcasting, or production on the stage from a novel or similar literary source."[7] At its core, then, to adapt is to alter or amend—to rework something (usually a text) from one medium to another. Because adaptation is so ubiquitous, we might already yearn to flex this definition to see how far it can stretch without breaking down. Must the something be a text (or, must the text be word-based), for example? Must the reworking be between media? Could it not be between cultures? Those of us who are historically inclined might also wonder how and when adaptation began and in what way and why it seems to be such a popular preoccupation in and across so many diverse populations and arenas. Luckily, for those readers who are already intrigued by these questions, there is a burgeoning field within academia grappling with the complex hybrid that is adaptation.

The field of adaptation studies, usually said to have begun in the mid-twentieth century, has experienced a remarkable uptick in scholarship in the last decade. In its earliest manifestation (often traced to George Bluestone's seminal 1957 text, *Novels into Film*), critics demonstrated a love-hate relationship with the concept of fidelity, usually defined as how faithful a movie adaptation was to its literary predecessor. Much as they attempted to move away from this basic mode of evaluation, their analyses belied a residual ethical judgment in favor of finding (and articulating) the ways that the film compared to the novel. "Virtually every adaptation theorist since Bluestone has agreed with the basic tenets of his argument," notes Kate Newell, adding that "most media are too distinct to allow faithful medium-to-medium transposition, and fidelity arguments are based on value judgments that cannot be substantiated and, therefore, are theoretically inconsequential."[8] However "inconsequential" these fidelity arguments might have seemed to Bluestone and his successors, they still could not seem to shake the expectation (either theirs or the public's) that adaptations should be evaluated according to their ability to faithfully reflect the sources upon which they were based. The conversation within the emerging field was fixated on this comparison. In addition, because the academic coursework for adaptation was traditionally rooted in English departments, it overlooked popular culture sources and other "lowbrow" entertainment in favor of the prestige of literature.[9]

These assumptions began to shift in the early twenty-first century. In 2008, the first volumes of two academic journals were published: *Adaptation: The Journal of Literature on Screen Studies* and *Adaptation in Film and Performance*, the former of which is connected to the Association of Adaptation Studies, an organization formed in 2005. The same year, one of the leading scholars in the field, Robert Stam, followed up his 2000 advocacy for "intertextual dialogism" with an introduction to an adaptation textbook titled "The Impact of the Posts." With the influence of poststructuralism and postcolonialism (as well as cultural and gender studies), Stam and his coeditor Alessandra Raengo suggested, adaptation studies was now duly aware that "audience pleasure in intertextual citation" should take center stage.[10] Following this trend, in 2010, Christa Albrecht-Crane and Dennis Cutchins edited a collection of essays called *Adaptation Studies: New Approaches.* With an overt mission to reframe the scholarship and move it away from its long-suffering dependence on fidelity ethics based in the primacy of Anglophone authorship, the scholars in this volume demonstrate a multivalent intertextual analysis that values popular culture equally with canonical literature.

As is evident from this brief overview, the majority of scholarship in adaptation studies has focused on the adaptation of literature into film. Exceptions exist, especially for certain figures and subjects for which adaptation is inescapable. Traditionally, this has included some branches of classical theatre (or drama), such as Ancient Greek plays and the works of William Shakespeare. The ambitious project "Play On!"—undertaken by the Oregon Shakespeare Festival (OSF) in 2015—represents an intersection of academic interests in translation and adaptation studies with theatrical practice. Using a team of playwrights and dramaturgs for each of Shakespeare's plays, OSF will produce new translations of the bard's canon. Notably, the company is adamant that "the Play On translations will not be adaptations. Everything to do with setting, time period, references etc. will remain unchanged."[11] While their approach to updating Shakespeare's canon might be conservative, their commitment to diverse contributors is anything but. "Under the leadership of O.S.F.'s director of literary development and dramaturgy, Lue Morgan Douthit, more than half of the selected playwrights will be women, and more than half will be writers of color."[12] This intervention alone, while not adaptation per se, demonstrates the ongoing desire to update and transform even the most sacrosanct theatrical texts.[13]

There are also scholars and critics who specialize in musical theatre adaptations, both historically and with a contemporary focus.[14] Within popular culture more broadly speaking, it is virtually impossible to consider *The Wizard of Oz*, *Harry Potter*, *Star Wars*, or any artifact from the Walt Disney conglomeration without attention to adaptation.[15] Nor can one study video games or comic books without considering how these stories and characters are adapted for different platforms, companies, or eras. With its primary academic home in English departments, the field of adaptation studies is necessarily transdisciplinary—not just with film studies, but also with scholars of printmaking and book arts, cultural studies, popular culture, communication studies, and of course theatre and performance studies.

A Genealogy of Literary Adaptation for the Stage

The praxis of literary adaptation is rooted in the field of oral interpretation, a predecessor (along with anthropology and ethnography) of performance studies. At Northwestern University, where the genealogy of elocution to interpretation to performance studies can be mapped via the transfer and development of technique and philosophy from teachers to students (who then became teachers), a central pillar of the School of Speech (now Communication) has been the study and practice of adaptation. From Alvina Krause to Wallace Bacon and Robert Breen, whose students included Paul Edwards and Frank Galati, to the founding of Lookingglass Theatre company among Northwestern undergraduate theatre majors who studied with David Downs (who was one of Krause's students), the influence of this lineage is still palpable today in adaptation for the stage.[16]

From this Northwestern-based tradition, there are several innovations that I would like to highlight as a means of better understanding the development of literary adaptation for live performance. The first is the work of Wallace Bacon and Robert Breen, both of whom were invested in the notion that students (or the general public) could experience literature most fully through interpretation—that is, performance. For Bacon, who wrote three different essays about the "dangerous shores" of text and delivery (the first of which was published in 1960), it was vital to recognize and appreciate both "shores" equally—"studies of interpretation have been concerned with both of the 'shores,' and it is as true now as ever that one may be grounded on either."[17] While this holistic approach is not reducible to a question of fidelity, per se, Bacon's approach to adaptation was as a means of deepening one's appreciation of the text and as such was not about altering the language but rather using the spoken word as another means of engaging with literature.

Bacon's colleague and collaborator, Robert Breen, comes closer to an articulation of adaptation theory in what he dubbed "chamber theatre," an approach to staging literature that embraces the narrative voice as a vital part of the performance. As later critics would point out, in Breen's manual for this technique, *Chamber Theatre*, he seems torn between recognizing adaptation as an art in its own right and disavowing any such power it might have.[18] Early in the book, he suggests that "Chamber Theatre is *in the service of* literature; it makes manifest for an audience the structure, the theme, and the tone of literature."[19] In one of the last paragraphs of the same book, however, Breen claims "there is no obligation on the part of the interpreter to respect the author's intentions. Once the story is made, the reader looks to *it* for meaning, not to the author's intentions; he or she is responsible to the text, not to the author."[20] Recognizing the distinction Breen has made between author and text, what at first seemed to be a servile role (the interpreter) by the end of the book appears to have creative power. To locate Breen and his chamber theatre approach with regard to fidelity, then, is difficult if not impossible—what is clear is that both Breen and Bacon see adaptation (or interpretation) as a means of elevating the text itself.

But what is that text? Is it the words on the page, or the text's tone? Is it the rhythm of the story, or its theme? Not surprisingly, the answer will vary depending on who is doing the adaptation, but if one intends to adapt a novel for the stage, one must contend with point of view as well as narration. This particular challenge of adaptation is precisely what drew Breen to formulate his approach. "Chamber Theatre is interested in presenting stories that depend for their value on the point of view expressed in the narration."[21] The practice of enacting narration, especially when the narrator speaks from an omniscient point of view, ensures a kind of metatheatrical acknowledgement—it makes it impossible for spectators to forget they are watching actors perform. This approach borrows from Bertolt Brecht and Erwin Piscator's epic theatre, although for Breen the technique is not meant to be didactic or political. Instead it is used—as is Brecht's *verfremdungseffekt*—to "deepen, not to terminate, their involvement in the [story]."[22] Although Breen did not share Brecht's Marxist goals for defamiliarizing the experience of theatre, others who use the chamber theatre approach of adaptation might do so as a means of political critique.[23]

One of Breen's students, Frank Galati, is perhaps the best-known contemporary representative of literary adaptation for the stage, having won a Tony award for his theatrical version of John Steinbeck's novel *The Grapes of Wrath* (*Wrath*) in 1990. A hybrid between chamber theatre and nonnarrative drama, Galati's adaptation features four different narrators that speak descriptive passages, but their appearances are limited and easily overshadowed by the more traditional dialogue between the many characters.[24] Galati taught classes such as Presentational Aesthetics within the department of performance studies at Northwestern for over three decades, and continues to adapt literature for Steppenwolf Theatre in Chicago.[25] In his words:

> Adapting works of narrative fiction for the stage, it is suggested, is a matter of excavation, of editing, of removing everything that is not a play so that what is left, probably most of it dialogue, can be 'bodied forth' by the actors on stage. Of course some narrative works are better suited to stage adaptation than others. Novels tend to be long and sprawling, abundant often in descriptive detail, analysis of character, and action, anchored in the persona, and form the point of view, of the narrator. The theater, by contrast, craves action, velocity, momentum, inexorable forward motion.[26]

Several of the founding members of Lookingglass Theatre were inspired by Galati's approach to adaptation, especially after seeing the professional run of *Wrath*. As theatre majors, they also took classes in performance studies with Paul Edwards and Dwight Conquergood—in each of these instances, the appeal of adapting literature grew.

As one of these founding members recalls, it was "not long after starting the company [that they] saw a student production of the *Odyssey* directed by Northwestern University grad student Mary Zimmerman."[27] After they persuaded Zimmerman to premiere her epic adaptation with their nascent company, she joined the ensemble, "and a unique Lookingglass aesthetic began to emerge."[28] It was this promising aesthetic in Zimmerman's *Arabian Nights*—lyrical and dreamlike—that first ignited my own passion for adaptation when I saw it performed in Chicago in 1993. Typically, Zimmerman creates her adaptations in rehearsal with her actors, a flexible approach that necessitates early conversations with designers (and means that she typically writes to fill their choices, rather than the other way around). "What does exist on that first day is her relationship to the source material."[29] Zimmerman's abiding reservoir of inspiration and desire to bury herself in different translations of the source material, as I will discuss in greater detail in relationship to other adapters throughout this study, is deeply dramaturgical.

Tracing this genealogy between oral interpretation, chamber theatre, and the more theatrical approaches of Galati, Zimmerman, and the Lookingglass ensemble enables a richer history of the practice of adaptation to emerge than that which we might typically assume, given the prevalence of adaptation theory that has emerged from the perspective of literature-to-film transformations. In particular, because the media of film and theatre (not to mention literature) are distinct and can approach the question of narration and point of view so differently, concentrating on the way literary adaptation has been taught and practiced for live performance brings the crucial question of adapting *telling* into *showing* into sharper focus.

Contemporary Theories of Adaptation

Surveying the trends within theatre and performance studies, the work of Katja Krebs and her collaborators overlaps most closely with the concerns of this book, as does the focus of the International Federation for Theatre Research's working group "Translation, Adaptation, and Dramaturgy." However encouraging it is to acknowledge these intersections, the majority of this work is written by scholars and practitioners from the perspective of theatre adaptations occurring overseas; there are few contributions from and about the United States. One recent exception is Vincent Murphy's *Page to Stage: The Craft of Adaptation*, a practical guide for how to adapt literature to playscripts. While this text is a welcome addition to the burgeoning field and succeeds in providing useful processes for how adaptations for the stage can be crafted, it nevertheless omits a full consideration of dramaturgical research, outreach, and feedback in its overview. Similarly, while the December 2014 issue of *Theatre Journal* is dedicated to theatre and adaptation and features several valuable interventions to how we discuss and understand stage adaptations, none of the contributors specifically address the role of the dramaturg in their analysis.[30]

Perhaps the most frequently referenced book on adaptation is the aforementioned *A Theory of Adaptation* by Linda Hutcheon, now in its second edition. Although Hutcheon's focus remains mostly on film, her focus includes theatre as well as digital media and popular culture, with references to theme parks, contemporary music, and video games. Hutcheon's contribution to the field of adaptation studies is difficult to overstate, for she was among the first to insist that adaptation was not merely derivative and to advocate for the creativity adapters must bring to the task. That said, her inclusive definition of adaptation as "repetition with variation" has limited applicability in theatre since (as Krebs notes) it "might as well [describe] theatre's relationship with text."[31] Indeed, as groundbreaking as her book has been, Hutcheon's purview of theatre remains limited. While she acknowledges the imaginative power that theatre holds over its audiences (citing Peter Brook), the example plays referenced are restricted to mainstream knowledge, such as Broadway musicals and productions like *Marat/Sade* that have been distributed as film. In contrast, her overview of film demonstrates a nuanced understanding of the range of screen adaptations, from the classics to cult-fan favorites and independent cinema.

Whereas Hutcheon's references to theatre are infrequent, Julie Sanders demonstrates a broad knowledge of theatrical (and literary) classics in her influential volume *Adaptation and Appropriation.* As the title suggests, at the heart of Sanders's analysis is a distinction between the acts of adapting and appropriating, one that she acknowledges often overlaps, but nevertheless defines separately. Simply put, if the production openly acknowledges its source text, it is an adaptation; if it does not, it is an appropriation. Like Hutcheon, Sanders persuasively argues against the reductively linear theory of comparing an adaptation to its "so-called source"; instead, she favors an approach introduced by Gérard Genette (who culls from horticulture and musicology), noting his observation that "any text is a hypertext, grafting itself onto a hypotext, an earlier text that it imitates or transforms."[32] With a central section devoted to literary archetypes (including myth, fairy tales, and Shakespeare), Sanders grounds her analysis in the recognition that storytelling and performance are at the root of all adaptive texts, ultimately making a case for "the pleasurable aspect of recognizing the intertextual relationships between appropriations and their sources."[33]

While both Hutcheon and Sanders published their theories of adaptation in 2006, a more recent analysis of adaptation as a cultural practice is Simone Murray's *The Adaptation Industry: The Cultural Economy of Contemporary Literary Adaptation.* Arguing that "literary adaptations are products of an intricate, hugely complex institutional and industrial system," Murray shines light on the materiality of adaptations, as well as the sociological context of their making.[34] This approach to adaptation studies is a welcome shift, moving the interdisciplinary field away from its previous limitations of comparative aesthetic analysis into methodologies gathered from cultural studies and intersecting with the political economy approaches originating with the Frankfurt School in the early 1930s. Although Murray concentrates on the book-to-screen adaptation and thus does not devote much focus to theatre per se, her attention to the "staging" of books as potential adaptations and her focus on audiences nevertheless tread territory familiar to performance studies scholarship.[35]

In addition to these theoretical volumes, two edited collections published in 2014 address stage adaptation: *Theatre and Adaptation: Return, Rewrite, Repeat*, edited by Margherita Laera and *Translation and Adaptation in Theatre and Film*, edited by Katja Krebs. Both collections take as a point of departure Sanders's consideration of appropriation as a kind of adaptation—for Laera, these two are interchangeable ("adaptation as a synonym of appropriation")[36]; for Krebs, it underscores the connective threads between the practices and products of translation and adaptation. While Laera's collection contains seventeen interviews with leading practitioners of stage adaptation, Krebs's volume consists of ten essays written by theatre/translation practitioners as well as interdisciplinary scholars of film, performance, literature, and pedagogy. The contributors to and topics addressed in both books represent an international focus, demonstrating both the variety and patterns of adaptation across the globe.[37]

Within filmcentric as well as theatre-based contemporary studies on adaptation, then, the major shift in the last decade has been away from fidelity and toward intertextual (or transtextual) analyses. In keeping with the critical trend of adaptation studies, though, the field tends to take "two steps forward and one back," as Murray notes. Namely, while adaptation scholars have increased attention on reception and audience, they have largely overlooked questions of production and the power structures governing the processes of making, marketing, and distributing adaptation products.[38] Promising trends within media studies offer methods of reconsidering theatrical adaptation in ways that are not literary (or text)-based.[39] Typically, adaptation scholarship tends to default to the methodology of analyzing case studies or, especially in the case of theatre, showcasing practitioner interviews (as a kind of case study) within collected volumes. Notably few of the essays or (especially) books about adaptation theory are written from the perspective of practicing adapters.[40]

In his 2007 review of Sanders and (mostly) Hutcheon's books on adaptation, Paul Edwards (who is part of the aforementioned oral interpretation lineage and teaches as well as practices adaptation at Northwestern University) provides a way of summarizing adaptation theory that underscores the goals of this present study. Recognizing connections between Hutcheon's 2006 book on adaptation and her earlier works on parody and irony, Edwards explains, "To be experienced *as adaptation*—an adaptation requires what Hutcheon calls a 'knowing' audience."[41] Moreover, he continues, it is necessary to recognize the "context of creation"[42] and attempt "to understand the very 'urge to adapt,' to break and remake specific works of art in specific contexts, before we can understand what it is that the adapter creates: "We need to know 'why,' which is to say 'why now,' or 'why here, for this audience.'"[43] These crucial questions—why now? why here, for this audience?—are precisely why any adapter for the stage should better understand dramaturgical praxis, and why dramaturgs should better understand adaptation. For they echo the ur-question of the practice of dramaturgy itself: why this play now?

Indeed, what all these understandings of adaptation have in common is the recognition that adaptation is both process and product, both creative and protective—it requires the theatre artist to hold to contradictory ideas (something new, something familiar) in mind at the same time. There are a number of ways to grasp the challenges of such a task, but whether adapters realize it or not, in order to adapt for the stage, they must embrace the craft of dramaturgy.

Adaptation, from a Dramaturgical Perspective

My working definition of adaptation draws upon these welcome trends within the ever-growing field of adaptation studies, but is necessarily influenced by my experience in and passion for dramaturgy as practice and theory. As such, I begin by considering adaptation (in terms of both process and product) with primary attention to *audience*. The reception of the adaptation—whether it is to be read (written words), seen (visual art), heard (music), or some combination of the above (stage or screen)—must be the guiding principle for dramaturgical practice. By shifting attention away from *what* is adapted to questions of *how* it is received, our understanding of adaptation expands to consider cultural context as well as material concerns of accessibility.

Considering this dramaturgical perspective, I define adaptation for the stage as any "text" (not necessarily made of words) that the author (or company) recognizes to be based on another text—this material (upon which the adapted work is based) we will call the source. The outward recognition is useful as a distinguishing factor between adaptations and appropriations, although in saying so I refrain from evaluating one as better (or worse) than the other. By specifying a one-to-one relationship between the adaptation and the source I also hope to clarify to some extent the possible confusion between adaptation and devised work, given that the latter usually involves pulling from multiple sources and remains process driven. Most importantly, as discussed above, because I focus on adaptation dramaturgy as both theory and practice, in classifying adaptations I choose to emphasize the reception of them in recognition of the overriding importance the audience holds for dramaturgy.[44]

A one-to-one adaptation could be created between (or within) several different kinds of media including, but not limited to: fiction, nonfiction (from either primary or secondary sources), film, theatre, opera, dance, painting, sculpture, music, video games, theme parks, toys and souvenirs, installations, comic books, and poetry. Nor are these categories themselves discrete—quite the opposite, especially for contemporary or experimental adaptations. The immersive theatre trend in particular tends to merge these media into one experience, while simultaneously adapting from other media. The New York remount of Punchdrunk's *Sleep No More* (adapted from *Macbeth* and inspired by a film noir soundtrack) demonstrates this practice to blend media and receptive modalities.[45] As we can see in popular culture, the same story also gets recycled in different media, a practice that can emerge from both adapters and the audience. With the much-anticipated 2015 release of *Star Wars: The Force Awakens*, for example, the popular toy company Hasbro released several action figures in the likeness of their onscreen counterparts. Starkly missing from the initial array of possibilities, however, was the figure of Rey, the young woman lead. Audiences were understandably disappointed with this omission, leading to several fan-based opportunities to create (and sell) Rey action figures on entrepreneurial artisan sites such as Etsy.[46] Here we see the power of adaptation with dedicated followers; its ripple effect ignites artwork and merchandise not sanctioned by the adapters or their producers, but demanded by consumers. Once shared, the adaptation cannot be contained.

Clearly, the limits we have established thus far venture only into the shallow end of the adaptation pool—as we have seen, it is not enough to specify the kinds of media being adapted, for that is only a fraction of what artists might consider adapting. The adaptation could be from one culture into another; it could reframe the same characters and language into a different time period; or it could reconsider the source's story from another point of view (especially one that in the original was marginal or underdeveloped).[47] One might even stretch the definition of adaptation to consider sequels and prequels, especially those taken on by fan fiction.

Given this admittedly wide-ranging definition, it would be possible to cover a massive range of performance media and genres; however, I have further delimited my focus for this volume to consider *literary adaptations for the stage*, with an emphasis on three case studies that will be referenced throughout the chapters. Within the taxonomy briefly covered above, then, the primary transformation under consideration in these adaptations will be between media—from a book meant to be read silently (and privately) into live performance experienced communally. To be sure, this one mode of adaptation triggers several other changes worth analyzing, but, as we will see, most of them are (or at least, intend to be) intratemporal and intracultural: the same time period (or culture) is performed onstage as is depicted in the book, for example.[48]

The decision to limit my focus to adaptations made of literature for theatre invites our recognition of the classical distinction put forth by none other than the progenitor of dramaturgy himself, Gotthold Ephraim Lessing.[49] In *Laocoön or the Limits of Painting and Poetry*, Lessing offers his thoughts on the subject of inter-art adaptation, comparing a work of marble sculpture with how the event it represents has been described in writing. According to a museum curator, in this classical artwork—usually dated from the first century C.E. and attributed to Greek artists—"The Trojan priest Laocoon . . . [is] entangled by the snakes which had been sent to punish him for his hostility to the god Apollo." Because this scene is depicted in literature (in the second book of Virgil's *Aeneid*) and as three-dimensional art, analyzing it gives Lessing an opportunity to compare the same moment as it appears in words and image.[50] Lessing sought to specify the differences between these two forms of art, claiming that although they are both imitative arts, "*painting* uses figures and colors in *space*," while "*poetry* articulates tones in *time*."[51] Through detailed aesthetic analysis, he arrives at the conclusion that whereas Virgil describes Laocoon producing "hair-raising shouts like the roars of a bull," the Greek artists showed restraint in crafting the scene. This is due to the observation that "producers of visual representations tend to tone down the unpleasant features, and that is why, according to Lessing, Laocoon is not roaring like a bull: his jaw is tightly constricted in a position that would enable him to utter only a low groan."[52] This reflection leads Lessing to conclude that poetry is the superior art form, because it depicts the imaginative and invisible, while visual art must represent the natural and visible.

Such distinctions would hardly hold sway today. Certainly we can conceive of paintings and sculptures that suggest something invisible. Yet at the heart of much adaptation theory has been the desire to compare the adapted artwork to the source to discover either what is different or what is similar (rarely both). Lessing's *Laocoön* conclusions are clearly "normative rather than descriptive," but they nevertheless showcase a central concern of an early and influential dramaturg when looking at the question of (what he assumed to be an) adaptation.[53]

Whether or not we can verify that Lessing's subject in *Laocoön* was adapted the way he thought it was, this eighteenth-century example encapsulates a familiar theme, one that remains a central question for any study of adaptation between art forms, especially intermedial ones such as literature and performance (the dangerous shores): What gets lost (or what is gained) in translation? What can live performance show and/or tell that deepens and/or complicates our conversation with the source and its author? How does the experience of seeing and hearing the theatrical version of this novel compare to reading it silently?[54]

Throughout the following chapters, my use of "theatrical" implies scripted adaptations written for a cast of actors, intended for a full stage production. This may seem obvious, but in saying so I mean to distinguish what we might call theatre from performance or workshop-based stagings of adaptations, as well as to specify that in this book I will focus primarily on word-based scripts. In so doing, I purposely eliminate the possibility of including musical theatre (itself a major genre where adaptations flourish) and dance theatre, as well as improvised or sketch-based work. In addition, I exclude adaptations of (and by) Shakespeare from consideration, since writing on this topic is abundant enough to be considered a subfield within adaptation studies.[55] Instead, I have chosen to focus on three adaptations of the American literary canon: novels written by white patriarchs, the plots of which are typically considered to be "required reading" for secondary education. These novels include: *Moby-Dick* by Herman Melville (1851), *The Red Badge of Courage* by Stephen Crane (1895), and *The Sound and the Fury* by William Faulkner (1929).

There are several advantages to limiting my scope (mostly) to these three examples. For one, these novels are old enough that there are likely several generations of readers who are at least superficially familiar with the stories they tell. This cultural fluency is especially important for dramaturgs as liaisons to audience members. Because of their familiarity, these narratives have had decades of repetition, whether through their primary mode of reception (reading) or via previous adaptations (on film, for television, in popular culture, or even as stories told orally)—therefore, spectators of these stories arrive with varying degrees of previous knowledge about them. Given the primacy of recycling to adaptation (and the concomitant relevance of a *knowing audience*, as will be discussed in greater detail in chapter 3), I limit my focus to fiction that was well established within US culture. Canonical works such as these offer multiple opportunities for intervention from the margins, whether aesthetically or politically. In addition, as we have noted above, limiting the focus to adaptations of literature for the stage assures that we are also focusing on the transformation of an experience that is individual and imaginary (reading) into one that is collaborative and embodied (theatre). While there are a few exceptions to these limits, for the most part they apply throughout, allowing us to concentrate our attention less on the variation of intermedial adaptation and more on the adapturgy itself.[56]

Finally, these three case studies stem from both a concrete and a conceptual rationale: practically speaking, I was part of the creative team for the premieres of the first two adaptations, as dramaturg for *Moby-Dick*, adapted by John Gentile and as co-creator of *Red Badge of Courage* with Michael Haverty. I also had the opportunity to sit in on rehearsals for Elevator Repair Service's *The Sound and the Fury* as well as to interview company members during the remount of this adaptation in 2015. Moreover, each of these adaptations has been staged multiple times, with different variables (space, language, casting, etc.). Using them as our primary examples of the adaptation of literature for the stage, then, allows us to see how Hutcheon's maxim (*adaptation is repetition without replication*) holds sway with theatrical remounts.[57] The conceptual rationale has to do with two aspects: the different reception modalities for each of the three source inspirations; and the problems each production had to solve, as well as the way those challenges created possibilities for dramaturgical contributions. Strategically, my methodology for locating viable case studies is itself rooted in dramaturgy: I have ensured that the variety herein is based in how the staged adaptations emphasize different aspects of spectatorship (what we see, what we hear, but also what we feel and imagine), and I have isolated examples that highlight the difficulties often encountered by those who create theatrical adaptations. These problems necessitate dramaturgical intervention.

Source Texts and Reception Modalities

While on the surface each of these three sources shares the same medium and mode—they are fictional novels, meant to be read—the way each source inspired the adapters in turn had significant influence on how the reception modality was emphasized in performance. In order of appearance in this volume, the first case study under consideration is adapted from Faulkner's *The Sound and the Fury.* Not surprisingly, given the modus operandi of Elevator Repair Service (ERS) as a company (to solve problems through performance), their adaptation is of the first chapter, "April Seventh, 1928." Often described as impenetrable, this chapter is told from the mentally disadvantaged point of view of the youngest Compson sibling, Benjy, who has no way of distinguishing the past from the present. There are several different scenes in time occurring between the span of 1898 and 1928 within this chapter, but because Faulkner writes from Benjy's perspective the reader has no immediate way of logically ordering or otherwise making sense of the prose, other than the fact that the author varies between italic font and regular font for each shift. This first case study emphasizes *sound* as an organizing principle, along with casting and movement, and is discussed most fully in chapter 4 but reappears in chapters 8 and 9.

The second case study analyzed in this volume is that of Herman Melville's epic, *Moby-Dick; or, the Whale.* Considered by many to be "the supreme American novel," it is the story of Ishmael's pilgrimage as he boards the Pequod and observes Captain Ahab's singular quest for the great white whale to whom he lost his leg.[58] At over two hundred thousand words, it is a book that revels in language and whaling knowledge, with biblical and classical references throughout. Fittingly, the adaptations examined here (two different productions by John Gentile, one by David Catlin of the Lookingglass Theatre Company, and one by Blair Thomas and Company) highlight *language* in their scripts, although each of them must also contend with space—chiefly, how to represent the hugeness of the ocean, the whale, and the ideas Melville presents. The primary case study for the sixth chapter, *Moby-Dick* is also considered briefly in the eighth and ninth chapters.

In contrast to Melville's tome, Stephen Crane's *The Red Badge of Courage* is often called a novella for its brevity, featuring several vivid passages that describe how a young Union private (Henry Fleming) copes with his first encounters on the battleground of the American Civil War. Known for its odd mixture of realism, vivid imagery, and irony, the story delves into the youth's troubled mind, showcasing the psychology of fear and trauma common to men and women who have survived war. To meet the challenge of depicting this story, cocreator Michael Haverty and I chose to highlight *spectacle* in our adaptation, discarding narration in favor of a visceral, multimodal performance experience. Our decisions to blend dialogue with animation, original music, and a faceless puppet will be examined in greater detail in chapter 7, although references to *Red Badge of Courage* also appear in chapters 8 and 9.

In summary, we have three different affective approaches to what has been called the "surgical art" of adaptation for the stage for each novel: with ERS's *The Sound and the Fury*, while the adaptation includes Faulkner's narration and prose, the production uses sound and stage choreography to tell the story; whereas for *Moby-Dick*, the adapters emphasized the storytelling, highlighting Melville's language and narration; and with *Red Badge of Courage*, our adaptation stems from imagery rather than words, so there is relatively little of Crane's prose spoken in performance.[59]

Much like the process of staging an adaptation, however, we must begin with the dramaturgical research. In the next chapter, I survey the scope of dramaturgical practice in the United States, with special attention to the developments of the last twenty years. Chapter 2, then, serves two functions: for readers less familiar with dramaturgy as a crucial role in the creation of live performance, it provides a survey of possible configurations of how a dramaturg might function therein. For readers with differing levels of experience with dramaturgy, though, the next chapter also ensures that we are "on the same page" regarding our understanding of the range of roles a dramaturg fills. From this basis we can better understand the significance of and demand for adaptation dramaturgy.

2. THE RISE OF AMERICAN DRAMATURGY

The challenges presented by theatrical adaptation combine intellectual and artistic rigor, requiring theatre practitioners to hold at once a nuanced understanding of the source, its author, and original context while simultaneously remaining open-minded and creative regarding their approach to transforming the source for the stage. While parts of this task are handled by the adapter/s and director/s (or a combination thereof), the navigation of this duality of scholarship and creativity is the distinct province of the dramaturg.

But who exactly is the dramaturg? As discussed in the first chapter, while dramaturgy can be defined more broadly "to mean any purposeful arrangement of events," the role of someone acting as a dramaturg is something more specific, yet less commonly known.[1] According to a perspective widely accessible to many young theatrically minded adults, a dramaturg is a script doctor. I refer, of course, to the third episode of the second season of *Smash* ("The Dramaturg"), a musical drama television series broadcast on NBC in the United States from 2012 to 2013. This episode, however poorly received it was by critics, nevertheless served as an introduction of that "funny word" *dramaturg* into the lexicon of contemporary popular culture.[2] In this odd episode, Peter Gilman (Daniel Sunjata) has been brought onboard to overhaul Julia's book, with the expectation that his ghostwriting will "fix" whatever problems her musical has. His lack of compassion provides (sexual) tension with Julia (Debra Messing), but otherwise contradicts the receptive and collaborative role actual dramaturgs play. Ironically, as one blogger quipped, "A good dramaturg is EXACTLY what *Smash* needs."[3] Quite the opposite from how it was depicted on *Smash*, Canadian dramaturg Brian Quirt explains his role this way: "There are no rules here. The work requires a tremendous sensitivity to language, history, politics, gender, race, and modes of storytelling. It demands a lot of listening. I find that exercising that level of sensitivity makes me a more effective dramaturg."[4] This perspective—that dramaturgs are highly attuned listeners, mediators, even empaths—encapsulates the labor and talent of the leading practitioners of dramaturgy today.

In the past two decades, the practice of dramaturgy has enjoyed a revolution in the United States. As editor D. J. Hopkins noted in his preface to a 2014 special issue of *Theatre Topics* devoted to dramaturgy, "All of the many submissions emphasized expansions or refinements of perspective and innovations on practice rather than questions of professional identity. This discursive development in itself suggests that dramaturgy in North America may have passed a significant milestone."[5] In the past decade alone, several dramaturgy textbooks or guidebooks have been published, helping to carve out space for the academic study of dramaturgy for both undergraduate and graduate students. Each of these offers permissive and multivalent definitions of dramaturgy, helping to move the field of study and practice forward, while continuing to frustrate and inspire students who crave a precise definition.

As an academic whose title once included "resident dramaturg," I have been called upon numerous times to define dramaturgy, and each time find myself answering the question a bit differently, as my experience (and the field) continues to morph in response to aesthetics, industry, audience taste, and culture. And yet a definition of dramaturgy is a crucial launching point for a book of this nature; thus, in what follows I present what I consider to be the most relevant and convincing definitions of the work dramaturgs do and the practice of dramaturgy. Following this gloss, I offer my own definition to the mix, shaped (of course) by the contributions I have mentioned but with my own "critical proximity"[6] that stems from the perspective of working as an adaptation dramaturg and teaching classes that explore adaptation dramaturgy.

Defining Contemporary Dramaturgy

Michael Chemers's *Ghost Light* inspired this book and could be considered a companion volume to this one. With a primary focus on production dramaturgy (which will be defined later in this chapter), Chemers offers a cogent yet thought-provoking introduction to dramaturgy while also arguing persuasively for the increased importance of dramaturgs in theatre making. Drawing on history as well as the working metaphor of the ghost light, Chemers argues that dramaturgs shine a light "usually alone, into dark places for the benefit of others, to illuminate potential hazards, prevent missteps, and navigate across that most perilous of all terrains, the living stage."[7] In addition to providing an overview of dramaturgy, *Ghost Light* includes examples of in-class activities and questions at the end of each chapter that can guide academic instruction as well as on-the-job training for emerging dramaturgs.

Equally helpful for those new to dramaturgy is Felicia Hardison Londré's *Words at Play*, a collection of curated program notes (or dramaturgical essays) from her years of experience in the field as a production dramaturg for Missouri Repertory Theatre, Nebraska Shakespeare Festival, and the Heart of America Shakespeare Festival, from 1979 to 2003. While the impressive collection of essays can serve as a model for research and writing, the book also works to persuade readers that dramaturgy is an art form, with creative demands not entirely dissimilar from the rest of the production team. Of particular value to this book is the way it captures Londré's fallibility, insofar as she includes multiple entries for some plays (e.g., *Hamlet*) that demonstrate her development and maturation as a writer. Before each essay, she offers a reflective paragraph about the production in question and her take on the essay included. In this way, *Words at Play* captures the process as well as the product of dramaturgy.[8]

The Routledge Companion to Dramaturgy (edited by Magda Romanska in 2015) encapsulates the recent groundswell of interest in dramaturgy; it contains eighty-five short essays by established and emerging practitioners and scholars alike. A quick survey of the eight sections into which the volume is divided speaks to the aforementioned shift from defending dramaturgy to embracing its interdisciplinary power, as well as its increasingly global focus. The fifth section, entitled "Dramaturg as mediator and context manager: transculturalism, translation, adaptation, and contextualization," most connects to this project, although contributors reference adaptation frequently throughout the volume.[9] As Romanska indicates in her introduction, this book "is intended to serve as a primary sourcebook for dramaturgy students, practitioners, and academics."[10] With the aim of scaffolding the field "in the contemporary context," *The Routledge Companion to Dramaturgy*'s breadth testifies to "ever-expanding" variety of dramaturgical approaches and concerns.[11]

Similarly, Trencsényi and Cochrane's *New Dramaturgy: International Perspectives on Theory and Practice* frames the field globally, recognizing the diverse and nevertheless distinctive qualities of dramaturgy in different cultural contexts. This collection takes as its premise the fact that there has been a shift in dramaturgical thinking: namely, in the editors' words, that the practice "is now considered to be the inner flow of a dynamic system." Free from traditionally word-based research, dramaturgy is now "synonymous with the totality of the performance-making process."[12] As representatives of practice (Trencsényi, a freelance London-based dramaturg) and theory (Cochrane, an academic based in Australia and the UK), the editors are well positioned to capture the essence of this transformation, and they do so through five parts: "Towards a New Theory," "Text," "Devising," "Dance," and "Spectatorship." Within this structure, there are brief mentions of adaptation as an artistic undertaking, but the contributors' focus does not incorporate adaptation fully into their definition of new dramaturgy, per se. Instead, they use as a framework three (at times oppositional) qualities of new dramaturgy: it is intercultural; it focuses on process; and it embraces "the decline of mimesis as the dominant dramatic model and, by extension, the decline of representational theatre culture."[13] These three aspects transform our expectations of dramaturg behavior, Trencsényi and Cochrane explain, from that of an interloper who offers critical objectivity into a facilitator who helps to curate the variety of cultures and symbols of the performance. Far from an outsider role, they argue, the new dramaturg is at the very center of theatre making, and can help illuminate the company's methods "by articulating, challenging, or, at times, disrupting the creative process(es)."[14]

A year after this collection was published, Trencsényi published *Dramaturgy in the Making: A User's Guide for Theatre Practitioners*, a survey of dramaturgical praxis that attempts "to spin together . . . two threads, Apollonian and Dionysian dramaturgy, theory and practice, arguing that they are the two sides of the same thing."[15] Also transnational in focus, Trencsényi's single-authored book divides her focus into three arenas where dramaturgical labor can be analyzed: within the institution, at the level of productions, and for dance performances. In the first section, she delves into the role of the institutional (or resident) dramaturg and the related work of literary management, as well as the development of new scripts and the commissioning of translations. Of particular interest in this arena is her astute reading of dramaturgy through the lens of museum curators, a metaphor that has gained traction in the field at large.[16] Throughout this otherwise instructive volume, the references to adaptation—and especially its dependence on dramaturgy—are infrequent, usually serving other purposes.[17] As in her coedited book, Trencsényi advocates for an understanding of dramaturgy that upends the outdated model of a text-based (if not library-dwelling) individual who endangers (or upholds to the detriment of the director's vision) the sanctity of the playwright's intention. Instead, she closes the book with an eloquent (if pithy) observation: that, ultimately, dramaturgs "'Support' and 'Challenge.' The order is important."[18] Our role, she maintains, "is always a secondary one," and thus our modus operandi "is questioning, not statement."[19]

My own definition of dramaturgy coincides with Trencsényi's for the most part, but at the center of how I define my work is the equally complicated idea of adaptation. In the following chapters, this intersection will become more clear, but for now we might agree to accept the premise that both adaptation and dramaturgy share part of the definition (of dramaturgy) that Adam Versényi offers in *The Oxford Encyclopedia of Theatre and Performance*: namely, that it "can be understood as an attribute, a role, or a function."[20] Fittingly, the meaning of dramaturgy *adapts* to its context, such that it can mean the "aesthetic architecture of a piece of drama, the individual person who is assigned to cultivate an understanding of that architecture, and also can refer to the functional means by which that architecture is discovered in rehearsal."[21] In other words, dramaturgy (like adaptation) is both product and process, noun and verb. It is work that we do with scripts (whether word based or not) and their authors, with productions (both in rehearsal and in meetings), and with spectators and public relations (before, during, and after a run of performances). That "work" is both product and process—it is both material (e.g., program notes or lobby display) and ephemeral (e.g., conversations or suggestions made during the creative practice).

The fact that dramaturgy resists definition and represents an intersection of several different fields is at once its strength and its greatest challenge. Like many interdisciplinary subjects, dramaturgy requires a big-picture worldview as well as attention to detail—it demands attention to both the forest and the trees. Those who begin to explore dramaturgy can easily feel overwhelmed or lost even in their excitement to explore this territory; happily, guidance from professional organizations is available. In particular, for North America this guild is the Literary Managers and Dramaturgs of the Americas, or LMDA.[22]

Dramaturging the Profession

LMDA formed in 1984, the same year that Macintosh desktop computers were introduced into the marketplace.[23] In the early years it was a fledgling organization (originally Literary Managers and Dramaturgs of America) that served the Northeast region of the United States, but by 1990 the "A" in LMDA changed to reflect the inclusion of Canada in the association, although LMDA Canada (formed in 1997) continues to operate as a subdivision of LMDA as well as an organization in its own right. One of the core goals of LMDA is to "encourage cooperation among the practitioners and theoreticians of dramaturgy," meaning that the organization's annual conferences feature a balanced mix of academic and professional dramaturgs.

During the first two decades of LMDA's existence, much of the focus remained on advocacy. In the 1990s dramaturgy had little to no recognition in the United States, and this lack of visibility was made more complicated by the litigation surrounding the authorship rights to *Rent* in the wake of Jonathan Larsen's untimely passing. Lynn Thompson, who was one of several dramaturgs participating in workshop performances that later became Broadway shows, had a significant role in the development of *Rent,* but was initially cut out of any royalty payments; she sued the commercial producers who had taken over *Rent* after Larsen's death, and one of the results of this high profile entertainment lawsuit was that the role (and rights) of the dramaturg became part of the conversation. In the 2000s these goals began to shift, as dramaturgy became more of a common and recognized practice, and its advocacy shifted from supporting dramaturgy as a legitimate part of theatre making to broadening how dramaturgy is defined and what dramaturgs can (or should) do in the creative process.

Part of that expansion has included the adoption of several subgroups within the larger association that will be referenced later in this book, such as early career, dance, and dramaturgy for devised work. While these categories are fairly self-explanatory, it is nevertheless worthwhile to explore them briefly here, to establish a common vocabulary. In particular, the notion of categorizing the newest members of LMDA as early career (sometimes also called emerging) dramaturgs demonstrates the organization's dedication to mentorship and expansion. The organization's formal commitment to emerging dramaturgs is a recent development, allowing the more established members of LMDA to welcome newcomers with dedicated portals of social media, a fund to help defray the cost of attending conferences, and panels that focus on their interests and needs. It is these emerging dramaturgs who, in turn, have encouraged the guild to evolve according to the shifting dynamics of contemporary performance demands. Of these changes, perhaps the most significant (for what has been considered traditional dramaturgy) is the move away from word-based text as the script for performance.

Another change to the scope of both LMDA and the field at large is the recognition of the unique demands of dance dramaturgy. As contemporary choreography has taken new shape, the need for and value of dramaturgy has sharpened. "Dance dramaturgy may be a new strand, but its contribution to contemporary dramaturgical articulations and understandings figures large in today's evolving dramaturgical field."[24] The fact that most (but not all) dance occurs without speech or script contributes to the mutually beneficial relationship between contemporary dramaturgy and choreography; working with dancers challenges dramaturgs to interpret performance differently, as they cannot analyze the script. This is particularly true for choreographers who embrace dance theatre, a method of movement creation that is similar to devising insofar as it is made *with* the dancers (rather than choreographed *for* them). Dance dramaturgs' research methods shift as well. Although they can still work outside of the rehearsal room (by watching videos of the company's previous work, for example, or conducting research on concepts that influence the choreographer), the need for them to witness the ever emerging language of performance is heightened with dance. As European dramaturg and mentor Lou Cope explains it, "It is my job, as she who sits on the outside of the inside looking in, to also look outwards and see ways in which the material being developed speaks, and is linked to, the growing worlds around it—the world of the piece, but also the world outside the cosy rehearsal room."[25] Thus the dance dramaturg can be seen as an integral part of the creative process—an individual who is present for most of the rehearsals (inside) to observe and ask questions, but who also conducts research (outside) connected to the choreography as it develops.

The inside/outside creative role of dance dramaturgs is similar to that of the dramaturg involved with devised performance. While the nature of devised work varies according to the collaborators involved, to devise basically means that the company members (the actors, designers, director, and often the dramaturg as well) create the performance together, through the process of rehearsal. In other words, like dance, there is no script to analyze before the rehearsals begin (although the devised work might be inspired by a text or collection of texts); the shape of the piece emerges through the decisions made during the process. In this way, as Cathy Turner and Synne K. Behrndt acknowledge, "Devising implies that the dramaturgy of the work is not defined before the work commences."[26] The fact that the work is shaped during rehearsal means that dramaturgy is always part of devised work (although not all companies who devise have a specified individual called a dramaturg). Devised work can also be understood as a process focused "on a certain playful openness: to a range of stimuli; to creative risk and experimentation; to the views and input of a variety of participants," as Alex Mermikides and Jackie Smart suggest in *Devising in Process*.[27] This spirit of play demands both trust and vulnerability from the devising company, including the dramaturg. Such an "emotionally intelligent" and "emotionally ethical" definition further expands the role of dramaturg from the traditional understanding of an objective external observer to an empathetic engaged participant.[28]

Artists who work in highly collaborative performance genres such as dance and devised work frequently incorporate aspects of adaptation into their practice in ways that are particularly instructive for dramaturgs. Whereas the "fine art" of dance has become a welcome subject for academics and dramaturgs alike, the less established art of devised work remains relatively underrepresented in the field. In recent years, LMDA conferences and discussions have begun to consider the impact of dramaturgy for devised work, but the conversation within the United States is nascent compared to the complex ways that devising has been part of the dramaturgical landscape in Europe. Arguably, part of the reason we are late to the party is that dramaturgs in the USA usually receive training according to the continuum of new play and production dramaturgy.

The New Play/Production Continuum

There are several programs designated to training dramaturgs in the United States; the most well known and established of these is the Yale School of Drama, which offers a doctor of fine arts in dramaturgy, followed by Carnegie Mellon University's program (founded by Michael Chemers in 2012), which offers a bachelor of fine arts in production dramaturgy.[29] The concept of dedicating a degree program to dramaturgy as a fine art is relatively new; most of the pillars of the American dramaturgical community (e.g., Felicia Hardison Londré, Mark Bly, Anne Cattaneo) did not have the option to earn an official degree in dramaturgy. That being said, the kind of university or otherwise academic study that prepares one for dramaturgy is innately interdisciplinary and arguably does not have to result in a degree dedicated to the field. An increasing number of colleges and universities in the United States offer courses in dramaturgy at both the undergraduate and graduate level, helping to introduce the craft to students who otherwise might not realize the possibility of becoming a dramaturg.

At the heart of most American-based dramaturgy courses and programs (as well as the basis of most professional dramaturgy opportunities) is what I call the continuum of new play and production dramaturgy specialization.[30] In what follows, I provide an overview of this continuum, by focusing on the unique demands of both kinds of dramaturgy, combined with examples of the process and products of new play and production dramaturgs, generally speaking.

While the tendency to specialize in new play dramaturgy may be more robust in Canada than the United States,[31] there are nevertheless several avenues for developing plays in America, many of which recognize the value of dramaturgical assistance. Just as it sounds, new play dramaturgy is based in the stewardship of playwriting; dramaturgs who identify on the new-play side of the continuum tend to combine the skills of an editor with those of a writing coach or mentor, focusing their efforts on helping playwrights reach their aesthetic and cultural goals. Some of the programs and retreats that make this work possible include the New Play Dramaturgy Intensive at the Kennedy Center and the National Critics Institute, a summer conference at the Eugene O'Neill Theater Center that runs concurrently with their National Playwrights Conference.

On an institutional level, new play dramaturgy can take the form of literary management—a literary manager is an individual (usually with dramaturgical training and/or experience) who curates a company's season selection process, usually by soliciting and reading new (as well as established) scripts. Literary managers function as gatekeepers and advocates for playwrights, especially those who have not yet been produced elsewhere. Annual events like the Humana Festival (Actors Theatre of Louisville) help introduce emerging playwrights to literary managers from across the United States, but some theatres dedicated to producing new work also hold their own festivals or contests to encourage local participation as well as to target diverse voices. Recently, the process of searching for scripts has been streamlined significantly with the launching of The New Play Exchange, an online database that connects writers with literary managers and dramaturgs as well as theatres, festivals, and contests.[32] Not only has this database made the process of finding new plays more accessible and less reliant on outdated submission modes, its search and filter options allow users to tailor their research, a function that enables intentional parity of racial, ethnic, and gender representation in American theatre.[33]

While many playwrights seek out dramaturgical assistance, the relationship between author and dramaturg can be volatile; one of the primary organizations to advocate for authorial rights in theatre is the Dramatists Guild, an association that has taken a public role in questioning the limits of creative rights for dramaturgs who work directly with new plays. In part because the Dramatists Guild was involved in the aforementioned *Thompson v. Larsen* case as an advocate for the defense, their stance regarding dramaturgy is noticeably wary, especially with regard to any claim of collaboration a dramaturg (or director) might have that could result in shared royalties.

At LMDA's thirtieth anniversary conference in New York City (2015), the question of copyright was at the heart of a session entitled "Authors' Rights," with panelists from Dramatists Guild, Samuel French, and Dramatists Play Service, as well as author Amanda Green (who wrote the lyrics and music for the musical adaptation *Hands on a Hard Body*) participating in the conversation. Ralph Sevush, an attorney who spoke on behalf of the Dramatists Guild, specifically avoided answering a question from the audience about the potential for the dramaturg to intervene on behalf of the playwright's rights, stating, "The less I say on that, the better."[34] Sevush is on record, however, regarding the "ongoing danger for playwrights that dramaturgy can sometimes present" in his 2014 essay, "The Guild and Dramaturgy," published in *The Dramatist*.[35] In this polemic he echoes some of the sentiments expressed in the LMDA authorship panel, that academic theatre programs might be "particularly hostile environment[s] in which to cultivate the singular vision of a new playwright" because they encourage "the European model of theatrical 'auteurism,' where the director is deemed the 'author' of the work."[36] These lingering concerns about fidelity to authorial intention will resurface throughout this book, but will be discussed in the most detail in chapter 3.

There is considerably less controversy surrounding the work of production dramaturgy, which may explain why most introductory handbooks focus on this side of the continuum. Whereas the new play dramaturg works most closely with the playwright, the production dramaturg works with (some might say for) the director. The job of the production dramaturg is to help the creative team achieve the director's goals, or production concept, for staging an established script. Because this kind of dramaturgy results, by definition, in a production being performed for an audience, much of the work on this side of the continuum has to do with communication with the audience. This could take the shape of program notes, a lobby display, a website, pre- or postshow discussions, or any combination thereof. In addition to helping to communicate the intentions of the director to the audience, a production dramaturg works before and during rehearsals with members of the creative team, starting with the director, but extending to the designers and the actors and often including the front-of-the-house management team.

Some companies and academic theatre programs go as far as to hire (or appoint) a resident dramaturg who works with all the productions in a season. Resident dramaturgs have responsibilities that somewhat overlap with those of literary managers, insofar as they help shape the season as well as the publicity for it, and as such the resident dramaturg usually works closely with the production manager and artistic director of the company or academic program.

While this continuum is useful for articulating the different roles (and training) for dramaturgy, an increasing number of plays being produced in the United States are neither entirely new nor established; they are adaptations. That is to say, the role of the adaptation dramaturg combines the elements of both new play and production dramaturgy. Because of this proliferation, coinciding with the emergence of adaptation studies as a field of study, more scholars are analyzing theatre adaptation; however, little of this scholarship focuses specifically on adaptation dramaturgy, per se—an odd omission, given how much the fields of dramaturgy and adaptation have to learn from each other. In particular, the capacity of dramaturgs to empathize with spectators enables us to see stage adaptations with a clarity that frequently escapes students whose interest in adaptation centers on literature or film. The next chapter explores this overlap in greater detail, by offering a new model for understanding dramaturgical practice, as well as a dynamic system for analyzing theatrical adaptation that emphasizes audience reception rather than source or author fidelity. In it, I suggest several ways of seeing and understanding the transformative work of adaptation for the stage, all of which are empowered by adapturgy.

3. THE POWER OF ADAPTURGY

My experience and research suggest that a new model of dramaturgy has emerged: adaptation dramaturgy, or what I call *adapturgy.* This kind of dramaturgy applies to both definitions of the term previously discussed: dramaturgy as the analysis of script structure and aesthetic, and dramaturgy as practice. Whereas the guiding question for dramaturgy has been *why this play now?*, for adapturgy I suggest a modification of the question, so that it becomes *why this source as theatre now?* This adapted question, so to speak, encompasses the key elements under dramaturgical consideration for any adaptation for the stage.[1] In particular, the emphasis on "as theatre" will help guide dramaturgical curiosity to always consider the languages of the stage, and the particular ways that a source thrives with (or perhaps is challenged by) theatricality.[2] The removal of "text" from the more commonly used "source text" within adaptation studies is intentional, signaling the wide possibility of materials viable for creating theatre. Finally, the use of "now," as with the original question, implies both time and space—that is, it signals a consideration of the "here and now," since a full understanding of contemporary concerns must respond to one's audience. This is not to suggest that dramaturgs should be myopic, ignoring global concerns, but that the macro question of "now" should filter such transnational readings of contemporary culture through the lens of how and why the adaptation matters on a micro level, to their local and current audiences. Dramaturgs and adapters share a practice that makes the past present; dramaturgy does so by articulating how and why a historical event matters to today's spectators, while the adaptation reframes a previously created source anew. Adapturgy traffics in re-presentation.

Visualizing Adaptation in Perspective

Focusing on the audience is crucial for dramaturgs, whether their work is with new plays or productions. The model of adapturgy allows students as well as practitioners to consider and experience both new play and production dramaturgy, since adaptation dramaturgy always falls somewhere between the editing and feedback role of new play dramaturgy and the research and contextual role of production dramaturgy. Exactly where on that continuum adapturgy falls will depend on the specific nature of each production—if the adapter is in residence (and requests feedback on their script), the dramaturg's work will more closely resemble new play dramaturgy. If the adapter does not consider the script a work in progress, the dramaturg will function more like a production dramaturg, with primary focus on the director's vision and the cast's questions or needs. That being said, this continuum is more dynamic than a linear model suggests, and so perhaps it would be best to consider the range of adapturgy in two stages: first, as a Venn diagram with three intersecting circles (figure 3.1), and then as a Cartesian coordinate system, in three dimensions.

Venn diagrams excel at demonstrating points of comparison and contrast, but can also be used to stimulate higher levels of thinking, including visualizing logical arguments. These schemas become more complex when three circles are used, however, because doing so creates eight regions of information (if one includes the space beyond the three circles as the eighth zone). For our purposes, using three circles to signify the intersecting areas of new play, production, and adaptation dramaturgy sheds light on the distinct ways that each of these types of dramaturgical praxis operates, as well as the zones in which they share interests. Not surprisingly, at the nexus of this diagram—that is, in the portion shared by all three circles—is the consideration of the audience, a constant for all dramaturgs, especially (but not only) when plays are produced for paying spectators.

Notably, there are portions of this model where new play and adaptation dramaturgy overlap (staged readings, scripts revised during rehearsal), where new play and production dramaturgy coincide (playwright's vision), but the largest area of commonality is where production and adaptation dramaturgy intersect (adapter's vision, director's vision, critical response, and the relationship to the source). This comes as no surprise when one recognizes that some adapters prefer to rewrite their adaptation for specific productions, thereby working closely alongside the rest of the production

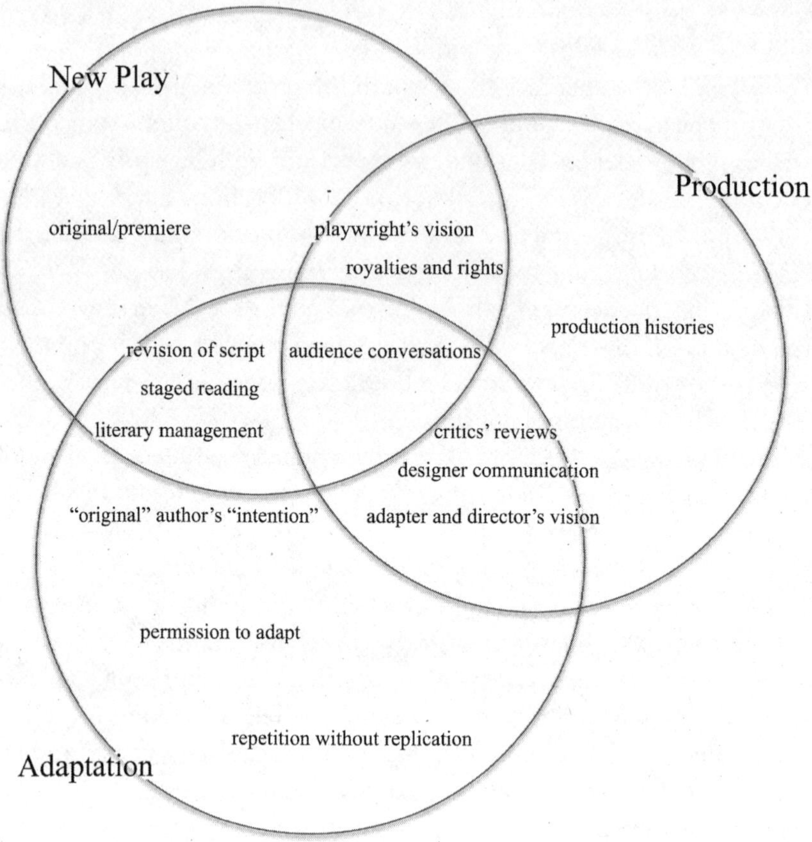

Fig. 3.1. Types of dramaturgy. *Created by author.*

team with a specific understanding of the venue and how its limitations and/or opportunities shape the work (much the way a director does). As adapter of literature for the stage John Gentile explains, "I like to re-adapt the work in a sense, or at least revise my adaptation, given the circumstances of a specific production and a specific director."[3] Gentile's preference also reminds us that all live performances must adapt to their audiences and that directing can be akin to adaptation, even when the production honors every word exactly as written in the script. Theatre is, by definition, adaptation.

To acknowledge the ubiquity of adaptation in theatre making does not diminish the need to uncover the dramaturgical labor behind adapted scripts—quite the contrary, this knowledge heightens the urgency of our focus, especially since the work of adapturgy occurs whether or not there is a specific person designated as dramaturg. If the adaptation is directed (or codirected) by the adapter(s), the dramaturgical research has likely been so interwoven into the creative process that it may not be easily untangled from the adaptation and directing of the project. The same may be said about production dramaturgy: the entire creative team, especially the director and designers, partake in dramaturgical thinking and investigation.[4] However, it is far less likely that a director or designer would suggest that they helped shape the script they are producing, unless that script is an adapted one. In some ways, this is due to the nature of adaptation itself—"to make fit"[5]—a process that occurs with any type of theatre making, whether the lines spoken onstage are adapted from an acknowledged source or not. But it also illuminates adapturgy's connection to new play and production dramaturgy. Because adaptation dramaturgs function as liaisons between the adapted script and the production thereof, they have the potential to contribute to both levels of creation. The same can be said when no specific person is given this role—even plays without dramaturgs need dramaturgy. This is even more applicable when we consider stage adaptation. There is no adaptation for the stage without dramaturgy.

We can see why dramaturgy is so crucial to adaptation in figures 3.2 and 3.3, a model of spectator-based adapturgy.[6] Whereas all produced plays—whether new or established—require dramaturgy to clarify the choices particular to a specific mounting of that script, when the script in question is one that has been adapted from something else, new variables enter the equation. In particular, the dramaturg must contemplate how staged versions of the source have differed from the source on which it was based. As reviewed in the first chapter, there are copious ways to consider these changes, including a useful taxonomy distinguishing the intertextual possibilities.[7] To both simplify and exemplify this classification method, I have adapted it to a Cartesian coordinate system, so that readers can begin to imagine two crucial dramaturgical clues: (1) how the production in question relates to the source, and (2) the other possibilities for how it might have been adapted and/or staged. Especially for dramaturgs new to adapturgy, the latter point can be difficult to imagine without some guidance and a framework within which they can map this relationship.

As you can see, spectator-based adapturgy contains the basic coordinates of an x- and a y-axis, where the x-axis is horizontal and the y-axis is vertical. The addition of a third axis, the z-axis, transforms the diagram

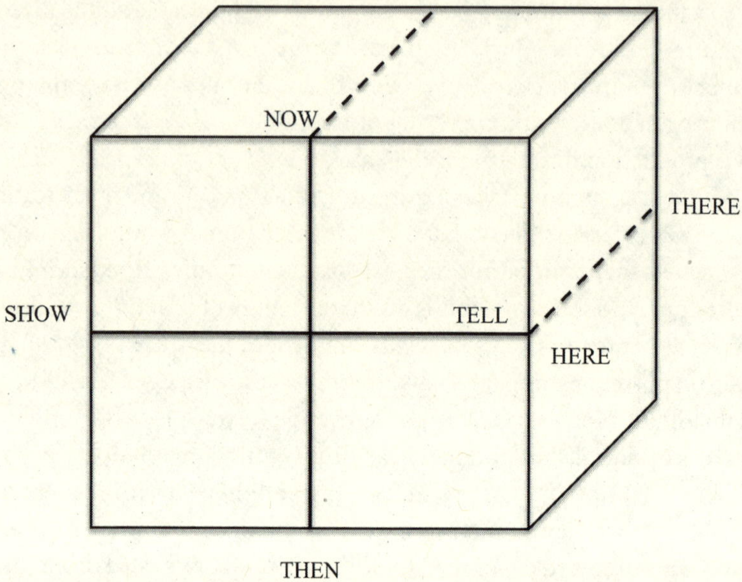

Fig. 3.2. Spectator-based adapturgy, as a cube. *Created by author.*

from the flatness of two dimensions to flexible three-dimensionality. The z-axis means that instead of quadrants there are now eight areas—in other words, the dramaturgical considerations have doubled. But what do these coordinates represent? To keep the model intuitive, let us suggest that the z-axis points toward and away from the user and means much the same thing: *here* (closest to user) and *there* (furthest away). The x-axis, meanwhile, runs between the left and right, and likewise signifies similar societal values: *to show* is left of center (Dionysian); and *to tell* is right of center (Apollonian). The final line, the y-axis, represents time: above the x-axis means *(beyond) now* and below it means *then*. Thus, with these three axes we capture elements relevant to all literary adaptations for the stage: space (here or there), point of view and narrative voice (show or tell), and time (now and then). Significantly, the model is designed to "make sense" *to the user*—it is designed from the point of view of reception, not authorship.

Such a model allows dramaturgs to organize their thoughts about particular adaptations without defaulting to the familiar trap of fidelity as it is typically understood: as a value wherein proximity to what is presumed to be the original is considered better than distance from it. Instead of determining value based on "origin," this model locates the adaptation in relation *to the spectator's point of view.* Not only does this model shift our thinking about adaptation from a linear consideration between the source and adapted script to one that is three-dimensional, but it does so by fully embracing the very *perspective* that three-dimensionality permits. Thus, whereas the coordinate system requires an origin point (0, 0, 0), in this model the user or spectator occupies that position, rather than the source's author. Where a spectator in rural Montana might locate an adaptation in this model might turn out to be quite different from where one in Manhattan might locate the same adaptation, because what is considered "here" for each differs, both geographically and culturally. Moreover, older spectators might consider "now" differently from how young adults would, because their understanding of time (and culture) is relative to their accumulated experience (or lack thereof). And while virtually all performances include both showing and telling, in the case of literary adaptation, this axis relates to the primary (not the only) mode of action used by the production. If the piece emphasizes the visual more than the aural, it belongs somewhere on the "show" side of the axis; if it is more word- (or sound-)based, it goes on the "tell" side. While a good rule of thumb for literary adaptations may be the question of narrative voice—that is, whether the actors speak lines other than dialogue from the source—there are some productions that include narration but are otherwise mostly visual. This is why the points along the axis become useful: users can indicate the intensity of the value by where they locate it along the axis. That said, there are no absolute values to be determined here; nor is there a right or wrong way to locate the adaptation. Instead, to recall Trencsényi's summary of the dramaturg's job, the model exists to facilitate conversation and questions.

Locating a particular adaptation within this model, then, allows dramaturgs to envision other viable choices that the adapter and/or director could have made. Considering this notion—*the road not traveled*—helps us explain the significance of the choices that were made, especially for audiences whose range of theatre experience is limited, or whose attachment to the source (and how they have imagined it thus far) is particularly strong. In addition, visualizing the location of a particular adaptation in this system in relationship to other versions enhances our understanding of that interaction, which can inform the dramaturgy throughout the rehearsal process. Most crucially, this approach encourages us to practice and model empathy with spectators from diverse backgrounds, upon whom the growth and very survival of theatre practice rely.

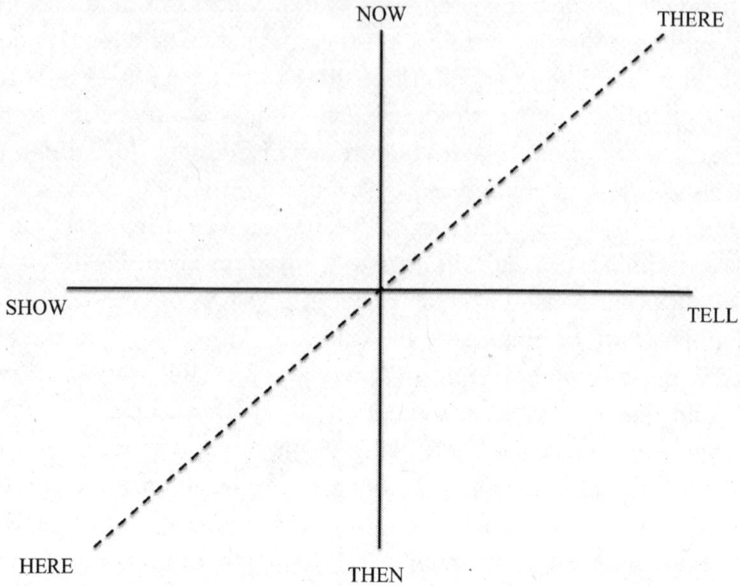

Fig. 3.3. Spectator-based adapturgy, as coordinates. *Created by author.*

The Yellow Brick Road Not Traveled

Let us consider two musical adaptations of L. Frank Baum's 1900 children's book *The Wonderful Wizard of Oz*, to query how they would register on the three-dimensional model in question: *The Wiz Live!* (2015) and *Wicked* (which opened in 2003).[8] While both are examples of the musical genre, *The Wiz Live!*, a television event broadcast on NBC, is perhaps best known for its 1978 film version, starring Diana Ross and featuring Michael Jackson, which itself was based on a stage musical that debuted on Broadway in 1975 after opening in Baltimore in 1974. *Wicked: The Untold Story of the Witches of Oz* was adapted from a 1995 novel written by Gregory Maguire, *Wicked: The Life and Times of the Wicked Witch of the West* (itself an adaptation—a prequel to Dorothy's arrival in Oz).[9] For the purposes of this example, we shall focus on the 2015 live-TV production directed by Kenny Leon and the 2003 Broadway show starring Idina Menzel and Kristen Chenoweth. As will become apparent, however, users will find it difficult (if not impossible) to chart an adaptation in isolation. This is "not a bug; it's a feature," since the model is built on intertextual analysis rather than a fidelity assessment.[10] As Thomas Leitch has argued, "No intertextual model, however careful, can be adequate to the study of adaptation if it limits each intertext to a single precursor."[11] The purpose of the model is to show connections between and distance from both other versions of the story, as well as how it is located relative to the source and the user.

For the y-axis (*time*), we can locate *The Wiz Live!* as taking place "now," as several cultural references were updated in this adaptation, penned by Harvey Fierstein. In Fierstein's version, Dorothy (Shanice Williams, a New Jersey teenager cast from open auditions) used the phrase "what had happened was," identified by several critics as an example of contemporary African American vernacular.[12] For the 1978 film version directed by Sidney Lumet, the point on the y-axis would change to "then" for twenty-first century audiences, but would have been considered "now" when it premiered. The question of where to place *Wicked* on this axis depends even more explicitly on other adaptations; since the action onstage occurs in the years leading up to (and including) the arrival of Dorothy in Oz, we can assume it is "then," but our assessment of how far back in time the tale goes depends entirely on when we would date its source/s. There are parts of Maguire's tale that stem from Baum's book, but the most recognizable choice (the fact that Elphaba has green skin) is pulled from the film. Whereas we might consider the film (and the book) "timeless" because of its continued appeal, the fact that Professor Marvel travels by a horse-drawn wagon indicates the setting cannot be later than the early twentieth century.

As for the x-axis (*action*), with a tale like this one especially in its musical version—there is little doubt that most users would place both examples in question on the "show" side rather than the "tell" side. It is worth noting, however, that although the primary source—Baum's 1900 tale—is a book, it is not so easily classified on the "tell" side of the axis. The illustrations for this book were drawn by W. W. Denslow, who collaborated with Baum on several projects and shared the copyright royalties for both the book and the 1902 stage extravaganza. Although not as fully image laden as a graphic novel, *The Wonderful Wizard of Oz* can nevertheless be considered closer to the "show" side than one might initially expect for a fictional novel. As for the degree of action depicted through spectacle rather than narration, both musicals could be placed virtually anywhere on the "show" side of the axis, depending on the user's perspective and (crucially) the other texts under consideration.

When turning to the z-axis (*space*), our reliance on individualized points of view for this exercise comes into sharper focus. For many readers, the world depicted in *The Wiz Live!* is a familiar one, at least in terms of Dorothy's home base in Kansas. However, depending on one's race and cultural background, the milieu depicted may be more or less recognizable. Ratings for the live event peaked in African American households, according to Nielsen reports, which indicated the highest ratings for "Richmond (16.1), Norfolk (15.0), Baltimore (14.8), Washington, D.C. (13.2), and Atlanta (13.2)."[13] Fluency with the musical styles in *The Wiz Live!*—including gospel, hip-hop, and R & B—will also influence the placement on this axis. As television critic Eric Deggans summarized, "Make no mistake, NBC's 'The Wiz Live!' was fully and fearlessly filled with blackness."[14] In short, the choice of where to place this musical depends on whether users locate themselves inside, on the perimeter, or outside of contemporary American black culture.

Thus, the z-axis can be understood as shorthand for what Lawrence Venuti calls "foreignization" and "domestication" within the related field of translation studies. When translators (or adapters) use time- and space-specific cultural idioms, they domesticate the source, making it more familiar to their peers.[15] From the perspective of African Americans, *The Wiz Live!* has the potential to turn a memorable story (about white culture) into something more recognizable, less foreign. Not all African Americans would find this to be true, of course, any more than all spectators of any race or ethnicity could be assumed to share any other singular point of view. But the adaptation technique at play in this example is akin to making the source either closer to home (domestication) or less well known (foreignization), depending on who's analyzing the musical. This tactical shift, from the source to the user as the point of reference for analysis, invites a recognition of privilege and how relative one's interpretation of an adaptation will be, based on where (and what) one considers "home."

In *Wicked,* the point of view is no longer Dorothy's, but Elphaba's—and her home is not in Kansas (or Harlem, for *The Wiz*), but in the fantasy world of Oz.[16] As such, we might be tempted to assume that it would occupy a spot far along the "there" side of this axis, but before deciding, we might also consider the experiences of this young woman with green skin. She experiences prejudice and alienation, and as a result holds herself back from her full potential, in an effort to blend in. As the ongoing popularity of this musical demonstrates, there are many adults who identify as outcasts or underdogs, and may find parallels to their experiences in this musical. In addition, there are several recognizable characters and situations that Stephen Schwartz (music and lyrics) and Winnie Holzman (book) pull from Maguire and Baum.

In sum, we have *The Wiz Live!* located on x-, y, z/z- (depending on perspective), and *Wicked* on x-, y-, z (the degree of z also depending on perspective).

Meanwhile, Baum's book would be on x, y-, z-/z (depending on perspective). In order to determine the placement of each story, the following questions became crucial: Whose point of view encapsulates the narrative of the story? How does that point of view—with regard to time, place, and action—relate to my own? How is it likely to relate to members of this particular audience? And how does it compare to other adaptations of this story?

Admittedly, the system I offer here for mapping adaptations in relationship to others as well as their source/s relies upon a semiotic binary mentioned in chapter 1, defended by Lessing himself: that of words (tell, related to time) and images (show, related to space). As Kamilla Elliott asserts in *Rethinking the Novel/Film Debate,* a critical blindness about "the unbridgeable word and image divide" persists alongside "the indissoluble form and content union."[17] This stubborn insistence that the sign system of words (the province of literature) differs from and can never adequately translate into that of image[18] restrains adaptation theory from understanding the potential exchange between both realms, and more importantly, the way that traveling between them changes both source and adaptation. Moreover, the resistance to unhook form from content stymies creativity and contradicts the very nature of theatre itself: to rehearse and to design, after all, is to restage (or recontextualize) content—to *play* with the form.

While the spectator-based adapturgy model relies upon Aristotelian rules for unity in drama (time, space, action), the use of it nevertheless challenges these very categories, because it encourages the kind of analogy that resists the binary of word/image as well as the notion that content and form are inseparable. By placing different adaptations of the same source in the same ecosystem as the source itself, the model assumes that they share resources, thereby upending the territorialism that Elliott critiques. This approach to knowledge—finding analogies between and making connections across disciplines—is both deeply dramaturgical and ultimately reliant on speculation, rather than structural analysis. Arguing for interconnectedness is not the same as suggesting universality, however, because (as we have seen) every user will have a different point of view, according to their relative experience and cultural worldview.

The Specter of the Source

Yet to engage in dramaturgy, one must rely on some level of both speculation and analogy. This is because dramaturgy (and, I would add, adaptation) traffics in what Marianne van Kerkhoven has evocatively called the "twilight zone between art and science." As she remarked in 1994, "Dramaturgy is *always* concerned with the conversion of feeling into knowledge, and vice versa."[19] To be a dramaturg, she concludes, "demands an investment from all the senses, and, more especially, a firm trust in the path of intuition."[20] Confidence in one's intuition is especially necessary for adaptation dramaturgy, in part because of the additional layer of responsibility one takes on with adapturgy—the specter of the source.

The word *specter* (or "ghost") has come to have negative connotations (as terrifying or something dreaded, for example), but the Latin root of the word is *specere,* meaning "to look," as well as *spectrum,* which meant (and still means) "an image or apparition." That we might draw upon a metaphor about specters in a book about theatre practice (or dramaturgy) is hardly surprising; folklore about ghosts haunting playhouses abounds, and scholars have theorized the stage as a place of disappearance, surrogation, and ghosting.[21] Moreover, since *specter* is at its core a word about an encounter (to look, [to see] an image or apparition), the notion that the possibilities for such an encounter would be heightened in a theatre (a seeing place) or an auditorium (a hearing place) makes sense.[22]

Nor is it entirely unusual to consider adaptation a kind of ghosting, given the inescapable and highly charged relationship between the source and the adaptation. As Elliott notes, there is ample precedent in adaptation theory for understanding the process of change between novel and film as one that requires the adapter to extract the soul from the body in order to translate it into another medium. She delineates six approaches to adaptation that rely in various ways on this corporeal model of the source: psychic, ventriloquist, genetic, de(re)composing, incarnational, and trumping. As "the psychic concept of adaptation argues," for example, "to be true to the spirit of a text, an adaptation must leave behind the literary corpse."[23] Whereas from this perspective the spirit or soul is considered to be set free, in the incarnational concept, based on a Christian perspective of transforming word into flesh, the process of giving material form to something once ephemeral can be seen "as carnalization, a sordid, morally reprehensible corruption of spiritual and transcendental signification and of a romanticized 'divine' imagination."[24] What has been seen cannot be unseen, and therefore after seeing an adaptation onstage (or on the screen), it is difficult to recapture the freedom experienced by the reader of the novel.

Elliott's observations about the field do not consider live performance, but they intersect with my perspective in ways that will be borne out in the following chapters. In particular, as we shall see, she and I agree that adaptation is "reciprocally transformative," such that the resulting performance is "not translation or copy, but rather metamorphoses the novel and is, in turn, metamorphosed by it."[25] This reciprocal transaction—wherein both the literature and the drama might evolve, *because of the dramaturgy required to adapt one into the other*—speaks to the power of adapturgy. It is dramaturgy that informs and ensures the logic of metamorphosis between source and adaptation, which is to say that adapturgy has the capacity to change not only the performance but also how audiences (re)encounter the source itself.

Conjuring the Numinous

At the heart of every theatrical adaptation and therefore at the core of adapturgy itself is a process of transformation that is often experienced as both numinous and uncanny. The concept of theatre as an activity and place where something sacred occurs is familiar enough, since the earliest purpose of theatrical activity was likely religious, as part of a larger ceremony or festival.[26] With full recognition that the purpose of most theatre practice today is no longer religious (or even sacred), the process of adaptation for the stage nevertheless stirs up a kind of numinous energy, one that is often read or interpreted as uncanny.

In 1923, Rudolf Otto postulated the concept of the numinous in his book *The Idea of the Holy*.[27] Somewhat related to Mircea Eliade's concept of hierophany as the revelation of the divine ("*something sacred shows itself to us*"), Otto defines numinous as an experience or quality that evokes *mysterium tremendum et fascinans*.[28] This "paradoxical combination of fear and fascination experienced in the non-rational perception of the mysterious and sacred"—the numinous—is an affective reaction that is difficult to capture or conjure and is thus a frequent topic explored by art.[29] Because the experience of it is irreducible to logic, the Dionysian art of theatre is an especially apt medium for exploring the numinous. Authors of fiction and poetry also evoke it with words, so it is not uncommon to feel the presence of the numinous when reading such works—however, this encounter occurs privately in the reader's imagination. Translating such literature into the language of the stage allows for this to be a communal experience, magnifying the potential for emotional responses and/or numinous experiences to spread throughout the crowd.

Adapters are often drawn to a challenge they believe can be best explored through their home medium; theatre artists, for instance, might be attracted to a source upon which the embodiment of live performance can shed new light. In literature, events that resist logical explanation provide fertile ground for encounters with the numinous; in turn, these numinous events are fecund sources to adapt into the medium of theatre. That said, even when the source under consideration for stage adaptation has nothing remotely mysterious or otherworldly about it, the process of adaptation itself can nevertheless evoke the numinous.

There is something within that very process that invites the recognition of that which is awe-inspiring or numinous. More to the point, especially when the adaptation is a single source written by a single author, the regard of the adapter (and director) for the source/author is frequently admiring, even reverential. By speaking the author's words repetitively in rehearsal and ultimately in performance, there is a kind of conjuring that occurs—of what? Of the spirit of the piece, perhaps, or even of the presence of the author, who is usually no longer alive.[30]

In turn, the nature of adaptation—insofar as it is "repetition without replication," or the presentation of something that is not the original, but also not-not the original—is itself uncanny or *unheimlich*. In saying so I do not mean to embrace Sigmund Freud's overarching psychoanalytic theory so much as capture what he has said about fiction in his 1919 essay on the uncanny. Namely, I am interested in the paradox that "*in the first place a great deal that is not uncanny in fiction would be so if it happened in real life; and in the second place that there are many more means of creating uncanny effects in fiction than there are in real life.*"[31] Although Freud does not specify theatre in this explanation, it is not difficult to make the leap from reality to theatre, insofar as both are embodied and live(d) experiences.[32] The doubling inherent in adaptation, a doubling that is never entirely exact, recalls Freud's observation that "the 'uncanny' is that class of the terrifying which leads back to something long known to us, once very familiar."[33] Because the work of adapturgy includes the task of helping assure that spectators have some grounding in the source, triggering that potentially shared familiarity, it enables uncanny recognitions to occur. While (we certainly hope that) not all theatre experiences need be "terrifying" in order to be memorable (especially as adaptations), most performances have some element of surprise or intensity; certainly this is true of the case studies considered in this book.

In suggesting that the numinous and uncanny are part of the stage adaptation experience and process, I build on observations that scholars and practitioners have already made, especially when speaking about the essence, energy, spirit, or soul of a piece. Karin Coonrod, whose adaptation of Flannery O'Connor's short stories will be discussed in chapter 8, is representative of this trend. In a short documentary about her adaptation-oriented company Colombari made in 2011, company member Michael Potts is asked to discuss Coonrod's approach to adaptation. His response, that "it always is about speaking to the human soul,"[34] is echoed by other adapters, especially those who work with theatre. When we adapt (or practice adapturgy), we seek to conjure the spirit of the original, to share that experience of communing with the source and/or its author—which is frequently numinous and/or uncanny—with the audience.

As a result, the experience of watching an adaptation unfold in live performance can be immensely pleasurable, especially when spectators glimpse something onstage that reminds them of other iterations of the story. The potential to enjoy adaptation exponentially grows when spectators have the tools to make sense of the theatrical language used in the production to signal these other versions of the tale (including the source); when they can decode these different layers of meaning, their experience becomes that much richer. One way of understanding these multiple layers is to consider them a palimpsest, as will be explored in the next chapter.

PART TWO
THEORIZING PRACTICE

4. PALIMPSESTUOUS PLEASURES

In 2006, when Linda Hutcheon cited Scottish poet and literary critic Michael Alexander and his use of the word *palimpsestuous,* the term was so evocative that several other scholars working in adaptation studies (mostly in film) referenced it in their own gloss of adaptation theory.[1] As Hutcheon acknowledges soon after introducing the term, what Alexander calls palimpsestuous the French literary critic "Gérard Genette would call a text in the 'second degree.'"[2] As one might expect, these types of text are "derived from another preexistent text," a relationship that Genette calls "hypertextuality."[3] Written in 1982, Genette's influential book *Palimpsests* does not discuss adaptation per se, and of course predates the widespread use of the Internet, making his use of "hypertextuality" quite different from how it might resonate today. Thus Hutcheon spends little time on Genette's theories, instead introducing the phrase "palimpsestuous pleasures" to capture the distinct enjoyment that spectators experience when viewing an adaptation. Such pleasures are particularly evident when the audience members are familiar with the source on which the adaptation is based, because they recognize the references throughout, a feeling that may extend to considering themselves a type of "insider" to the process of the adapted medium's creation.

A palimpsest is an object, often made of parchment, paper, or similar fiber that has multiple layers of "text" written on it. The text in question is usually assumed to be writing (words), but it may also be images or hieroglyphics, or any kind of symbol; the term palimpsest does not suggest the type of message in any way, but rather the material on which it is inscribed. In the ancient world, when paper was rare and expensive, writers (artists) would recycle paper that had been previously written on, covering what existed with what they created. Inevitably, the coverage was incomplete—they could not entirely erase what had been previously inscribed on the paper—and the resulting material, with layers of writing (or images, etc.) was called a palimpsest. The reader (or beholder) would therefore read (or take in) both the current creation on the top layer and the remains of what had existed before. Sometimes these layers ran deep, and the effect of taking in a palimpsest might include fragments of creation dating from preceding generations.

In considering the palimpsest, there is a kind of nostalgia evoked—a desire to recover or recapture the feeling of the past. Contemporary examples of a palimpsest might include (for those of us old enough to remember such things) the practice of posting over previous advertisements for music or performance shows—using paste or glue to attach the new poster to a wall or signpost in (usually urban) areas heavily trafficked by pedestrians. More often than not, the mounting of one poster on top of another did not result in perfect coverage, with a corner of the previous flyer peeking through; or passersby might rip off the poster incompletely, revealing part of what was there before.

The word *palimpsestuous*, though, resonates on a different level of desire. Sounding like *incestuous*, it suggests the taboo, the forbidden. The pleasures signified by this word are unspeakable, even ruinous. Here the focus shifts to what is hidden below the layers rather than peeking out from beneath. Here too the entanglement of family dynamics complicates and troubles the nostalgia, in ways that prove productive when considering the depiction of family favored by William Faulkner.

Peeling Back the Palimpsests: Layers All the Way Down

Michael Alexander first used the term *palimpsestuous* in his discussion of Ezra Pound's modernist epic *The Cantos,* and for those students of *The Cantos* who recognize just how deep the rabbit hole goes for Pound, this was an apt term indeed.[4] As Alexander emphasizes, "It becomes clear that Pound has a faculty for what might be called palimpsestuous-ness, the literary romance of the past carried to new depths of verbal resonance."[5] This "literary romance of the past" itself strikes me as dramaturgical, since much production dramaturgy preparation involves "going long" with historical research.[6] The fruits of this research are typically shared with the director and/or creative team and ultimately the audience with the enthusiasm and gusto of discovery, hopefully with some measure of "verbal resonance." While Alexander's description has its limits (the subject of this palimpsest is literary, not sociological or cultural or scientific, for instance), the quality he describes rings true for dramaturgs, especially when working on adaptations.

Significantly, when Hutcheon references Alexander's neologism, she does so via the work of Elizabeth Deeds Ermath, a cultural theorist who applies the term to a reassessment of agency within postmodern identity.

> Identity is not something essential and atomic, like the vestigial "soul" of early modernity; identity is sequence and palimpsest. Its singularity exists in the unique and unrepeatable sequence of a life, but not in some essential "subject." Its palimpsestuousness derives from the multiplied discursive condition in which each moment involves a complex subjective specification of multiple codes.[7]

Here, the palimpsest is a metaphor for a larger political question about how such a multivalent understanding of agency might revolutionize and revitalize democracy. Citing Václav Havel in her conclusion, Ermath argues that the end game of politics that understand individuals as Cartesian subjects is totalitarianism, "and these [agendas] might include those of either the Religious Right or the Dogmatic Left."[8] No less urgent than Alexander's description of Ezra Pound's remarkable facility with literary history, Ermath's use of *palimpsestuous* speaks to the human yearning for the texture and complexity of a palimpsest's layers as they might speak to a postmodern, politicized sense of self.

Given these two strikingly different examples of how the concept of a palimpsest might be used to unpack literature and articulate political theory, it is intriguing that the word has subsequently become such a touchstone for both adaptation studies and theatre criticism. What is it about the palimpsest that connects such disparate fields of inquiry? Surely part of the appeal stems from the fact that a palimpsest is both one and several objects. It can be read simultaneously or sequentially—that is, (to an extent) one can isolate layers for consideration, or take in the entirety of the palimpsest at once. In addition, it is unlikely that any two people will read a palimpsest exactly the same way. Unlike performance, it is not ephemeral, although it is not exactly reproducible or mass producible, so it has some qualities in common with performance. When considering the palimpsest, the emphasis is on *reception*, since it can have such different resonances for different readers (or spectators).

Reception is central to how Hutcheon uses the palimpsest as it pertains to adaptation. She extends the metaphor to include pleasure, which adaptation spectators (and certainly dramaturgs) take in the discovery of each layer as it reveals itself to them. Much has been written about pleasure and theatre, but considerations of the pleasure of dramaturgy are notably less frequent.[9] Perhaps this is due to the persistent stereotype of dramaturg as "the smart kid in class"—that we are (or should be) the studious ones, spending our free time in the library with our noses in books.[10] "If dramaturgy is to serve the theater," Geoff Proehl contends, "and if pleasures—simple and complex—play a central role in theater's effectiveness, then dramaturgy might well be guided by whether or not it produces parallel pleasures for its participants: dramaturgs themselves, but also directors, designers, actors, and audiences."[11] For the adaptation dramaturg, much of this pleasure comes from the cartography of the palimpsest so that it might be more easily navigated by the creative team and understood (and likewise enjoyed) by the spectators.

As Simone Murray asserts, however, this pleasure exists within a larger adaptation industry that thrives on the consumption of byproducts of palimpsests as adaptations. The proliferation of Harry Potter-themed items and activities exemplifies this market for adaptation consumers, as does the expanse of "fanfiction" responses to Potter's world, among (many) others.[12] Once we begin to consider the wider impact of adaptation, as others have discussed, media like video games, theme parks, and cosplay (to name but a few) enter the conversation. The role of dramaturgy in these other media, while certainly intriguing, is beyond the scope of this present study.[13]

Within theatre and performance studies, the word *palimpsestuous* serves Karen Jürs-Munby in her introduction to the English translation of Hans-Thies Lehmann's groundbreaking *Postdramatic Theatre*. Jürs-Munby claims, in her cataloging of the theatre companies that owe a debt to the Wooster Group (and Elizabeth LeCompte), that their work features a "palimpsestuous intertextuality and intratextuality [that] are a significant quality of much postdramatic theatre."[14] Among other qualities, the key distinguishing factor about the postdramatic is the focus on elements other than the script or drama; thus, often the type of text that is layered in such performances is necessarily adapted into the medium of theatre (from literature, from film, from poetry, and so on), although the overall performance itself may not be (called) an adaptation, exactly.

One of the best-known examples of adaptation-savvy theatre companies stemming from the Wooster/LeCompte tradition is, of course, Elevator Repair Service (ERS). John Collins, the artistic director of the company, once designed the sound for the Wooster Group, working closely with Liz LeCompte. He credits that experience as having greatly influenced his own development as an artist, stating in 1999, "In college I was influenced a lot by going to Wooster Group shows, and I probably unconsciously imitated them. Now I have a completely different relationship with them, since I've been working for them for five years."[15] Part of the "downtown scene" in the 1990s, ERS performances are known for their awkward affect, as well as their distinct choreography, especially evident in their earlier works. With a movement vocabulary that includes everyday gestures and an emphasis on extremities (hands, head, feet), their choreographic style has been linked to Judson Dance Theater and the innovations of Yvonne Rainer.[16] One of the earliest members of the collective, Katherine Profeta, is listed as a movement dramaturg on their website and in programs, although after discussing this with several of the members, I would clarify that dramaturgical research for their work is done collaboratively among all members of the team, including the designers and actors.

ERS is perhaps best known for their production of *Gatz,* featuring a verbatim performance of F. Scott Fitzgerald's *The Great Gatsby* set in a drab, vaguely contemporary office space. Given that every word of the novel is part of the performance, this work challenges how we think about adaptation with regard to the tendency to otherwise compress the duration and scope of literature for the stage. As they describe the show on their website, "*Gatz* is by far ERS's most ambitious endeavor yet—not a retelling of the Gatsby story but an enactment of the novel itself."[17] Two other works can be considered part of this "trilogy of literary adaptations" within their oeuvre: *The Select* (*The Sun Also Rises*), based on Ernest Hemingway's *The Sun Also Rises* (1926) and *The Sound and the Fury,* an adaptation of the first chapter of William Faulkner's fourth novel, published in 1929.[18]

Having earned international acclaim for the adaptation phase of work (2004–2011), in their early days ERS used even more of a collage approach that could be interpreted as palimpsestuous, combining inspiration from videos of odd movement patterns with classic texts and accidental sounds or gestures and affects that became solidified as part of the piece. Generally speaking, their repertoire is created collectively, in a manner similar to devising, although there are some unique qualities that differ from most devised approaches. Chief among those is the primary influence of the sound designer, who attends and contributes to all rehearsals, including those that occur before the company knows what it will perform.[19]

This audio focus stems from Collins's history as a sound designer, including the early phase of ERS when he codirected with Steve Bodow while simultaneously creating the soundscape for performances. Whereas a traditional theatre production calendar might integrate sound during "tech week," or shortly before, for ERS sound is a building block of the dramaturgical creative process. Integrating sound into our understanding of the kind of "text" that can make up the palimpsest of adapturgy accomplishes (at least) two goals: (1) it opens the word "text" productively, encouraging the consideration of modalities other than words, dialogue, and drama; and (2) it allows us to likewise expand the understanding of dramaturgical work to include sound, which in turn might inspire dramaturgs to consider other modalities such as touch, smell, and three-dimensional visual installations.

In the summer of 2015, ERS was invited to remount *The Sound and the Fury* for the Public Theatre, a few of the rehearsals for which I had the privilege to observe. *The Sound and the Fury,* as performed by ERS, is memorable for the innovative way that the company clarifies the multiple moments in history that are jumbled throughout the narrator's mind. The text is verbatim from the first chapter of Faulkner's signature novel, a chapter that is widely considered "impenetrable" by most readers, since it is written from the perspective of Benjy, the youngest son of the Compson family. "Mute and mentally handicapped, Benjy cannot distinguish between past and present."[20] Upon deciphering the nearly three decades of Benjy's flashbacks, the cast decided to help the audience recognize distinct periods of time by having different actors play certain characters when they occur in the narrative. This dramaturgical research process was taken on collectively by the entire company, but serendipitously and significantly facilitated by an extensive website hosted and edited by the University of Saskatchewan that had detailed the memory shifts with hypertext.[21] In fact, during my interviews with company members, whenever I asked for examples of dramaturgy they conducted, the actors, including Collins himself, referred to the website and their gratitude for it. The ERS program for the 2015 remount of *The Sound and the Fury* states, "The company relied heavily on a hypertext version of the novel for help with decoding the chronology of the story." There is no mention in the program, however, of dramaturgy as such.

The hypertext edition of Faulkner's novel, created by a team of scholars under the leadership of Peter Stoicheff, is an astounding resource in both breadth and depth. It uses color-coding to make the changes in time clearer for the reader, a technique that Faulkner apparently wanted to use in the first

Fig. 4.1. Adapturgy in Elevator Repair Service's *The Sound and the Fury* at the Public Theater, May 2015. Actors, *left to right*: Greig Sargeant, Ben Williams, Susie Sokol, Lucy Taylor, and Daphne Gaines. *Photo copyright © Paula Court.*

chapter, but "he was told publishing was not advanced enough to accomplish [multicolor printing of text]."[22] Faulkner's compromise was to use italics to indicate a shift of time, but since there are so many different moments jumbled in Benjy's flashbacks, italics are not nearly as helpful as having the text color-coded. Using hyperlinks, one can navigate between the regular text and the colored text, allowing readers to study the narrative for clues as well as check their interpretation against the colored text. In addition, the Benjy chapter (as it is frequently called) is available in two formats on the University of Saskatchewan site: as originally written by Faulkner; and rearranged in chronological order, giving readers (and adaptation dramaturgs) further flexibility in their mode of reception.

For readers who crave more visualization tools, the website also includes nine "visual displays," including a map of the Compson property and other charts and graphs to further explain the complicated mélange of memory that characterizes the novel. One graph goes line by line through the text, charting the nineteen different events (between 1900 and 1929) that Benjy relives, so that readers can get a birds-eye view of this troubled young man's vivid cognitive process. Such insight into "the patterns of association between events and the frequency of those events" allows readers (and performers) to better understand "Benjy's psyche."[23] There are also two illustrations of how Faulkner uses time in the novel, one that graphs the chronological and narrative time two-dimensionally, on an axis, and another that displays the relationship of these two types of time to the proportion of memories and flashbacks within the novel three-dimensionally.

Rounding out the typical inclusions of a bibliography and external links, the website features nine different "intertexts" to which Faulkner alludes throughout *The Sound and the Fury*, ranging from biblical references to Sir Walter Scott and William Wordsworth. From an adapturgical point of view, these intertextual resources are especially useful tools for both research and communication (with the creative team as well as the audience), as they simplify the process of linking the novel with its sources, a process that could be replicated for the stage-adaptation text itself.

One might argue that the Internet itself, with its variable reception that can be accessed in different sequences and somewhat (with multiple windows) simultaneously, is a digital version of the palimpsest. But with Stoicheff's hypertextual website, the effect of palimpsestuousness is magnified, because *The Sound and the Fury* is already palimpsestuous. Because he is unable to separate then from now, Benjy embodies the extreme version of the postmodern identity that Ermath describes: his is the epitome of "the multiplied discursive condition in which each moment involves a complex subjective specification of multiple codes." More to the point, Faulkner's great experiment in this novel is with time and point of view, and as such each chapter captures how different members of the family recall the same events distinctly. As Jean-Paul Sartre put it, "As soon as we begin to look at any episode, it opens up to reveal behind it other episodes, all the other episodes."[24] This palimpsestuousness is evident not just in the fictional world of the Compson family, but also in Faulkner's intertextuality.

Like Ezra Pound, Faulkner also calls upon a myriad of sources with mythic and religious connotations.[25] The title itself refers to Shakespeare's Macbeth and his soliloquy in Act V, "To-morrow and to-morrow and to-morrow," which ends with the lines, "Told by an idiot, full of sound and fury, / Signifying nothing."[26] The failure of a single sign (or tale) to mean anything once again calls to mind Ermath's postmodern self, and reinforces the necessity of a multilayered palimpsestuous approach to signification.

Palimpsestuous Performance: *The Sound and the Fury* on Stage

What the Stoicheff hypertext website heightens digitally, Elevator Repair Service amplifies in performance. One of the ways that members of ERS describe the company's modus operandi is that they want to solve problems with their creative work. As Sara Jane Bailes puts it, based on her several years of observation, "In their method of collective authorship the *discoverability* of theatre, that is, its searching, processive, and deeply unstable ontology, is exploited in order to craft emphatic and complex texts that bring the present to some sort of layered and unanticipated fullness."[27] ERS is drawn, therefore, to work that appears at the outset to be unstageable or impenetrable—like the first chapter of *The Sound and the Fury*, "April Seventh, 1928." The company's solution to the problem of staging Benjy's jumbled memory, as previously mentioned, was to transform the idea of different colors for the chronological changes into different actors to play those characters at different times in Benjy's life. Thus, everyone in the cast except Susie Sokol, a founding company member who plays Benjy for most of the performance, plays multiple roles and/or years. That is, some actors play the same character in different years (such as Tory Vazquez, who exclusively plays the Compson daughter Caddy, but represents her in six different years of Benjy's memory).[28] Other actors, perhaps most memorably Vin Knight, play multiple characters—for example, Knight embodies seven different characters, three of which he also represents in two different years of memory. The frenetic effect of these frequent changes, which mostly occur onstage, is madcap comedy, and at first only reinforces the confusing nature of Faulkner's palimpsestuous text.

However, the frenzy of stimulation this creates accomplishes its goal: to represent the events "exactly as Benjy remembers them."[29] At several points, Sokol (Benjy) puts her hands over her ears to attempt to stop the flashbacks, the cacophony. To exacerbate the frustration Benjy experiences, he is mute—he cannot contribute to or otherwise alter the ongoing conversation with words; instead, he relies on unintelligible sounds and furious movement, like that of a toddler pitching a fit. The duration of the performance—lasting nearly three hours—both supports Faulkner's focus on time throughout the novel and allows the layers of the performed palimpsest to rise to the surface for brief glimpses. In an interview during the rehearsal period for this remount, Vin Knight suggested that the best way to experience an ERS performance is to "let it wash over you," and not to try to make sense of everything with my mind.[30] He was right—the palimpsestuous pleasure of the company's dramaturgically complex work is best experienced without the expectation of linear or obvious logic. It is like experiencing performance in a foreign country where we might know key phrases and words but can't speak the language; we can still understand the gist of what's happening, but we have to use a different mode of reception, and sometimes that allows us to experience aspects we might have missed if we did know the language.

As previously discussed, this focus on elements other than language (or the script) is the hallmark of the postdramatic theatre as theorized by Lehmann, but it also allows us to reframe the word palimpsest for stage adaptation, especially from the perspective of a dramaturg. Because theatre engages the senses and brings words on the page into live action, the stage palimpsest will necessarily be more image and sound based (with some productions also including smell, taste, and touch). Like the material palimpsest, the performed palimpsest can be experienced both sequentially and simultaneously, but the sequence is usually predetermined for spectators of theatre.[31] If we consider Elevator Repair Service's adaptation of *The Sound and the Fury* as our example, focusing on the opportunities for palimpsestuous pleasure within the company's dramaturgical praxis, we can zero in on three key elements of their adapturgy: (1) the embodiment of the text; (2) the rehearsal methodology; and (3) the ephemera of the production.

Embodiment of the Text

One of the distinguishing characteristics of the ERS approach to performance is the company's choreography, which includes everyday gestures as well as "found object" dance moves that are ultimately set by Katherine Profeta, their "movement dramaturg." As many theatre artists do, one of the first things ERS members do after reading a text is "get it on its feet," or experiment with movement. In the case of *The Sound and the Fury,* the first step taken by the company was to read the text of the first chapter aloud, to experience the aural sensation of Faulkner's language. It was when they read the chapter aloud that Collins first heard the rhythm and musicality of the novel, leading the company to embrace the centrality of sound to how they would unlock the mysteries of Benjy's chapter. According to Collins,

> The first important sound that we heard was the sound of [the first chapter] being read aloud. That was when we decided to do it, was when we heard the actors reading it. That's when I heard the humor in it, and I—and it sort of lifted off the page then . . . that's when I understood it in a different way. . . . [and when I knew] that sound was going to be the key to unlock it.[32]

Soon thereafter, Ben Williams discovered a PBS documentary, *The Dancing Outlaw,* that he brought to the company. This 1991 film follows a West

Virginia flatfoot dancer, Jesco White, whose father was "this kind of legendary flat foot dancer who was shot down by his neighbor."[33] Within that PBS movie, Williams continues, there was

> archival footage [of D. Ray White, Jesco's father] . . . from a Smithsonian documentary from back in the '80s and that's the really fascinating stuff. This lanky skinny guy who would just like dance on a piece of plywood out in the yard, you know, like do anything—it was just something simple and fascinating about the way he moves. So, that stuck.[34]

With keen dramaturgical instincts, Williams tracked down the Smithsonian film (*Talking Feet*), which ultimately became the basis for many sounds and movements within the production.

Before detailing the connections between these found objects (films) and ERS's embodied text, it is already apparent how palimpsestuous the company's adapturgy is. Williams's research process resembles the peeling away of layers from a palimpsest, albeit from video, a medium wholly unlike paper or written words. He finds archival footage in one documentary, which leads him to the documentary *Talking Feet,* and ultimately it is this 1984 dance ethnography film that informs their sound and movement the most—"I would say like 90% of the choreography from the entire show comes from that documentary."[35] In addition, much of the music ERS incorporated into *The Sound and the Fury* stemmed from *Talking Feet,* according to Williams. There are recognizable banjo sequences from D. Ray White's section of the film, and the sound effect of tapping feet that accompanies Benjy whenever he runs is also pulled from this source. The sound effect of laughter throughout *The Sound and the Fury* is that of Stanley Hicks, a North Carolina storyteller who is also featured in *Talking Feet.*[36]

To create the main dance that gets repeated in the show, Williams worked with company member Mike Iveson to mimic parts of D. Ray White's flatfoot dancing, combining it with "hand gestures [another person's] mother is using when she's telling a story," and other marginal movement occurring throughout the documentaries.[37] The foot-focused, percussive dancing that White performs is fast and complicated, especially for performers who are not trained tap dancers. But ERS is not interested in perfecting White's choreography—they seek out found objects, "identify the things that [they] can do, and all the things that would be interesting to do" instead.[38] Once they had found a sequence of movement that Collins found intriguing, they invited

Katherine Profeta in, so that she could help them sharpen and fix the dance. With her assistance, they solidified a memorable, gawky dance sequence to be performed by Iveson and Williams, with other members of the company joining for selected parts of the movement later in the performance.

The awkwardness that characterizes much of ERS's movement vocabulary and performance style has been discussed at length by Sara Jane Bailes, who draws productive connections between their choreography and that of Yvonne Rainer and the Judson Dance Theater. As she recognizes, "Sources are rigorously 'treated,' brought into collision in the group's skillful dramaturgy in innovative ways and with often hilarious consequences."[39] This "treatment" of what Collins calls "found objects," such as the video mentioned above, or Faulkner's text itself, involves an adapturgy that is especially cognizant of sound and movement. In Collins's words, "I mean, my medium is language, but it's the language of *theatre*. So it's the language of movement, it's the language of sound, it's the language of all of those things being coordinated together in time."[40] Although Collins mentions these two elements of theatrical language in the same breath, they are not always developed or added at the same time. Following their approach with the movement, sound elements are also treated as found objects, brought to the table—or, in the case of *The Sound and the Fury,* added just before their first audience sees the working "draft" of the performance.

Fig. 4.2. Dance in Elevator Repair Service's *The Sound and the Fury* at the Public Theater, May 2015. Actors, *left to right*: Lucy Taylor, Daphne Gaines, Susie Sokol, Randolph Curtis Rand, Vin Knight, Greig Sargeant, Aaron Landsman, Ben Williams, and Mike Iveson. *Photo copyright © Paula Court.*

The first public showing of *The Sound and the Fury* was only about forty minutes long and presented as a work in progress in 2008 at the New York Theatre Workshop. Shortly before going public, sound designer Matt Tierney offered ERS several tracks of sound and Collins "ran them during the show," quickly realizing that these sounds "*really* transformed things, right away." For the first time, Collins admits, "our approach started to make sense to me . . . it gave it a kind of smoother texture . . . [and] helped sew everything together."[41] Knowing that the sound would continue to inform the performance so crucially, Tierney began to solidify his design. Ultimately, "he created different aural signatures for each of the different episodes" for the production, using the different signature sounds to "mark all the changes" in time and memory as experienced by Benjy. For example, during the cemetery visit scenes (in 1912), there is a track the company referred to as "funeral music" that was somber and vaguely religious, with church organ tones, but for more chaotic scenes "this crazy banjo music comes in" to underscore the hyper-charged energy of those moments from Benjy's perspective.[42]

Importantly, both the movement sequences and the sounds are strategically repeated in *The Sound and the Fury.* While there is plenty of repetition throughout Benjy's chapter (indeed, part of what challenges readers is the nonlinear and seemingly random way Faulkner bounces between the nineteen different episodes he recalls), in the pattern of repetitive embodiment choices made by ERS we can most clearly see their adapturgy. Unlike many adaptations, where the decisions are more text-based, such as eliminating narrative markers like "he said" or compressing the length by cutting sections, ERS approaches adapting by embracing the challenge of the text "exactly as it was written."[43] The company seeks out problems to be solved, using the tools of live performance to grapple with and attempt to solve those puzzles.[44] "We didn't want to make an adaptation that sort of told the same story but shied away from [Faulkner's] incredibly complicated *way* of telling the story," Collins explains. "We were actually most interested in the incredibly complicated way."[45] Not only is their attraction to conundrum a recognizable trait of dramaturgy, but it also is fueled by the *pleasure* they take in embracing (rather than smoothing over) thorny, dense sources to adapt.

The Rehearsal Methodology

The ERS rehearsal methodology sheds more light on how they merge the joy of discovery with the rigor of precision. As mentioned, the dramaturgical research is done collectively, by the cast and creative team. For these early discussions, the creative team for ERS includes the director and the sound designer, but not the costume, set, or lighting designers. As Williams shared, "The sound designer has to be there. For every rehearsal. In the room . . . before we even know what the show *is.* We're just sitting there talking about the show, what we're interested in."[46] While this is unusual, it is not surprising, given Collins's emphasis on and background in sound design. As discussed above, this sound focus has a direct impact on the type of found objects the company collects, and how they embody the text.

The space in which the company performs also informs the adapturgy, quite literally. One of the problems that Collins prefers to embrace is the tendency of literature to have multiple locations, without succumbing to the solution of representing those locales individually. He explains, "I'm more interested in just watching the problem play out by having a singular setting. . . . We did that with all of our novel adaptations." Part of this single set tendency stems from Collins's practice of replicating the rehearsal space in production; *Gatz* was set in an office "just because [they] were in an office" when rehearsing. Similarly, the set for *The Sound and the Fury* reflects the early work ERS did in "a little theatre on 4th street that's in New York Theatre Workshop."[47] The set pieces that happened to be left in that space when they began rehearsing there are replicated in the original production as well as the remount, except for what Collins jokingly called the "grouch," a couch that had grass on it. (As a compromise, they used a green couch.)

This desire to replicate the experience extends to blocking and was especially evident when I attended two rehearsals a few weeks before they opened at the Public. For this remount, ERS hired four actors who were not in the original production.[48] These performers had the challenge of learning this complicated chapter and its hectic character changes in a fraction of the time the first cast used to create it. The typical ERS rehearsal period (for the trilogy of adaptations) was a year and a half to two years, although Collins "very deliberately" sequenced these rehearsals, working approximately six weeks intensely, then taking time off. These intervals away from the project were crucial, allowing the company members time to "absorb and see [the adaptation] from a different perspective."[49] To assist the cast, particularly the newcomers, in (re)acquainting themselves with the performance, Collins used a video recording as a reference point throughout the first rehearsal that I observed. The attention to detail was meticulous, on the part of both the performers and Collins, and the goal was to duplicate the movement exactly as it was before.

This precision of performance is a hallmark of Collins's directing style; his desire to keep everything—from the movement to the props and furniture to (especially) the sound—exactly as ERS has set it in initial rehearsals stems from an attention to detail his performers have come to expect. Unlike some directors, "John doesn't know how to say, 'just do this for now,'" and fix it later.[50] He demands precision. Given the interlocking nature of the actor/character changes throughout *The Sound and the Fury*, such perfectionism is necessary. Their embodied text, set through detail-oriented rehearsals, is a bit like a house of cards: to disrupt one aspect of the structure risks it collapsing in on itself.

One of the delicate balances that the company managed to strike was the way that they expanded their initial ensemble of about seven performers to twelve (plus two understudies/stand-ins). Part of this growth was due to the fact that the initial work in progress of *The Sound and the Fury* that was performed as *Hand Panic* in 2006–2007 was built primarily around the dance routine, and thus its smaller ensemble was ill equipped to handle the multiple character changes, once that approach was added to the piece. But more crucially, ERS wanted to represent Faulkner's fictional Yoknapatawpha County more accurately in terms of race.[51] Among the five artists who joined the production, three were actors of color: Kaneza Schaal, Greig Sargeant, and April Matthis. In addition to having more truthful racial representation, having African American actors also helped the company tell the story through the embodied text adapturgy they had developed. "It was important that the image of the actor changed, to help us see that we were moving to a very different place in time," Collins explained. Instead of aligning the characters' races to that of the actors, he "embraced the problem of exaggerating that rather than smoothing it over." This amplification took place with both types of visible difference within his cast—in Collins's words, "We don't even tether [the actors] to their own race or gender. And that was partly a way of again taking something that was present in the book and running with it. Like Benjy doesn't really identify characters by race."[52] Thus, at several points in the performance there is a collision between the character and the actor. For example, Sargeant plays Mother, crossing both race and gender expectations as a black male portraying a white matriarch. Williams plays Luster, one of Benjy's black caretakers, and this clash is made more evident by the dialect Faulkner uses to distinguish the manner of speaking between the Compsons and their live-in housekeepers, the Gibsons.

When Matthis, who played several of the Gibson characters, was unable to join the ensemble for the remount at the Public, Collins knew it was necessary to replace her with an actress of color (Daphne Gaines). "Because we had very carefully calibrated the way the characters would switch and the different races they would play, and that—that's a delicate subject."[53] This calibration, in other words, was a vital part of the ensemble's adapturgy, an approach that made the palimpsest of the performance that much more visible, especially in the moments when the casting was noticeably, even uncomfortably in conflict with the role as Faulkner had written it.[54] To help spectators keep track of these potentially uncomfortable or confusing changes, ERS added several layers of ephemera to the production.

The Ephemera of Production

By ephemera, I am referring to both the notes and inserts included in the program for the Public remount of *The Sound and the Fury*.[55] Frequently, when theatre programs contain notes, they are written by the dramaturg (or director), but for the 2015 production, the section titled "Program Notes" contains three different quotations that are meant to function dramaturgically. The first two quotations are from Faulkner himself, and the final one is the aforementioned soliloquy spoken by Macbeth ("To-morrow, and to-morrow, and to-morrow"), that ends with the sentence "It is a tale / Told by an idiot, full of sound and fury / Signifying nothing." This Shakespeare reference helps locate the title of the novel as well as the adaptation, particularly when read alongside—that is, palimpsestuously—the two Faulkner excerpts.

In the first excerpt, taken from an interview where he is asked to explain how he wrote the complicated first chapter, Faulkner shares that he began with the scene ("a story without plot") of children who were unknowing witnesses to their grandmother's funeral.

> And then the idea struck me to see how much more I could have got out of the idea of the blind, self-centeredness of innocence, typified by children if one of those children had been truly innocent, that is, an idiot. . . . I wrote that same story four times. None of them were right, but I had anguished so much that I could not throw any of it away and start over, so I printed [the novel] in the four sections.

This admission that Faulkner never felt he was able to capture the story he wanted to tell and that the effort behind the writing was full of such angst is surprising and memorable, particularly when coupled with the next quotation. Taken from an explanatory introduction he wrote about the novel in 1972 for the *Southern Review,* in this excerpt Faulkner claims that "I wrote this book and learned to read." He elaborates, boasting that upon finishing it, "I discovered that there is actually something to which the shabby term Art not only can, but must, be applied." Every other novel or newspaper story he had read, he never fully took in, Faulkner confesses.

> After *The Sound and the Fury* and without heeding to open another book and in a series of delayed repercussions like summer thunder, I discovered the Flauberts and Dostoievskys and Conrads whose books I had read ten years ago. With *The Sound and the Fury* I learned to read and quit reading, since I have read nothing since. Nor do I seem to have learned anything since.

Read together, these statements reflect not only Faulkner and his musings about the art and struggle of writing—they reflect the philosophy and methodology of ERS. In what was a perceived failure (the four sections or attempts to tell the one story of the Compsons), Faulkner reached the apex of comprehension. Through embracing the problem, he learned more than if he had sidestepped it. By including these excerpts, even (one might argue, especially) without explanation, ERS encourages spectators to make their own connections between the layers they have presented.

There is one further piece of ephemera to consider, however. The ERS program included an invitation to patrons to become donors. This in itself is commonplace—soliciting donations is a necessary part of creating art in the United States. But when the glossy, full-color flyer is unfolded, it reveals a poster with Susie as Benjy (mid yowl) in the center, with her body "composed of hundreds of pictures taken of ERS in rehearsal, on tour and on stage over the last 10 years." This mosaic is, as stated on the outside of the poster, "an appropriately chaotic and joyful visual representation of how our shows are the sum of our experiences together as an ensemble." Indeed, what is a mosaic but a different approach to a palimpsest? Instead of words, mosaics use images or colors, but, as is true of palimpsests, the joy taken in beholding them is in seeing both the parts (or layers) and the whole, and appreciating how they work together.

This appreciation is at the heart of Hutcheon's concept of palimpsestuous pleasure, and has the potential to occur with all adaptations. For stage adaptations, dramaturgs (or a dramaturgically savvy ensemble) can increase the possibility of that pleasure in the palimpsest being shared by both the creative team and the audience. For ERS, the decision to emphasize the palimpsestuousness of adaptation is engrained in their praxis. As Collins put it, "We try to bring some kind of clarity through layering on rather than by simplifying." They do so because they want to honor "the soul of the book," a concept that will be explored in further detail in the next chapter as well as in chapter 7.[56]

5. HOW TO DO THINGS WITH BIRDS

Perhaps the most recognizable scene in the 2014 film *Birdman or (The Unexpected Virtue of Ignorance)* is the one that marks the height of Michael Keaton's character Riggan's humiliation—he gets locked out of the theatre in his underwear and has to reenter the space through the front doors, down the aisle of the house. This scene takes place a little over midway through the film, during the last preview of his Broadway performance, just after "things are finally going well."[1] It begins with his witnessing his daughter Sam (Emma Stone) in the wings making out with his costar Mike (Edward Norton). He asks a stagehand for a cigarette and heads for the stage door. There is a large lock on the door, located just above his head; he reaches up to unlatch it, steps outside into the rainy alley, and the door shuts behind him, catching the corner of his terry robe inside. Banging on the door fruitlessly, he then attempts to pull his robe out, also to no avail, leaving him no choice but to leave the robe in the doorjamb and proceed into the alley in his underwear and moccasins, his character wig in hand. In this pivotal moment, which turns on Keaton's stage-bound journey from the wings to the load-in door, to the alley, through the cacophony of Times Square, before entering the lobby and finally the auditorium aisle, cowriter/director Alejandro G. Iñárritu reveals as much about the challenges of adaptation as he does about the viscera of theatre making itself.

Using this film about stage adaptation as a case study, this chapter discusses the risks and rewards surrounding adaptation dramaturgy. I offer a model for understanding the complexities of how dramaturgy intervenes in the transformative process of adapting a text for the stage. Although in this instance my reference to text includes film and literature, this approach can be modified for other genres of text, including visual art, music, and other non-word-based media. My analysis of this case study takes inspiration from the Roman god Janus, whose faces look ahead and behind, associating this ancient god with doorways (*januae*), archways (*jani*), and beginnings (January). A powerful guardian god within the Roman pantheon, Janus was usually the first acknowledged in any prayer or ritual. He was a gateway god who helped connect humans to other more popular and memorable gods, such as Jupiter and Apollo. The Janus effect, then, is the transformation that successful dramaturgy makes within the process and product of adaptation for the stage. Recognizing this effect helps us unfurl the multiple layers of interstitial research and creative decision-making that adaptations require, especially when crafted for live performance.

Understanding Janus

Despite his significance and power, physical evidence of Janus worship is virtually nonexistent—"no positively identified statues, or even statuettes, of the god survive."[2] Nor are there remnants of temples or altars to Janus left to examine; instead, our evidence regarding him stems almost entirely from literary sources, where "Janus is something of a fetish-figure."[3] From those sources, we can determine some common characteristics: Janus typically has two faces, although earlier depictions of him featured four; he holds keys in one hand and a staff in the other; and his shrine's gates were open when Rome was at war and closed during (the rare experience of) peacetime.[4]

Janus's bifrontality remains his most recognizable feature—indeed, it is this dual or multiple (quadrifrontal) nature that ignites much of the fetishistic imagination in literature. While on a practical level, it is believed that his two faces allowed him to see both gates in his shrine at once, he was also said to see the past and the future at the same time. In Ovid's *Fasti*, which features an extended discussion/interview with Janus, the god offers two explanations for his odd shape. The first is historical and suggests that the god was once Chaos, which Steven Green interprets etymologically, arguing that his name derives from the same root of the word *chaos*, which stems from the Greek verb "to gape" and the Latin word *hiare*).[5] Because he was once "a featureless spherical hulk" with an indistinguishable "homogenous shape, / [Janus looks] the same both coming and going."[6] It is in this section that Ovid's Janus claims to be an "ancient thing," aligning himself with Chaos, the very beginning of the world, according to Greek mythology. In this section, Ovid also conflates two prevailing systems of thought regarding the creation of the world: mythological and philosophical. On the one hand,

Chaos and Janus are both gods, and (according to Hesiod) Chaos made it possible for the gods to be born. But Janus also refers to the separation of the elements, an idea in keeping with the prevailing cosmogony during Fasti's lifetime.[7] Doing so gives him a primordial weight, but it also connects him with human philosophers—in keeping with his threshold status, Janus embraces both theogony and cosmogony.

On initial reading, Janus's second explanation for his bifrontality appears more profane than sacred: as a doorman, having two faces helps him see both the inside and outside without turning his head. Referencing Hecate/Diana of the Crossroads, Janus explains, "I too can stay put and see two things at once / without wasting time by turning my neck."[8] While light-hearted in affect (he avoids the labor of turning his neck), this description of himself as a "doorman of the heavenly hall" nevertheless solidifies his status as a liminal god, connecting the human world with that of the divine.[9] Further, by connecting himself with Hecate (sometimes translated or understood as Diana), he establishes his role in the decision-making that accompanies one's arrival at the figurative (and literal) crossroads. At the same time, by referring to himself as a doorman, Janus associates himself with an earthly man of "the lowest status, unfit for other duties," a rank clearly at odds with his previous explanation of being on par with Chaos.[10] The word *janitor* (which historically meant a keeper of doors, like a doorman) derives from Janus, further connecting these roles.

With regard to his unusual shape, then, both explanations ultimately refer back to Janus's liminal position between the sacred and the profane, but in tellingly different ways. In the first, he straddles the divide between two seemingly irreconcilable systems of thought: (poly)theology and (emerging) science. In the second, he stands between high and low statuses, adopting the stance of a lowly doorman as well as a threshold god, and using humor to explain how having two faces helps him do his job without as much effort. It is the Roman historian Macrobius who offers the most oft-cited rationale for Janus's bifrontality, however: "he is said to have had two faces because he both knew past events and foresaw the future."[11] In each of these cases, we see Janus as a liminal god—standing betwixt and between two places or categories considered incompatible.

Adaptation dramaturgy requires similar skills: to think between and among different fields of learning, to perform both mundane and creative acts, and to see the source as well as the adaptation with clarity. At the nexus of this (deeply problematic yet strangely persistent) binary between the auteur-based and writer-based approach to theatre making we find the adaptation dramaturg, who—like Janus—occupies the threshold between the source and the adapted script, between the writer and the director. Thus adapturgy calls upon the skill sets of both new play and production dramaturgy, requiring editorial assistance for the newly adapted script as well as audience preparation (e.g., program notes, lobby displays, dramaturgical websites, etc.) for the concept envisioned by the director and design team. Not only do adaptation dramaturgs embody the interstitial position of Janus, they also take on the doorkeeper functions, of providing the "keys" to unlock the content and context of both the source and the adaptation texts for the production team as well as the audience. But there are other characteristics Janus possesses that also relate to the work of the adaptation dramaturg.

Aside from his two-faced appearance, Janus is also known to carry keys in one hand and a staff in the other. While the keys are relatively self-explanatory (they support his role as doorman or janitor), it is useful to acknowledge how his keys were thought to be able to unlock the mysteries of life and death, as well as actual gates and doors. The staff he carries, and the purpose of his shrine, deserve more attention here, especially with regard to the interpretation offered by classicist Rabun Taylor in 2000. In an article titled "Watching the Skies: Janus, Auspication, and the Shrine in the Roman Forum," Taylor suggests that "Janus Quirinus, the god of the shrine, must have been involved in another aspect of divination: auspication, the observation of signs."[12] He arrives at this hypothesis after carefully studying the obscure data from the period, focusing on Janus's staff and shrine. "Among the votive objects excavated by Giacomo Boni in the vicinity of the shrine," Taylor says, "was an archaic bronze figurine holding an augur's staff, the *lituus*"; while this was not a figure of Janus, the recovery of this artifact supports the notion that augury was practiced in (or near) Janus's temple.[13]

Augury did not begin in Rome, but most definitions of the practice cite the Romans, since early Christian records of the custom originated there. A human augur was a diviner who read the patterns and sounds of birds in flight. The Latin word *auspicium* derives from *auspex*, the roots of which are *avis* (bird) and *spex* (observer), meaning one who looks at birds. Augurs used their *litui* to delineate sacred sky space. They were, as Taylor puts it, "the 'carvers' of space into realms."[14] The staff they used to carve a *templum*, or sacred space, was the *lituus*, a staff with a coil on the end, much like the crosier used by Catholic priests today. As mentioned, the remarkable absence of Janus relics (whether archeological or object-based) makes it difficult to reach solid conclusions about the god, but the few remnants that do exist (mainly coins and statues or carvings found outside of Rome) show him holding a staff in one hand. While this staff does not resemble a *lituus* (it appears instead to be a walking stick), Janus does use it like a magic wand that "has apotropaic power."[15] In addition to his staff functioning like a wand, Taylor surmises that Janus's shrine had no roof in part because of the Romans' frequent reference to the space as a *sacellum*, which Festus defined as "roofless places consecrated to gods."[16] Janus's status as a liminal god would make access to the sky expected, but if we accept the theory that he is an augur, the open air would have been even more crucial to his work.

Thus, in addition to the reading of Janus's temple as an indicator of war (or peace) based on its gates being open (or closed), following Taylor we can interpret Janus as an augur, one who interprets the patterns of birds in flight, functioning as "a good translator" and helping to establish "a two-way channel of communication, directing signs to the gods by way of prayer and signs to mortals by way of omens."[17] In keeping with the notions that augurs "carve out the sky," we might consider this ritual task somewhat akin to the research adaptation dramaturgs perform: from the seemingly endless material related to an adaptation for the stage (whether regarding the source being adapted or the approach taken by the director, or both), they "carve out" the space that will inform this particular production. Furthermore, they interpret the signs from that section of the sky, so to speak: dramaturgs summarize complicated and possibly conflicting material and offer their readings to the director and creative team. What the team decides to do with that material usually depends on the will of the director, but (like augurs) dramaturgs don't mandate behavior; rather, they interpret the signs, allowing others to do with it what they will.

With regard to Janus's affiliation with doors, it is also worth mentioning that the door itself is an *ur*-sign of space, especially in theatre design. As Arnold Aronson reminds us, "On the stage, the door is a sign of the liminal, the unknown, the potential, the terrifying, the endless."[18] The strange *potential* of the door also helps us understand Janus as he affects adaptation dramaturgy: as the god of the doorsill, Janus perches between before and after (time) as well as here and there (space). This lack of fixity—how can he be in both places/moments at once?—is both powerful and problematic. In the pantheistic Roman culture, Janus's liminality was a distinguishing characteristic that gave him a power unique among the gods. In a monotheistic

Euro-American context, however, his lack of commitment to time or space reads quite differently.

In today's culture, the fact that Janus has two faces is understood as a mark of dishonesty or hypocrisy—a "Janus-faced" individual is someone who says one thing and does another. Such critiques of duplicity are all too common in reviews of adaptations. Because adaptation relies by definition on a source upon which the adaptation is based, critics' bias has skewed to favor fidelity, which is to say accuracy (as defined by the critic) to the original author's intent (as understood by the critic). As discussed in the first chapter, it is difficult to align this fidelity model with poststructuralist ontology, yet the desire to get the source "right" persists. And what does getting it "right" mean?

In the 2014 special issue of *Theatre Journal* titled "Theatre and Adaptation," editor Joanne Tompkins cites recent critical controversy in Australia for igniting her interest in this topic. There, the perceived preference for adaptation over original writing has reignited the "deep schism between advocates of director's theatre, where the text serves the auteur's whims and ideas, and a more traditional writer's theatre, where the director and production team serve the writer's vision."[19] In so doing, adapters (along with the director) are considered to be "two-faced" by virtue of their dual allegiance to the source author (à la new play dramaturgy) and the concept guiding the director's vision (à la production dramaturgy).

This notion of Janus as a hypocrite is manifest most clearly in Ovid's *Fasti*, since we come to see him as a rapist in book 6, whereas he appears as a "wise avuncular god" in book 1.[20] In his pursuit of the virgin nymph Cranaë, Janus uses his other face to capture her when she attempts to escape, and after raping her he gifts her a whitethorn wand for protection.[21] As we have seen, Janus's shrine is associated with both war and peace, yet in *Fasti* he claims "*nil mihi cum bello*" ("I have nothing to do with war," 1.253). There is also disagreement about the nature of the faces themselves—some say they represented youth and age, others suggest a male and female face, while some suggest that there were four faces, one for each of the cardinal directions.

Overall, this association of duplicity with dishonesty, along with the remarkable obscurity of evidence related to and leading to conflicting definitions of Janus, rounds out the negative and problematic associations with the god. These, combined with the positive and powerful qualities of interdisciplinary liminality and the ability to "carve out" the research space in order to interpret the signs, form the basis of my association of Janus with adaptation dramaturgy. That we might also consider Janus a divine augur, or bird-watcher, becomes especially relevant when turning to my case study.

The Unexpected Virtue of Augury

We can see this Janus-like role play out in intriguing ways in Iñárritu's 2014 award-winning film *Birdman.*[22] While not about birds per se, a major antagonist in this film is the title character, Birdman, a superhero that haunts the main character, played by Michael Keaton. The plot concerns the Broadway opening of a new play; Keaton plays Riggan Thomson, the auteur (writer/director/star) of an adaptation based on a short story by Raymond Carver. Riggan's ability to open this nonmusical play at the St. James Theatre stems from the celebrity he gained performing the role of Birdman on screen, and this source of his fame taunts him throughout Iñárritu's film, personified by Keaton himself in full superhero garb. The metaresonances of *Birdman* are difficult to overlook. Keaton played the role of Batman in Tim Burton's films (*Batman*, 1989; *Batman Returns*, 1992); the Birdman costume he wears was built on Keaton's Batman mannequin; and other actors in the film have also starred in superhero films (Edward Norton as *The Incredible Hulk*, 2008; and Emma Stone as Gwen Stacy in *The Amazing Spider-Man 1 and 2*, 2012 and 2014).[23]

More striking than the industry commentary, however, is the meticulous cinematography (and theatrical blocking) that gives the perception that most of the movie was filmed in one continuous shot. This allows spectators to believe that they are "following his journey through these three days" leading up to the opening of Thomson's adaptation on Broadway.[24] The logic of the continuous shot means that the camera lens remains fixed on one actor at a time, and in *Birdman* that actor is almost always Keaton. We follow him from his dressing room to the stage, from the interior of the St. James theatre outside into Times Square, from onstage to offstage. This cinematography in turn makes the Janus effect more visible, since spectators are necessarily more focused on the comings and goings of characters, and thus doorways and thresholds take on increased significance. With *Birdman*, the interior scenes of the theater space encourage shots of hallways, an aesthetic choice that becomes more pronounced as the film progresses and Riggan's anxiety mounts.

The focus on hallways in particular accomplishes two results: for one, it exacerbates the limitations of interior shots, by drawing attention to the walls surrounding the characters, in a way that begins to feel claustrophobic, much like how a bird might feel if trapped indoors. In addition, the hallway scenes emphasize Iñárritu's focus on liminal spaces, the corridors that lead from here to there. This liminality, coupled with the perception of how frustratingly limited it feels indoors, support the emotional arc of the film as well as my analysis of the Janus-like qualities of adaptation dramaturgy.

The fact that the central event in *Birdman* is a theatrical adaptation is not a side note here. The dubious value of the production and Riggan's uncertain potential to succeed on Broadway is heightened by the fact that he has chosen to adapt a short story by Raymond Carver for the stage. Known primarily as an American short story writer, Carver has an uncanny knack for "real" human language and situations, and his cogent prose gives life to incredible detail with remarkable brevity. With what Miriam Marty Clark has identified as his use of a "monologic imagination," Carver "suppresses the folk energies that are the founding forces of heteroglossia" and creates portraits of solipsistic *askesis*.[25] His stories tend to feature working-class characters who seek to protect themselves from the furor and confusion of the outside world. They rarely interact with the carnivalesque, and with but one exception ("Will You Please Be Quiet, Please?"), Clark claims that Carver "never deals in street scenes or crowds, spectacles, merriment, holiday, adventure, [or] dreams."[26] Given these characteristics of Carver's oeuvre—that he is revered as a plain-speaking hyperrealist and that his style is memorable for its lack of dialogism and avoidance of spectacle—the fact that Riggan chooses Carver to adapt for his Broadway debut emerges as quite the obstacle indeed. So why, then, has Riggan chosen Carver?

We learn in the course of the film that Riggan's rationale for choosing Carver stems from a message he received from the writer when he was a high school actor. Scribbled on a cocktail napkin, the note reads: "Thank you for an honest performance. Ray Carver."[27] It was at that moment, Riggan reveals, that he decided to be an actor. The epigraph to *Birdman*, taken from the "Late Fragment" that graces Carver's tombstone, suggests that Riggan's quest throughout the film is simply "To call myself beloved, to feel / myself beloved on the earth." [28] Riggan's friend (and producer) Jake solidifies this theme when he reminds him, "This is about being respected, validated, remember? That's what you told me. That's how you got me into this shit."[29] For Riggan, adapting Carver's work is a labor of both homage to the man who identified his talent onstage and a reminder to himself that he still matters, with or without his Birdman franchise. It is also about repairing the damage he has done to his personal life.

Of all the Carver stories he might have chosen, Riggan adapts one that tackles the desire for (and definition of) love, "What We Talk about When We Talk about Love," written in 1981 and the title of a collection of stories published that same year. This story (like Carver's other work) contains little in the way of dramatic action, since it takes place at a kitchen table with four friends drinking and reminiscing. The stories that they share bear remarkable similarities to Riggan's own past, offering further insight into the appeal of this source text for him to adapt. In order to create stage action out of literary storytelling, Riggan, like all theatrical adapters, must grapple with the demands of time and space as they translate on stage. If he were to simply transfer the dialogue from page to stage, the play would consist of two couples getting drunk and discussing their past relationships; by adding flashbacks and dream sequences, Riggan manipulates time and space for dramatic appeal.

The metaframework of the film itself encourages methodological observations like these, insofar as Iñárritu calls attention to the making of theatre as well as the film industry in both the content and the format of *Birdman*. Further, the setting of the film inside a Broadway theatre, with all its backstage and corridors exposed, with film actors playing stage actors in broad strokes (indeed, verging on melodrama) makes it clear that in *Birdman* Iñárritu comments on the absurdity of the art and business of both film and theatre, encouraging us to do the same. In so doing, the film reminds us that theatre is always already a kind of adaptation; each performance is different, adapting to its audience, and each time the same show is staged by different directors, it is adapted to suit different production concepts.

Aside from this fact, however, the unique demands of stage adaptation are also multivalent: to make live theatre out of a source, one must create an event that can be taken in by spectators within a limited time frame. One can put down a novel and pick it back up, but one generally sees theatre in one outing, and typically (though not always) the expectation is that the event will be between one and three hours long, with intermissions expected after approximately an hour to an hour and a half worth of stage action. Thus, the very act of adapting a source for the stage necessitates a consideration of time—the compression of time as it occurs in the novel, but also the concentration of attention as it must occur for spectators watching the event unfold. In addition, adapting for the stage requires attention to space: how to distill the imaginary possibilities of the novel, say, into the practical limitations and abstract implications of stage and light design.

As we have seen, at the heart of any stage adaptation is adapturgy: the dramaturgical intervention that connects the audience to the choices that the adapter and director have made for the production in question. There are two stages of these choices: at the outset, where new play dramaturgy usually occurs (between the playwright and the dramaturg) and in the staging of the play, where production dramaturgy usually occurs (between the director, the designers, and the dramaturg). Whether this role is specified or not, the work of adapturgy occurs in all stage adaptations.

How We Adapt When We Adapt for the Stage

Although never fully realized within the context of the film, there are several glimpses of the stage production of *What We Talk about When We Talk about Love* (hereafter *What We Talk About*) that suggest Riggan's approach to the adaptation. Without doubt, Raymond Carver's story presents major problems for any adapter, given the monologic limitations addressed previously. The major dramatic action of the source consists of two couples—Mel and Terri, Nick and Laura—telling stories at a kitchen table about Terri's abusive ex-boyfriend Ed. The only activity besides storytelling that occurs in Carver's story is the preparation and drinking of gin and limes. Every now and then the narrator holds his girlfriend's hand or touches her knee, or one of the characters leans across the table to make a point, but otherwise the story's static nature makes a "faithful" adaptation challenging to stage successfully.

How does Riggan solve that problem? For one thing, as Mike (played by Edward Norton) suggests, Riggan "took all the good lines for [himself]," conflating Nick (the narrator of Carver's story, played by Keaton) and his arc with the lines Carver gave to Mel (the cardiologist, played by Norton).[30] In Carver's story, Nick rarely speaks at all; he is the observer—readers witness the story through his eyes. Mel is the protagonist of Carver's story, insisting that Ed's display of devotion to Terri was not love, while Terri maintains that it was. In Riggan's adaptation of *What We Talk About*, the gathering appears to be set at Nick's house (rather than Mel's), and it is Nick who delivers at least two of Mel's gin-saturated speeches: "I'll tell you what real love is" and a story about the old couple who end up in the hospital, featuring a man whose "heart was breaking because he couldn't turn his goddamn head and see his goddamn wife."[31] In addition, in Riggan's adaptation, it is Nick who is chemically depressed, whereas in Carver's story Mel battles depression with pharmaceutical assistance. Perhaps most importantly, in

Riggan's version, it is Nick who says "it ought to make us feel ashamed when we talk like we know what we're talking about when we talk about love"; whereas in Carver's story it is Mel who delivers the title line.[32]

It is difficult to see these reassigned lines and traits functioning outside of the accusation issued by Mike: that Riggan's adaptation choices in this instance were fueled by ego, rather than aesthetics. That said, it is not unprecedented to take liberty with characters when adapting them from page to stage, and in some cases doing so serves a revisionist or revolutionary cause. In the case of *What We Talk About* within *Birdman*, however, any research leading to these changes appears to be hyperpersonal: in addition to making him the protagonist (and himself the star), by giving Nick the depression and the insightful reflections within the play, Riggan assures that his character aligns closely to his own life experience.

In addition to the conflation of the male characters, Riggan also stages two scenes that do not occur in Carver's story: a "surrealistic forest" scene where Laura soliloquizes about Nick's depression and her unwanted pregnancy, and the motel bed scene where Ed commits suicide. On the page, Ed attempts suicide alone in his room and is kept alive for three days. It is a "botched" attempt; he shoots himself in the mouth, but instead of dying immediately his head swells twice its normal size and Terri stays with him in the hospital until he passes. On the stage, Ed (played by Keaton/Riggan in a bad '80s wig and moustache) bangs on the motel door where Terri and Mel are spending the night, and enters the room to confront Terri, asking if she loves him (she does not). At this revelation, Ed says, "I don't exist. I'm not even here. I don't exist. None of this matters." Following this proclamation, he points his gun at Terri (Lesley, played by Naomi Watts), then at Mel (Mike/Norton), then at his own head, successfully killing himself and ending the play.

The choice to add both a dreamlike sequence (the forest) and a flashback scene (the motel) points to one of the key advantages of adapting literature for the stage: the ability to manipulate space and time. Both of these stage conventions—the soliloquy and the flashback—are methods of turning literary reflection and memory into dramatic action. In the forest (and in another scene where Terri speaks to the audience about her love for Mel), Laura's soliloquy verbalizes the narrative and descriptive parts of Carver's story. By changing the location of Ed's suicide to the motel with both Mel and Terri as witnesses, and performing it as the closing scene of the play, Riggan turns a memory into interaction with the highest possible stakes: life or death. Certainly these choices create more playable scenes for the stage, but because Riggan plays Ed in this climactic scene, it is difficult to interpret this adaptation choice as grounded in dramaturgical research—instead, it again appears to serve Riggan's ego.

Unlike the play, the short story ends when the gin does, never resolving the question about the nature of love, or even the expressed desire by Laura to eat something: "I don't think I've ever been so hungry in my life. Is there something to nibble on?" In answer, Terri says, "I'll put out some cheese and crackers," without doing so. According to Carver, she "just sat there. She did not get up to get anything."[33] The final lines of Nick's narration have been quoted elsewhere: "I could hear my heart beating. I could hear everyone's heart. I could hear the human noise we sat there making, not one of us moving, not even when the room went dark."[34] Thus, the story ends as it began, with the two couples sitting around the table, gin consumed and stories told, but otherwise without change.

The significant shift from a reflection—Nick's observation of stillness and "the human noise we sat there making"—to the "revelation" reached by Ed in his final lines of Riggan's adaptation ("I don't exist. I'm not even here. I don't exist. None of this matters.") changes the tone of Carver's *What We Talk About* from contemplative to tragic. Perhaps Riggan considered this shift necessary for his Broadway audiences, accustomed as they are to poetic justice in many commercially successful English-language plays. Arguably, there is an expectation within the adaptation industry for star vehicles like Riggan's to feature a more traditional climactic play structure, regardless of fidelity concerns.[35] The reasons for this transformation are not explicitly revealed, because the adaptation dramaturgy, like what we know about Janus, remains prominently obscure.[36]

What Would Janus Do?

While spectators of *Birdman* are not privy to the process that led to Riggan's adaptation choices, those decisions—and whatever research was gathered in the practice of making them—were (at least in part) guided by adaptation dramaturgy. The labor of transforming a source into a script involves dramaturgical thought, whether the adapter recognizes it as dramaturgy or not. That said, there is a distinction between theatre makers who self-consciously embrace adaptation dramaturgy and those who do not. In the case of Riggan, his quality of dramaturgical rigor may be questionable (indeed, the absence of rigorous forethought or research helps create conflict in the film), but the work surrounding the creation of the script, the director's concept, and its connection to the production team's design choices is what I call adapturgy.

That Iñárritu wants viewers to see this stage adaptation as lacking in quality is made clear by the contrasting attention given within the film to Riggan's (midlife) crisis of confidence and his intention for producing the play. Riggan's doubt is personified in the film by Birdman, who critiques his dream of being a respected theatre maker at first in voiceovers, unseen, but eventually in full costume near him. "All of us have a Birdman, no matter how big or small," Iñárritu explains, in his admission that this film was "an opportunity to explore my ego."[37] The kinds of things that Birdman tells Riggan (e.g., "What are you trying to prove? That you're an artist? Well, you're not"; and "You're an imposter here. Eventually they're gonna figure you out.") are classic articulations of the kind of doubt that most writers and artists know all too well. In its exploration of these doubts, *Birdman* calls attention to the Janus effect in adaptation dramaturgy.

A closer look at Riggan's jaunt through Times Square brings the Janus effect into clearer focus. As Riggan works his way around the alley to the front doors of the St. James Theatre, he encounters the rich variety of humanity. Mostly he passes tourists—some who recognize him as Birdman and others who do not—but he also weaves through performers, an essential part of the nightlife of the area. Among them the camera lingers on what appears to be a high school marching band (the film's drum score melds nicely with their marching beats) and someone dressed as Spider-Man. Meanwhile, as the crowd begins to recognize his fame, they ask for his autograph and begin recording the extraordinary event with their mobile phones (as the screenplay directions suggest, "a swarm of cell phones begin [*sic*] to glow like fireflies"). Their verbal recognitions of him culminate with a female tourist who remarks that "he looks so old in person" as Riggan passes her, the door of the theatre finally in sight.

Riggan presses into the lobby, but as he marches toward the house, his beeline is interrupted twice: first, by the sight of his erstwhile costar Ralph (the one Mike/Norton replaced) in a wheelchair, his lawyer beside him. The attorney threatens to sue Riggan, but he pushes through. "I've got a play to do," he says as he "storms toward the auditorium," only to have an elderly usher attempt to stop him again.[38] Riggan pushes the usher aside and goes through the house doors into the auditorium, where the actors onstage await his entrance for the motel scene. From the back of the house, he yells "knock knock knock!" and the surprised spectators twist around to see him, some of them laughing at him as he walks toward the stage, still in his underwear, covered in sweat and rain from the outdoors. His expected lines to Ed (Norton), "Fuck you. Shut up. *Fuck you*," are extended when he turns to an amused spectator, pointing to him to say, "Shut up!," blurring the divide between fiction and reality.[39]

In this brief but telling scene, it is difficult to overlook Iñárritu's emphasis on doors, locks, and thresholds throughout Riggan's trek. First, in order to reach the exterior he reaches above his head to unlatch the locked stage door; then, he finds himself in an alley—an exterior place that is like a street or a sidewalk, but is neither. The door here functions both as a site of passage (from interior to exterior) and containment (it traps his robe and locks him outside). His lack of clothing is also liminal—he is not quite naked, but he is not dressed either. When he finally circles around to the front doors of the theatre, his ability to enter the house is stymied in the lobby, a threshold (and often dramaturgically rich) space. When he does enter the auditorium, he uses his character's lines to speak to unruly spectators, further emphasizing his border-dwelling state between Ed and Riggan.

As cinema, *Birdman* emphasizes liminality in numerous ways. Perhaps, most noticeably, it does so in its embrace of the liveness of theatre within the recorded medium of film. The cinematographic choice to mimic a continuous shot for the majority of the film made theatrical blocking as well as one long take necessary. Unlike most films, where actors can provide several takes for scenes or lines, because the camera followed the actors, they were challenged to stay in character for exceptionally long takes, meaning that the pressure for performance was akin to live theatre. In addition, this film straddles the divide between a blockbuster and a limited-release "art film." The star power of the cast, along with the comic elements and sizeable budget of the film, suggest that it is a typical American blockbuster movie, but *Birdman* also resists that mode in several ways. It is a film about theatre making, limiting its appeal to those who appreciate the insider nature of the comedy; it critiques the movie industry while participating in it, perching between satire and parody; and its ending resists the American preference for poetic justice while simultaneously offering a kind of "happy ending." Finally, the prevalence of shots within *Birdman* that emphasize doors, hallways, interiors and exteriors, as well as the demarcation between onstage and offstage suggest that Iñárritu wanted to draw attention to thresholds.

For example, if we understand Janus as a divine augur, then we accept that one of his responsibilities is to "carve the sky," or to demarcate the area (in adaptation dramaturgy terms) worthy of research for a particular project. In the logic of the film, the sky becomes the shot—what the camera sees and how the sequence of shots progresses. The use of a continuous shot creates a different experience for everyone involved in the filmmaking as well as the audience. For *Birdman*, it was necessary to rehearse each scene on a simulated stage in order to set the blocking in advance, much like in theatre rehearsals. Ultimately, while they used as much of the actual St. James Theatre as possible, many of the interior shots had to be filmed on a mockup of the theatre's hallways, in order to create the depth needed for the camera angles. The continuous shot approach to filming means that the camera has to "choose" a character to follow, as they enter or exit, bringing the action into another space with other characters. Usually, this character is Riggan, although there are a few times when the camera follows his daughter Sam or costar Mike. For the actors, the continuous shot means that their experience on set is much closer to the stage, insofar as they must continue the scenes for the duration of the shot, and rarely have the luxury of choosing the best "take" from several attempts at a scene or line.

With regard to adaptation dramaturgy, the most significant aspect of the continuous cinematography in *Birdman* is when the established pattern breaks. This occurs on opening night, in the motel scene, when Riggan (onstage as Ed) uses a real loaded gun instead of a stage prop for his suicide. This moment is the equivalent of a blackout onstage, and after Riggan drops to the ground, receiving a standing ovation from everyone except the *Times* critic (Tabitha Dickinson, who has promised to ruin him with her review), the continuity established from the beginning of the film suddenly stops. Following a montage of images accompanied by a swell in the drum score, the story picks up in Riggan's hospital room, with a shot of the tile ceiling there.

The rationale for this abrupt change in the cinematography becomes clearer when we consider the final piece of the Janus effect: the reading of the signs. As discussed before, augurs interpret the sounds and patterns of bird flight, leaving others to decide what action to take based on those signs. This ambiguity might be understood as duplicity within the logic of what Janus-faced signifies today, and correlates directly to the advisory role that adaptation dramaturgs often adopt in theatre. Likewise, the ending of *Birdman* baffles viewers, allowing for multiple interpretations of the actions presented on camera. Once we arrive in the hospital, we learn that Riggan has survived the self-inflicted gunshot, and that his nose (which took the brunt of the shot) has been reconstructed. We also learn that Tabitha has given the show a glowing review, calling the type of theatre Riggan enacted "supra-realism." By his side in the hospital are his ex-wife Sylvia and his attorney and close friend Jake, both of whom are extremely protective of him. His daughter Sam arrives too, bringing his favorite flowers, and kissing his forehead sweetly before leaving to find a vase. When Riggan goes into the bathroom to remove the wound's dressing and view his crooked nose, Birdman sits quietly on the toilet, saying nothing. Free of his bandage, Riggan walks to the window and opens it, watching a pattern of birds in the sky before stepping on the ledge of the windowsill. From this moment, the camera pans away from Riggan to a bedside table, where we see a copy of Carver's *What We Talk about When We Talk about Love*, alongside family photographs.

Before addressing the final moments of the film, I want to pause to acknowledge how odd all of this is, especially compared to the previous parts of the film. Everything that occurs in the hospital room is suspiciously perfect: all of his visitors adore him, Tabitha's review of the show indicates respect for him as an artist, and Birdman is finally quiet. None of this makes sense, given what Iñárritu has established thus far. And then, after the camera has left the windowsill, with Riggan perched upon it, we see Sam enter the room, looking for her father. When she sees that the window is open, she cautiously approaches it, with trepidation as she looks down. Seeing nothing, she slowly shifts her gaze upward to the sky, whereupon "a smile, filled with pride, [begins] to wash over her face." This is how the film ends.

We do not see what she sees, because the camera does not follow her gaze.[40] Like Janus, we are left with these final moments to decipher ourselves. Did Riggan take flight? Were his telekinetic powers real all along? Every other moment of magic in the film has a logical rationale. When Riggan arrives at the theatre, for example, we see both his version (he flew there) and everyone else's version of reality (he took a taxi and walked out without paying). When Jake walks into his dressing room, we can tell that he's not moving things with his mind but with his hands, and so we are led to believe that any supernatural occurrence is a fiction of his distorted mind. Why, then, does Sam's final gaze suggest that Riggan can fly after all?

To follow the trail left within the logic established in the film—that is, to read the birds within this part of the sky, one interpretation of the ending is that it is Riggan's fantasy and not reality. In this reading, Riggan dies onstage from his gunshot, and the montage of image and sound are the flashes of his life that fire in his memory before his final breath; the hospital sequence is his imagination's way of resolving everything that mattered to him. Significantly, it also mirrors Ed's botched suicide attempt within Carver's story that Riggan altered to make more climactic. There are several moments that support this interpretation. For one, we see Tabitha leave the performance while the rest of the audience is giving a standing ovation.

Fig. 5.1. Fan art depicting the character Sam in a scene from *Birdman*. Digital painting. *Janah Adams, 2016.*

While this moment in the screenplay plays a bit differently, it's clear that Iñárritu wanted to emphasize the difference between her reaction (dazed, disgust) and that of all the other spectators (wild applause).[41]

Even so, there's no question that the ending of *Birdman* is ambiguous. The final moment, with Sam smiling at the sky, looking out the open window, is a striking departure for her character's pattern of gazing at the ground from the theatre rooftop and sulky disconnection from her father. From the perspective of analyzing adaptation dramaturgy using the Janus model, however, this image could hardly be more poignant: we are left with the vision of a young woman looking to the sky and finding clarity. Where her father struggled with augury, with the liminal stance of adaptation dramaturgy, perhaps she will succeed.

Overall, by telling a story about a stage adaptation wherein many stereotypes about bad adaptation are fulfilled, but within a film that demonstrates superior dramaturgical skill, Iñárritu gives insight into the precarious perch upon which adapturgy balances. By adapting Carver's story through the medium of the stage as told through the medium of film, *Birdman* encourages audiences to question the process of adaptation, and to recognize the challenging Janus-like border dwelling inherent to adaptation dramaturgy.

6. GEOGRAPHIES OF ADAPTATION

At its core, theatre can be said to consist of the equation Eric Bentley offered in 1964: *A does B for C.*[1] Peter Brook offers a similar perspective: "I can take any empty space and call it a bare stage. A man walks across this empty space whilst someone else is watching him, and this is all that is needed for an act of theatre to be engaged."[2] But these three elements (the performer, the character and/or performance, and the spectator/s) are not all we need for theatre to occur. As Marvin Carlson recognized, the word theatre itself alludes to the other necessary element: *theatron*, after all, means seeing place.[3] Therefore, we must add (the equivalent of) "*in X*" to Bentley's basic equation. "Theatre . . . cannot exist without space: there must be a location, a venue of some sort in which theatre can occur, or, rather, take 'place.'"[4] Just like the initial equation cited above, though, for decades scholars took the question of social geography for granted when looking at performance. Even Brook's amendment to Bentley overlooks key assumptions about space: that it can be "empty," and the means by which it can be "called" a bare stage.[5]

In approaching a literary source text for stage adaptation, some of the most crucial questions an adapter must ask revolve around considerations of geography. On both practical and philosophical levels, adaptations *rely on* the transformation of imaginary into theatrical space. Novels take advantage of the limitless possibilities of readers' imaginations; the action within them often occurs in several different locations, some of which are fantastical or immaterial. Novelists are not bound by the same practical concerns that playwrights (often) are: they don't bother to ponder if the action could be staged, and if it could, whether it would flourish best on a proscenium, thrust, or black box stage.

But first things first: how do we define *space*, and how is this word distinguished from the related concept of *place?* Defining these two essential terms, seemingly so simple, turns out to be more controversial than one might expect on first glance, in part because scholars continue to debate their definitions.[6] From a theatrically savvy point of view, space can be understood as a general concept, more amorphous than place. As Mark Augé notes, the meaning of space is tricky because it can reference both "a distance between two things" as well as a "temporal expanse (the space of a week)."[7] Likewise, for some, "*place* is overly particular."[8] These reservations, however, are helpful in distinguishing between the two words as they will serve adapturgy: following Joanne Tompkins, I will use "'place' for locations with specific geographical coordinates; and 'space' to indicate the more generic concept."[9] The specificities of space are made manifest by the recognition and acknowledgement of place; that is, as Peter Petralia puts it, "space is created by *activating* a place."[10] The place itself is simply the location; once meaning is attached to the site, it becomes a space. This more flexible word, space, becomes especially useful when analyzing theatre, which occurs in two adjacent spaces at once—the one created by mimesis onstage and the spectators' space, the "house." Dramaturgs are implicated in both of these spaces. Indeed, they help carve them out, and extend the space beyond the boundaries of the theatre experience itself. That is, the dramaturgy extends the physical and imaginary space of the audience beyond the doors of the house, into the lobby and online; it also extends the space of time in which the event occurs, with preshow discussions or talkbacks, among other options.[11]

Within theatre and performance studies, the scholarship on spatiality ranges from semiotic analyses of theatre buildings and surrounding locations to interrogations of sociocultural spaces.[12] Perhaps the most influential concept emerging from this work has been Una Chaudhuri's neologism of "geopathology" to refer to place-as-problem, a recurring theme within early modern drama.[13] Recent additions to this rich field include considerations of technology and multimodality, some of which challenge the semiotic and psychoanalytic biases of our field with promising considerations of phenomenology and cognitive science.[14] At the heart of these challenges is a call for a major shift in Western theory altogether: to replace the Cartesian duality bias (I *think* therefore I *am*) with a philosophy that synthesizes body and mind, resulting in embodied cognition.[15] Among other benefits, one advantage of these embodied approaches that privilege (subjective) experience over (objective) readings of space is that they encourage us to consider beyond the visual when analyzing geography. Our words for live performance privilege sight, as *theatron* means seeing place and *spectator* refers to one who looks.[16] But the experience of theatre engages more than just what we see—it involves what we hear, and can involve smell, touch, and taste, too. Most of all, the experience of theatre affects how we feel and what and how we think about the world around us.

In the case of adapturgy, these modes of reception become especially significant because the mode in which we have received the source (say, a novel we have read) must be transformed in order to be received as live performance. Therefore, the adaptation dramaturg has the opportunity (and even the responsibility) to recognize and offer feedback on this modal transformation. Here I would like to zero in on the question of how space transforms from the literary imagination to the stage, and how the adaptation dramaturg can facilitate this conversion.[17]

Practical Space and Adapturgy: Staging the *Pequod*

Our primary case study for this chapter is Herman Melville's *Moby-Dick*, which has been adapted for the stage several times, a handful of which will be discussed here. Because the story occurs on a ship in the middle of the ocean (and features a battle with a whale), the extraordinary challenge of adapting it for the stage makes it a useful example; if these methods helped to solve problems for *these* adaptations, perhaps other obstacles may appear surmountable.

While the novel may be at least superficially familiar to most readers, because of its length (and subject matter), many of us who have encountered it, when pressed, will admit that we did not finish the book. In meticulous (some might say excruciating) detail, Melville describes the hunt of the crew of the Pequod for the great white whale, Moby Dick.[18] Ahab's fixation and fascination with this nonhuman animal speaks to the residual power whales continue to hold for many activists—indeed, one of the first animal advocacy outcries was "Save the Whales," a slogan that helped establish a worldwide ban on whaling in 1986, when these mammals went nearly extinct. The word "whale" today refers to forty distinct species of marine animals, the largest of which (the blue whale) measures up to 112 feet long. Whales are ancient and modern monsters of the sea; they have captivated human interest for their practical use (the products made from their blubber, spermaceti, and bones) as well as for their mysterious power.

But what happens when we attempt to stage *Moby-Dick*—how/do we perform the whale? And how can a stage space best represent the vastness and power of the ocean, and the vessel upon it? These are practical questions that are particularly urgent for the adaptation dramaturg, who must understand why the director and designers make the choices they make to address these unavoidable concerns. But neither of these problems (staging the whale, representing the ocean and the ship) was solved in a vacuum. The choice of venue, the architectural container in which the performance would take place, likely affected the adapter's vision.

For John Gentile in 2008, then chairperson of the department of Theatre and Performance Studies at Kennesaw State University, that venue was the Stillwell Theater, a proscenium theatre configuration that seats about three hundred patrons.[19] To enter the space, patrons walk through one of several external doors, arriving at the house doors from one of two facing directions, with the box office located opposite the house door. In this vicinity, between the house door opposite the box office and the bathrooms and water fountain, was a bulletin board (later replaced by a flat-screen monitor mounted to the wall) that served as the lobby space for Stillwell performances. I detail this layout with such specificity because these liminal spaces, adjacent to the performance space, between reality and theatre, are inherently dramaturgical spaces. They are transitional spaces, and therefore they are *adaptive* spaces.[20]

Obviously, in this rather traditional space it would have been impossible to stage the water and the whale literally. Instead, the designer (Jamie Bullins) took an abstract approach, using a billowing white fabric attached along the upstage wall in sections resembling the sails of a ship. This draped, flowing fabric suggested wind and waves, allowing the audience to complete the picture in their own minds. To these sheets he added levels (by way of movable steps or blocks), to help create a sense of above and below deck scenes. As for the whale, the fact that it was never seen by the audience made sense, since Moby Dick is a mythic beast as much as a material one. The same approach was taken in the lobby space, where virtually the same white fabric that was used to frame the stage framed the bulletin board, inviting the spectators to connect the hallway design with what they witnessed onstage.

The simple abstraction of the stage design complemented the chamber-theatre approach that Gentile took to the script. Popularized at Northwestern University throughout the latter half of the twentieth century (see chapter 1), the chamber-theatre method featured rather literal translations of novels to live performance, including the defamiliarizing narrative tendency of fiction to include "he said" and "she said" before spoken dialogue. Today this technique has been embraced by playwrights like Tarell Alvin McCraney, where it signals an oral tradition that predates the twentieth century by millennia: that of primary orality.

As the original dramaturg for the 2008 production of Gentile's adaptation of *Moby-Dick*, I included a definition of chamber-theatre techniques in my dramaturgical notes that were included in the program. I wanted spectators to recognize the style and its history, and to help illuminate how this intersected with both the director's vision and the relevant scholarship about the source (and its author). To supplement this essay, the lobby display included renderings of the costume designs and quotations from the novel/script as well as the scholarship I cited in the program.[21] Finally, both the lobby and the program notes referred patrons to our extensive dramaturgical website, which included a photographic history of the adaptation's development as well as an interview with the adapter and codirector, Gentile.

Five years later, Phillip Justman, the actor who played Ahab, and his partner Marium Khalid remounted *Moby-Dick* as part of their new performance company, SAÏAH. The script remained virtually the same, but the experience was quite different, because SAÏAH produced *Moby-Dick* not in a traditional theatre, but in the found space of an abandoned warehouse. The Lifecycle Building Center, built in 1914 as a sprocket factory, is a sixty-thousand-square-foot facility located in West Atlanta, southwest of what was then Turner Field. The space—and here I mean both physical as well as durational space—transformed the adaptation, highlighting the pilgrimage aspects of the script as well as the material reality of it. As Gentile interprets it, Melville's story is one of Ishmael and Ahab's pilgrimage: "In *Moby-Dick*, the hierophany, to use Eliade's term for the breakthrough of the sacred, manifests in the unexpected form of the White Whale."[22] Inviting the audience to walk through the old factory, an industrial labyrinth of sorts, meant that the space spectators experienced was migratory, with the expectation of leading up to (or revealing) something (or some insight).[23]

The creative team behind this staging fully embraced the possibilities of the space, as site-specific artists typically do. This is one of the defining characteristics of site-specific theatre practitioners: "They speak of entering into a dialogue with the site, of engaging in a complex process of reciprocal animation."[24] As SAÏAH's Justman explained, "We have done our best to use the existing beauty of the space, building with it. For example, the soundscape has been created with the intention to blend with the distant sounds of passing trains."[25] Of course, the cast changed as well—there were new actors as well as some of the same performers playing different roles—but the transformation of this adaptation into a migrating, immersive performance, wherein the audience encounters the performance by walking through an industrial space changed the experience entirely.[26] As director Marium Khalid noted, "With the location of this show . . . we are trying to bring the vastness to our audience. And allowing them to see these men play in this space . . . you get a glimpse of the hard battle they fought—while at the same time realizing how small one man is."[27] In addition to the massive size of the building, its remnants (including oil and metal) complemented the industrial aspects of the story, immersing the audience's senses fully.

Another adaptation of Melville's classic also took advantage of ample vertical space: in the summer of 2015 the Lookingglass Theatre produced an adaptation of *Moby-Dick* written and directed by David Catlin. In keeping with their remarkably flexible performance space housed within the Water Tower Works building in Chicago, Catlin's vision for this adaptation was centered on the adventures of the high seas, with attention to the rigging and acrobatic feats that have become a specialty of Lookingglass performances. When I asked Catlin why he chose *Moby-Dick* to adapt, he related a story about reading it in a mad dash during the three days before final exams, and how the story transported him to another world, how this "feverish read" stuck with him, even as the novel sat on his shelf for years thereafter. Soon thereafter, in 2010, he was invited to join a grant funded by the Boeing Corporation, initiated by one of the cofounders of Redmoon Theater, Blair Thomas. This grant supported the simultaneous development of three distinct adaptations of *Moby-Dick*, created by Catlin, Thomas, and Shawn Pfautsch from House Theatre company (all Chicago-based theatre makers).[28] The adapters met periodically at a local pie shop, where they would share their emerging ideas and collaborate on how to shape their different stagings of Melville's novel, suggesting passages and sections to each other and providing feedback on early drafts. This extraordinary opportunity culminated in a two-week residency at the University of Chicago, where the adapters worked with actors and a dramaturg (Derek Matson) who circulated among the three companies, continuing to provide feedback on their work.

From this incubation period emerged Catlin's adaptation, highlighting the power of water, as well as the metaphor of rope (or rigging) as a connective tissue linking the men of the Pequod together. A central image that inspired Catlin, both in staging and scripting the adaptation, was that of the mother whale nursing her infant—the calm in the center of the churning of whales that readers encounter in "The Grand Armada" chapter, when the Pequod navigates the constricted straits of Sunda. "Starbuck saw long coils of the umbilical cord of Madame Leviathan, by which the young cub seemed still tethered to its dam." This moment proves transcendent for Ishmael, who remarks of it, "There I still bathe me in eternal mildness of joy."[29] Thus, for Catlin, the hemp rope also served to reference the umbilical cord from this passage, as well as serving to showcase the acrobatic talents of the Lookingglass actors.

From a dramaturgical perspective, the fact that the Lookingglass Theatre space is located within the Chicago Water Tower Complex is also significant. In a place once occupied by a steam generation plant, the Chicago Avenue Pumping Station (located on the Miracle Mile) was one of very few structures to survive the 1871 Chicago Fire. Even after the Lookingglass Theatre converted the part of the building that had been used for storage and repair, the other half of the building continues to function as intended, pumping water for Chicago's North side residents. Whereas for SAÏAH the found space of an abandoned factory was a temporary home that offered sensory benefits that complemented the story of *Moby-Dick*, the Water Tower is Lookingglass Theatre Company's permanent home. Indeed, it was built to exist acoustically apart from the massive plumbing within—"new concrete floors were poured over rubber isolation pads, a massive new ceiling was constructed suspended on spring isolation hangers, and walls were built spanning from the isolated floor to the isolated ceiling without ever connecting rigidly to the existing pumping station walls."[30] Thus spectators who recognize the industrial housing of the Lookingglass facility do so only visually and briefly, before entering the "room within a room" that is their theatre space.[31]

This notion of a "room within a room" echoes the uncanny opportunities afforded by puppet stages—frequently built as mini prosceniums, presented on the apron of a proscenium stage. As Blair Thomas suggests in "In Defense of the Puppet Stage":

> A deeper meaning is exposed as the puppet makes an entrance into this custom made world. The materiality of the puppet blends with the materiality of the stage, making the puppet and it's [*sic*] world one. This unified universe seems both strange and familiar, comforting and disorienting. Herein lies the puppet theater's allure, fulfilling a need for wonder in our age of reason and rationality.[32]

And what better source for exploring wonder and awe than *Moby-Dick?* Thomas, who initiated the Boeing grant that supported the development of Catlin's, Pfautsch's, and his various adaptations of Melville's masterpiece, has been exploring *The Whale* since 1990, when he first staged it on North Avenue Beach in Chicago, in collaboration with Redmoon Theater. Unlike this initial interpretation, that had been conceived as a large-scale performance in keeping with Redmoon's urban architectural aesthetic, in 2016 Thomas and his company presented a new adaptation in the Edlis Neeson Theater, in Chicago's Museum of Contemporary Art (MCA). *Moby Dick, or The Brotherhood of the Monastic Order of Ancient Mariners Purges the Ills of Society through a Reading of the Tales of Moby-Dick*, as this adaptation is boldly titled, "imagines a time after the rescue of Ishmael, when a group of men who are still wrestling with the issues raised by Ahab attempt to liberate themselves from torment by forming a Monastic Order of Ancient Mariners."[33] In the lobby of the MCA theatre, there were two dramaturgical spaces: the first was a table placed between both doors to the auditorium, featuring representatives from Thomas and Company and one of their puppets for spectators—especially the young (or young-at-heart) ones—to see up close. At this table they also sold copies of the richly illustrated book that accompanied the company's recent exhibit at the Ballard Institute and Museum of Puppetry, *Stages of Enchantment.* On the far wall from the entrance, a video loop of Blair Thomas talking about the making of *Moby Dick* also displayed (what appeared to be) clips from the performance itself, whetting our appetite for the spectacular and varied puppetry we (would expect to) soon behold.[34]

This production, framed as "part ritual, part religious service," featured several types of puppetry (Bunraku, shadow puppetry, tabletop, and other hybrids), animation, and objects to assist in the telling of Melville's tome.[35] The sea, for example, took shape both onstage and in the audience in different ways: onstage, the company used what appeared to be handmade paper to represent water, roughly textured and gently wrinkled throughout its generous width. As they created waves by lifting and lowering it, the sound of the thick paper mimicked that of waves hitting the shore.

But it was the opening moments of Thomas and Company's *Moby Dick* that most mesmerized me. Upon entering the house, the sound reverberated like wave after wave of tonal unrest. It was both soothing and nauseating, promising something epic, likely terrifying, and definitely more than human. After the lights dimmed, two puppeteers entered the space, carrying a boat aloft (in both senses of the word) above their heads. They were followed by the balladeer and the musician, who assumed places on either side of the stage. After the puppeteers passed the boat back and forth between them several times, one of them (Michael Montenegro) kneeled on the edge of the stage and handed it to a spectator in the front row. He gestured for the spectator to pass it along the row, and there was a collective "oh!" from the audience. We were delighted to take part. This little boat, made of dowel rods and paper, had a small light in it, and for quite some time, this was the only light in the theater. We were part of the sea.

That singular speck of light, carried overhead by members of the audience, immediately established the Pequod's journey as both dangerous and awe-inspiring. It also meant that, in a proscenium house where spectators otherwise face the stage, we were invited to recognize our neighbors in much the same way as one might when sitting in a pew during a religious rite.

Our acknowledgment of one another, along with the passing of the light (inside the paper ship), marked the liminality of Blair Thomas and Company's "part ritual, part religious service" performance, transforming our spectatorship into communion and our interaction into *communitas.* As Victor Turner puts it, within the liminal stage of rituals, when individuals are on the threshold of some kind of (usually sacred) transformation, they experience communitas, and in so doing offer "recognition to an essential and generic human bond, without which there could be *no* society."[36] For Thomas and Company's *Moby Dick*, this bond was established by inviting the audience to become part of the performance, using the material prop of the paper boat to extend the physical boundaries of the stage into the imaginary, even sacred, space of collective participation.

Thus we witness the shift from material to ethereal space, a threshold especially apt for puppet and object theatre to occupy. So far, our discussion of space/place theory in relationship to *Moby-Dick* has focused on the practical concerns of theatrical venue and the configurations of audiences relative to the performances. Special attention has been paid to the liminal and surrounding aspects of these architectural spaces, since these are often the domain of the dramaturg or are at the very least dramaturgically noteworthy. The practical architectural and spatial decisions are closely related to the decisions the creative team makes regarding the staging of imaginary space, and often overlap therein. Just because the space is literal (made of bricks and mortar) does not mean that it is empty (of meaning). For instance, an obvious way that both SAÏAH and Lookingglass used space (or, one might say, that space used them) for their adaptations of *Moby-Dick* was to embrace the phallic resonances of this tale. Because their versions of Melville's book were staged in buildings with rather tall ceilings, each production (in different ways) took advantage of those vertical possibilities. This observation acknowledges both the imminently practical (actors should explore all available space; ships have multiple levels, so vertical staging is in keeping with their reality) and theoretical implications (it is, after all, a story about men).[37] To explore these gendered implications further, we shall consider imaginary space.

Imaginary Space and Adapturgy: Staging the (Whiteness of the) Whale

By imaginary space, I mean to suggest the space of ideas and cognition, usually driven by the director's concept but equally influenced by the spirit of the adaptation. These metaphors and ways of thinking may begin as amorphous thoughts, but ultimately must take shape as part of the design of the performance, thus taking up physical space.[38] In the case of *Moby-Dick*, the productions' approaches to staging the whale become particularly useful examples of how imaginary space can take shape onstage. Of the three adaptations (and four productions) I discuss in this chapter, most used human actors to symbolize it; only one chose to portray the whale with an object. That adaptation, not surprisingly, was the one based in spectacle and puppetry; as Blair Thomas put it during an interview at the Chicago Humanities Festival, "Here we have a vocabulary where [staging the whale] is possible."[39]

But Thomas ultimately found that his earliest attempts to represent the whale were least satisfying when they most resembled the mammal directly. "There's a problem when it becomes so concrete," he explained. During the yearlong residency at the University of Chicago, he concentrated on the chapters where Ahab and his crew zero in on the white whale (the three days/chapters of "The Chase"), and through trial and error discovered that "if the picture is too complete, the audience doesn't have anything to do."[40] Moreover, in Melville's tales, the only whales that are actually seen by the crew are those that are captured (and dismembered and drained for oil). In order to evoke (rather than represent) a whale, Thomas and Company used a large illuminated paper blimp, which whalers could cut open onstage. The blimp made the scale as well as the brutality of the hunt evident, while still requiring spectators to use their imagination to connect the dots.

Thomas's beliefs about suggesting rather than directly showing Moby Dick resonate with the other adaptations as well. Khalid, the director of the SAÏAH found-space version of Gentile's adaptation, had this to say about whether (or how) to stage the whale: "Putting a 'whale' on stage could never be done gracfully [*sic*]. . . . For us the presence of what the whale represents . . . is so much more powerful."[41] Coincidentally enough, in both Catlin and Gentile's adaptations, the answer to how to represent the whale with grace was to transfer the idea of a whale onto the human female body.

Catlin claims that he "knew from the beginning" that he would have women play the whale/s in his adaptation. Without question, *Moby Dick* would be a "dude-heavy show," as Catlin put it, and thus from the start he wondered about those years on the ship, what it meant for the brief stints at home with their wives or (when applicable) female partners.[42] In addition, Catlin recognized that we use feminine pronouns for ships ("Thar she blows!") and the ocean can be seen as a feminine force, even as amniotic fluid of the earth. The following passage (from "Loomings," the first chapter) in particular inspired how Catlin envisioned the three female roles in his adaptation: "I cannot tell why it was exactly that those stage managers, the Fates, put me down for this shabby part of a whaling voyage."[43] Willfully conflating the Greek understanding of the Fates with the Furies, while also calling upon the multiple allusions to *Macbeth* (and, in this case, the Three Weird Sisters) throughout the novel, Catlin created a haunting and avenging role for three women (the Fates), who also portray the whale.[44]

The female actors' costumes provide the means for much of the whale symbolism—they begin in traditional Victorian garb, with voluminous layers. The sound of their parasols opening and closing, for example, represents the opening and closing of the whale spout. When Stubb kills a whale (Melville's chapter 61) in Catlin's adaptation, one of the Fates (played by Emma Cadd) is hoisted up onto the Pequod, wearing a black dress, her limp body slumped on the stage. Crewmen attach her feet to a rigging pulley, and she is raised upside down, her hooped skirt falling over her face and torso. The men unwrap the whale carcass as they might peel an orange, pulling the ribbon of clothing while the lifeless body spins above them. Finally, the dark skirt has been fully stripped away, leaving her underhoops dangling over her head and her pelvis and thighs fully exposed to their white leotard base. As this shell of the mammal is lowered to the ground, the actor's costume has gone from a proper traveling dress to her white whale-boned corset and

Fig. 6.1. The Fates of *Moby Dick*. Actors, *left to right*, Monica West (Fate #1), Kasey Foster (Fate #2), and Emma Cadd (Fate #3) in *Moby Dick*, adapted and directed by David Catlin and produced by Lookingglass Theatre Company (2015). *Photograph by Liz Lauren.*

the skeleton hoops of her skirt; from a Victorian perspective, she is naked. In her role as the whale, she has been gutted.

This scene is particularly disturbing for the ways it signifies sinister male group activities. Because all of the crew members are focused on one body, gleefully removing that body's clothes and exposing its underwear, it is difficult not to associate the butchery as sexual assault. Unsettling as it is, the resonance between the two events is not entirely misplaced—for animal and environmental activists, the brutal attempts of (hu)mankind to assert power over Mother Earth can be understood as a kind of rape. But the Fates in the Lookingglass *Moby Dick* are not powerless victims—quite the contrary, they control mortality itself, ushering the dead through a warmly lit door upstage left. When they embody the "White Whale," they do so in tandem, with grotesque makeup exaggerating their mouths and eyes as they open both unnaturally wide. In the final moments of the play, another of the Fates (played by Kasey Foster) stands center, her voluminous skirt extending around her to the limits of visible stage. As each crew member loses his life, he meets his Fate literally, walking up to her as she greets him with a kiss, before ducking under her enormous, billowing skirt, representing the vast mystery of the ocean itself.

With one exception (a split-second spectacle when the dark stage is illuminated by a huge white canopy that flips up and over the audience like a whale's tail), in the Lookingglass adaptation the physicality of the whale is left to our imagination, as symbolized by the gestures and use of women. By contrast, Gentile's adaptation of *Moby-Dick* features one woman playing The Whiteness of the Whale, a character Gentile created to embody the chapter of that name in Melville's novel. In this version, there is no attempt to depict the whale directly; instead, attention is paid to the numinous qualities the whale represents, with particular focus on Melville's exploration of whiteness in chapter 42.

Whereas in Catlin's adaptation the focus was on the fantastic and monstrous qualities of the sea voyage and Moby Dick respectively, in Gentile's version Ishmael's journey takes on the extraordinary qualities of a pilgrimage. Through Ahab's doomed quest for the great white whale Ishmael catches a glimpse of the numinous—"the paradoxical combination of fear and fascination experienced in the non-rational perception of the mysterious and sacred."[45] Much of that paradox finds articulation through Briana Brock's portrayal of The Whiteness of the Whale, a narrator who frames the performance (opening act 1 and act 2) with lines from this chapter, wherein Melville reflects on the terrifying purity of whiteness—"which strikes more of a panic to the soul than that redness which affrights in blood." Brock, costumed in regal white attire, corseted and with a high, stiff collar to accentuate her stature (she towers over many of the male actors and is virtually the same height as the actor playing Ahab), spoke this chapter's lines from a platform above the stage, underscoring the distance between her and the men on the ship, between the sacred and the profane.

Aside from Brock's embodiment of whiteness, the whale's body (or remnants thereof) is represented in Gentile's staging of chapter 94, "A Squeeze of the Hand." This memorable chapter, about the labor of squeezing solidified whale spermaceti into liquid, has been called "one of the most erotic scenes in nineteenth-century American literature."[46] Rather than omit the chapter (as Catlin does), Gentile embraces these implications, having the male actors sit in a circle chanting "squeeze!" in a moment that—according to his stage directions—"builds to a climax of bliss, transcendence, and *communitas* among the men." Without question, the sight of five men ("shirtless or fully nude") seated in a circle as they massage white cloth and proclaim the virtues of spermaceti solidifies their intramale bond and reads as a (homo) sexual release—thus, spectators witness a ritualized group orgasm.[47]

As indicated in Gentile's stage directions, however, the purpose for release is not merely physical. This shared experience is meant to be a rite of passage, and as such the scene falls at nearly the exact center of the script (but approximately three quarters of the way through the novel). To put it in traditional American actor-training terms, the objective driving the story—the grand hunt that these men undertake following the obsessive leadership of Captain Ahab—is about more than killing the whale. It is about discovering one's place in the world, as a man among men, but also as a human among other creatures—all of whom exist within a world governed by forces greater than our mortal minds can fathom.

In representing the whale (or its whiteness) through human female actors, both Catlin and Gentile appear to embrace the analysis other scholars have made about Melville's cetological assumptions—namely, that whales epitomize the mystical feminine, in contrast to the masculine energy of the shipmen.[48] As cultural critic Richard Slotkin argues, "Moby Dick is either an avatar of the nature goddess, embodying a principle of fertility, or else the objective correlative of the anima, the necessary feminine component of Ahab's own mind—or both at once."[49] Had either adaptation decided to represent the whale realistically (either by staging the production in an aquarium, for example, or creating a huge replica of the animal), it is doubtful that audiences would see the mammal as gendered at all.[50] By anthropomorphizing Moby Dick through the medium of women's bodies, Catlin and Gentile ensure that spectators will share this gendered vision of the title character.

In so doing, they also invite our recognition that the experience of space—both on- and offstage—is inexorably tied to gender.[51] This observation matters regardless of where and how the audience is positioned, but in theatres of encounter, such as the site-specific adaptation of *Moby-Dick* that SAÏAH created, the gendered dynamics of space come into sharper focus. While during the first portion of SAÏAH's production, the audience processed through the space, following characters (such as the Whiteness of the Whale and Ishmael), by the time Father Mapple gave his sermon (perhaps fifteen minutes into the performance), we were no longer transient. With some odd chairs and stools set up to face the dock they used as the

Pequod for the remaining action, some spectators sat down, leaving others to stand. While not set up in the same "survival-of-the-fittest" race that the immersive theatre troupe Punchdrunk embraces for their wildly popular *Sleep No More*, there was nevertheless a social negotiation that took place as the audience members recognized that there were not enough chairs for everyone to sit.[52] While some allowances were made for age and ability (chairs were offered to those who appeared more feeble), others were made to favor women over men, segregating the audience such that the able-bodied men stood, increasing their vision as well as their visibility.

In addition to the material ways that space is gendered, allowing men to take up more space with their bodies, our very concept of what is visible/physical and what is invisible/imaginary is gendered. The Fates in Catlin's adaptation and the Whiteness of the Whale in Gentile's version are not really beings so much as they are concepts. While the concepts themselves are crucial and fertile ground for adaptation dramaturgy to explore, the fact that they are made manifest through women's bodies also matters. How different would these adaptations be if men were cast in those roles? How important were the dresses and undergarments to Catlin's metaphors about the ways men dominate animals (and women), from whale-boned corsets to the skirt (and ultimately the womb) symbolizing the depths of the ocean, most of which remain unknown to humankind?

At the heart of any consideration of space for theatrical adaptation is this question: how do we transform what we have imagined into a story that can be performed by actors within the parameters of our chosen (or assigned) stage? And how does the material and social reality of our current world intersect or collide with that of the source? In the case of *Moby-Dick*, because Melville's subject is necessarily hidden—whether one considers it to be Ahab's hubris, Ishmael's pilgrimage, or the hunt for the great white whale (and all the power and monstrosity it comes to represent)—the challenge of performing this tale brings sharper focus to the artistic labor involved in giving shape to all theatrically adapted literature. Like the whale, the stories we imagine swim under the surface of the ocean, and without dramaturgical care the physical shape we give them can render them lifeless, a material body without soul. How then, can we preserve the spirit of the source? This question—which turns on the matter of how to transform literature's imaginary world using the language of the stage—is the subject of the next chapter, as we shift from "Theorizing Practice" to the final section of this book, "Practicing Theory."

PART THREE

PRACTICING THEORY

7. WORKING WITH THE SCRIPT (THE SPIRIT OF THE SOURCE)

By this point, it should be clear that dramaturgy is the very lifeblood of adaptation. How that blood flows through the creation of adaptations for theatre is the subject of this chapter. In 2014, Michael Haverty and I developed a new adaptation of Stephen Crane's 1895 novel *The Red Badge of Courage* for Kennesaw State University and 7 Stages theatre in Atlanta. The following year, I directed our adaptation for Auburn University's new black box theatre. Here, I reflect on these two productions to demonstrate some of the practical ways in which dramaturgical awareness is critical to the task of adapting literary works for the stage, with special attention to "the spirit of the source."

There were several factors influencing our decision to adapt this novel.[1] For one, the fact that Crane's novel was in the public domain was essential for us. Our earlier attempts to secure rights to other literature had been unsuccessful, so we embraced the freedom such a source offered. Because our source was not managed by an estate or living author, we could take creative risks and liberties that might not have been possible otherwise. For this reason as well as the financial reality of royalties, experimental theatre companies often gravitate toward adaptations of public-domain material. 7 Stages is one such experimental theatre, located in the historically hip Little 5 district of Atlanta. The Department of Theatre and Performance Studies (TPS) at Kennesaw State University (a public university with a history as a commuter school serving a culturally diverse population) supplements its regular curriculum and season offerings with courses and productions led by professional theatre makers from the Atlanta area; however, this was the first partnership of its kind for TPS. Michael and I had the opportunity of a "soft opening," as part of the TPS season—then, after two weeks off (during which time we revised the script), we had one week to rehearse the production in the studio theatre of 7 Stages, before our professional run began.

In addition to material concerns about public domain, producing *Red Badge of Courage* during a season that coincided with the 150th anniversary of the Kennesaw Mountain battle of the Civil War appealed to us for the possible publicity this might generate as well as the dramaturgical energy upon which we hoped to capitalize. We reasoned that if the city of Kennesaw were going to commit time and labor to commemorating this battle, our cast and crew could benefit from their research and outreach. These incentives alone would never motivate us to undertake such a challenge, however; there were also several aesthetic and personal reasons we wanted to adapt *Red Badge*. For Michael, who is a Civil War devotee, Crane's novel had burned a psychic imprint on his soul: he loved the language and the spirit of the Youth's story, and had long been fascinated with the prospect of making theatre about the Civil War. In my case, I was unfamiliar with *Red Badge* and Crane altogether, but as I encountered Crane's poetic language and recognized the dissociative patterns of trauma he was describing, I found myself drawn further into the literary and historical world the author had conjured.

In US public schools, *The Red Badge of Courage* is often a required text in junior high or early high school, and the basic story is fairly simple: a young man—Henry Fleming, first identified as "a youthful private"—joins the Union army during the height of the American Civil War, leaving his mother behind.[2] He doubts that he will have the courage to face the enemy in battle and indeed he does run away, eventually getting a head wound that others assume is his "red badge" earned in combat. Paradoxically, Henry is both a coward and a hero: he allows his peers to believe he has honorably fought and survived a shot to the head, but also comes to see the more refined and subtle ways of demonstrating courage, and the final lines of Crane's novel suggest the Youth has reached a peaceful resolution, that all is right with the world: "Over the river a golden ray of sun came through the hosts of leaden rain clouds."

Most of the scholarship surrounding *The Red Badge of Courage* focuses on interpretive strategies used to assess whether (and how) Henry is a hero, and if he is not, whether (and how) he matures over the course of the novel. Because Crane is deliberately ambiguous, the novel ultimately "tests us nearly as much as it does Henry Fleming, eliciting judgments that in turn judge us more than is true of most fictional texts."[3] Mixing detailed naturalistic descriptions with a knack for "the landscape of hysteria," the author invites the reader to experience the confusion and trauma of war.[4] His great innovation, and what drew us to the text, is the way Crane presents war "as a system of violent insatiability," emphasizing the perspective that combat "does not produce heroes; it produces mangled bodies."[5] Thus, it is an ironic vision of war: on the surface it appears to uphold heroism and manly battles, but upon reflection Crane's tone is unmistakably wry, even sarcastic.

How, then, might we adapt this text? How could we honor the bloody "crimson blotches on the pages of the past," while also embodying the irony in the author's voice?[6] At the heart of these adaptation decisions is a slippery concept that calls for greater attention, especially when considering the process and product of adaptation: "the spirit of the source." As discussed in chapter 3, this notion—that a source has a spirit, and that we might arrive at agreement about what the nature of that *spirit* is—is crucial to the approach I take as adaptation dramaturg. Above all else, it is this idea that becomes the decisive factor in my desire to collaborate on any project, but especially new adaptations such as the one Michael and I created with *Red Badge of Courage*. What I call *spirit* others might call *essence*—insofar as they also seek to communicate the most vital part of the source. While essence and spirit are both useful concepts to help articulate what guides the creative work of adapting literature for the stage, my choice of spirit stems from the word's meaning of "the animating or vital principle in man (and animals); that which gives life to the physical organism, in contrast to its purely material elements; the breath of life."[7] "The breath of life" can be seen as the transformation of a story from the singular experience of reading it on the page to the communal one of experiencing it performed live; by adapting it for the stage, we give breath and embodiment to stories. Also, unlike essence, spirit conveys a kind of *numinous* energy—an encounter with something beyond the material world (or things that might be experienced with the five senses) that both fascinates and terrifies the reader. Rudolf Otto's word *numinous* refers to the quality of a sacred encounter. As mentioned in chapter 3, Otto defined numinous as that which evokes *mysterium tremendum et fascinans*, or an ineffable experience to which we are powerfully drawn and of which we are simultaneously terrified. The paradox of being both attracted and repulsed suggests that this is an uncanny encounter, that perhaps it registers as familiar and wholly unknown at once, adding to the push-pull sensation of discovering the numinous.

In my experience as dramaturg of numerous adaptations, it is frequently this numinous and uncanny quality that adapters target for transformation into live performance. As we have reviewed, the stage is a place of disappearance, surrogation, and ghosts—so it makes sense that adapters would be drawn to these aspects when considering how to give breath to literature for theatrical purposes.[8] The centrality of breath becomes even more visible in adaptations (like ours) that use puppets, as the actors bring an inanimate object to life, making the puppet appear to breathe. As Dassia Posner argues, "Every puppet performance is, to some degree, a performance of the ür-narrative of life."[9] That is, by choosing to use puppetry (or to give life to an object), adapters emphasize the animating quality itself, an experience that is frequently uncanny for spectators. Add to this the ephemeral nature of the stage, combined with the collective memory of all who have walked the boards before—these factors might influence adapters' inclusion of numinous scenes. Or perhaps the nature of adaptation itself invites a focus on the uncanny. Either way, my research has suggested that by looking for the *mysterium tremendum et fascinans*, we can better see the dramaturgical research undergirding theatrical adaptations.

In the case of *Red Badge of Courage*, both Michael and I were particularly intrigued by the manner in which Crane narrates the introspection of the Youth (Henry Fleming)—the way that his imagination and inner monologues transform through his experience with the "fog of war," through encounters with death and the dying, and what we came to understand as a dissociative pattern not uncommon to survivors of (natural and man-made) trauma. Whereas other adapters have chosen to depict this inner life through monologues and character speech (including narration), we decided not to include word-based narration in our staging. Most extant theatrical adaptations of *Red Badge* are targeted for young audiences, a genre that often employs narration and storytelling techniques. In addition, these theatre-for-young-audiences (TYA) adaptations are frequently penned with the expectation of touring, meaning that the scenic designs for these tours are minimal.[10] Not only does Crane avoid using first person (with the exception of dialogue) throughout the book, but the descriptive passages about the landscape are so vivid that nature virtually becomes a character. Recognizing the primacy of image and sound for Crane, we sought to capture the spirit of this piece through three audiovisual narrative approaches: the portal, the projected animation and musical score, and the puppet.

Fig. 7.1. *Red Badge of Courage* at 7 Stages (2014). Actors, *left to right*, Laura Driskill, Megan Jance, and Bryan Mercer in *Red Badge of Courage*, with text by Stephen Crane, created by Michael Haverty and Jane Barnette. *Photograph by Chris Burk, Stungun Photography.*

The Role of the Portal

Our earliest conversations about the novel began with sharing the impressions that stuck with us the most. While we had slightly different examples, Michael and I both remembered the moments when the Youth encountered death as our pivotal images. This organizing principle—the perception that, when boiled down to its core, *Red Badge* is about the Youth's terrifying yet mesmerizing experience of facing mortality—influenced our scenic design with our inclusion of a portal. We knew we wanted this portal to function metaphorically in addition to serving as an actual entrance or exit: we wanted to signal a threshold between the world of the living and the dead, between the world that we experience with our five senses and what lies beyond.

Because we kept referring to the "hell of war," as well as the "fog of war," we decided to nudge those metaphors into the design. In early discussions, I brought into the mix images of the medieval hellmouth, as depicted in artwork as well as on vernacular religious drama stages, as inspiration. Hellmouths, usually crafted as gaping beast mouths with sharp teeth, featuring the scent of rotting animal flesh and filled with various (actors costumed as) demons, reminded audiences that hell is repulsive and terrifying, and coincided with the church-based message of this type of medieval theatre: to repent and be saved from everlasting damnation. While neither of us considered the source particularly religious (much less Christian), we were intrigued by the possibility of salvation that we saw in the Youth's encounters with death.

In our script, the earliest description of this portal states that it "is a large hole [about four feet diameter, raised about three feet from the floor] in the center of sheet [of fabric that stretches from the back wall over the heads of the spectators] through which set pieces and performers may come and go."[11] In consultation with our student set designer (Alyssa Brosy), the portal became a giant barrel of a gun, big enough for actors to crawl through.[12] The unnaturally large gun barrel, along with the use of miniature muslin tents in the opening scene, establish a warping of scale that unmoors the audience from what is "natural" or "real." By making the portal a larger-than-life rifle barrel, we absorbed the concept of the feudal hellmouth into an industrial capitalist vision of life and death. This coincided with other parts of our early conversations about "the spirit of the source," insofar as it represented a machine in the garden, mirroring Crane's consistent juxtaposition of the man-made world of firearms and war with the challenges of the natural world, which often prove to be just as inhospitable to the Youth.

Even so, the oversized barrel still functions as a sacred portal, and its selective use underscores how it can be seen as a threshold space of significance. For example, the first entrance through the barrel is made by the puppet, manned by three puppeteers standing behind the barrel. The sound effect is one of "distant rumbling," meant to be "like birthing, the BIG BANG."[13] The next entrance through the barrel is of another uncanny object—"paper trees with tops shaped somewhat like bullets, so that as they enter through the hole they seem like bullets exiting a gun barrel."[14] From the audience perspective, this moment first seems familiar (a bullet coming out of a gun), before the entire prop is seen. Once the objects are outside of the portal, they are recognized as trees (or tree-like items), a transformation that is both surprising and disquieting, as something that once appeared to be man-made (a bullet) has been understood to be a (prop representing) a living natural thing (a tree).[15] The next use of the barrel as portal is when the Youth has been wounded, when the puppet guides him through the barrel, as an exit rather than an entrance. Following this, the lights rise on him sleeping within the barrel after he has been discovered by his fellow soldiers. At the emotional climax of the play—what we call the "black rage" section—the Youth turns his back to the audience, faces the barrel, and continues to reload and shoot at the screen animation.

The way the Youth processes those challenges was of particular interest to us, insofar as it was both crucial to the source and (arguably) potentially the most difficult part of Crane's novel to dramatize. How do you stage a journey of the mind, in the midst of a story about the Civil War? In the medium of literature that is typically read individually and silently, the mental diversions and struggles of the Youth are immersive, even against the backdrop of the battleground scenes and his close encounters with death. But on stage, it is different. We could choose to have the Youth tell the audience what he was thinking, in a series of monologues, but since we had chosen to omit all other narration, this felt out of place. We wanted the experience of watching the play to be intense and visceral, a theatre of cruelty immersion—into the terrible truth of war that took inspiration from Antonin Artaud. Thus, we decided to privilege image and sound over language, and depicted the Youth's inner thoughts through projected animations, supported by original music composed by Damon Young.

The Role of Image and Sound

While there are also instances where animation supported the *mise en scène* more generally (e.g., establishing the time of day, weather, or location), its primary purpose with regard to the adaptation dramaturgy was to represent the Youth's dreamlike and nightmarish thoughts. The first time this occurs in our script is when the Youth daydreams about the circus, while the army waits for their marching orders. "What did they march us out here for?" he asks. "The battle's somewhere else. We're just a demonstration. I want to see some action!"[16] As if queued by his demand for action, on the screen we begin to see circus imagery and we hear the barker say, "If it's action you want, well then my boy, join the circus parade!" The barker is played by the same actor who plays the Lieutenant as well as Tall (or Jim Conklin), the soldier who becomes a fatherlike mentor to the Youth. The fact that one actor plays these three roles helps relay our intention that the advertisement of the circus acts sound much like the pitching of the military—that buying tickets is like signing up to join the army, that playing a shooting game is like being in glorious battle, and so on. The frenetic energy of the circus is matched by the chaotic rush to battle that follows on the tail of this divertissement, as the images on the screen transform from circus activities like a magician and animals playing instruments to a large red reptile—"the swollen red animal," in Crane's words. At this point, the music also changes from a circus parade to a war march, and the Lieutenant rushes onstage, saying, "You've got to hold 'em back!"[17] In the following sequence, as the Youth encounters his first actual battle, the animation continues to display his terror by morphing the red animal (a snake in the Atlanta shows and a dragon in the Auburn production), so that it eventually "vomits red bullets."

The next symbolic use of animation occurs near the end of the play, but before I turn to that moment, I want to zero in on how the music helps establish the pivotal death of Tall, who dies before the Youth's eyes in what Crane describes as a "hideous hornpipe" of a macabre dance that almost resembles a grand mal seizure. This encounter deeply affects the Youth, not only because he witnesses the gruesome death of his closest friend but also because Tall dies the way a soldier should die: from the wounds he has received during war, because he stayed on the battleground and fought, rather than running away from the danger (as the Youth has done). This extended death scene stood out to us in the source as an event that lent itself quite well to theatre. It is already dramatic and spectacular in the novel when described by language alone; when embodied in live performance, it is mesmerizing yet terrifying. Consider the theatricality of Crane's description of Tall's downward spiral (which we used as stage directions):

> *There is a resemblance in Jim to a devotee of a mad religion, blood-sucking, muscle-wrenching, bone-crushing. . . . Suddenly his form stiffens and straightens. Then it is shaken by a prolonged ague. For a moment the tremor of his legs causes him to dance a sort of hideous hornpipe. His arms beat wildly about his head. His tall figure stretches itself to its full height. Then it swings forward, slow and straight, in the manner of a falling tree. The body bounces on the earth.*[18]

Dramaturgical research revealed that the hornpipe is a folk dance of Celtic descent, with active legwork and folded or otherwise nonactive arms, sort of like a jig. The hideous (or grotesque) version of this might exaggerate the disconnect between the legs and the rest of the body, as if they were convulsing of their own accord, quite apart from the rest of his wounded body.

Fig. 7.2. Death of Tall (Bryan Mercer) in Kennesaw State University's 2014 production of *Red Badge of Courage*, with text by Stephen Crane, created by Michael Haverty and Jane Barnette. *Photograph by Robert Pack, Widescreen Video Productions.*

The music for this section supports the frantic pace of the hornpipe, with a forward-driving beat punctuated by a chord-playing fiddle. The chords increase in intensity throughout the song, played during the stage directions quoted above. Young's "Hornpipe" is surprisingly upbeat for a swan song, but fits the bizarre explosive dance that accompanies Tall's strange death. For those who have read Crane, this passage was probably memorable, and yet seeing it in a live performance, with an actor mimicking those spasms accompanied by such agitating music, is likely a more extreme experience. The result is a dance that is both spellbinding and horrific.

The Youth also gets wounded later in the story, but his injury comes from an exasperated soldier who bashes him in the head with his rifle butt, not from fighting the enemy in an honorable way. Nevertheless, when he is discovered and nursed back to health by the soldier called Loud, the Youth never corrects his assumption that the wound was sustained in battle, instead basking in the misplaced respect that his peers pay him. This pride boils over into the next symbolic animation sequence—of the Youth's "black rage" that rises when he and Loud charge the enemy and seize the flag. Because our adaptation pulled in parts of the lost manuscript from Crane's earlier draft of *The Red Badge of Courage*, featuring what we perceived to be a complete loss of moral compass, this moment of rage was important to symbolize as part of the Youth's descent into madness. By definition, rage is an uncontrolled and violent variant of anger. To symbolize this loss of control, the animation imagery gets chaotic, as does the music. For the Auburn production, the animation designer Matt Kizer created a swirling hypnotic effect for the black rage section that suggested a blurring of the lines between reality and fantasy, as if the Youth were undergoing (or spectators were invited to take part in) a surreal expansion of consciousness.[19] In so doing, the images projected on the screen encouraged a *psychedelic* experience—not in the modern sense of mind-altering drug usage, but from the Ancient Greek, meaning to make the soul visible.[20]

The Role of the Puppet

Crucial to our understanding of the Youth's journey was an analysis that his quest for courage is about more than physical or mental bravery. The Youth wants enlightenment, or to become his highest and best self, and the war provides a convenient *topos* for an extraordinary experience that might lead to this higher self. The puppet, therefore, became a physical manifestation of the Youth's heightened consciousness. The puppet, built with long rods and meant to be operated by two to three puppeteers, is costumed identically to the Youth and resembles him with the striking exception that it has no facial expression or fully recognizable face. Our request to puppet designer Tanner Slick was to build a "faceless" puppet; the resulting design achieved our goal by including eyes (with what appears to be a concerned expression on the puppet's forehead) but no mouth. The absence of a mouth allowed the puppet to mirror the facial expression of the Youth, to morph more easily with a spectator's imagination. This detail became so important that when

Slick was commissioned to build another puppet for the Auburn remount of *Red Badge*, we ultimately chose to use the original puppet, because the newly designed one was too expressive. Not only did he have a mouth, but his eyes were chiseled out and there were deep nasolabial folds that indicated age and wisdom, ultimately making the new puppet not functional for the spirit of our production. In complement to this design, the costume design in both productions featured a Kepi hat that could be pulled low on the actors' brow bones to hide their eyes, so that only their mouths were visible. Thus, when functioning as puppeteer, the half of the actor's face that remained visible completed the part of the puppet's face that was absent.

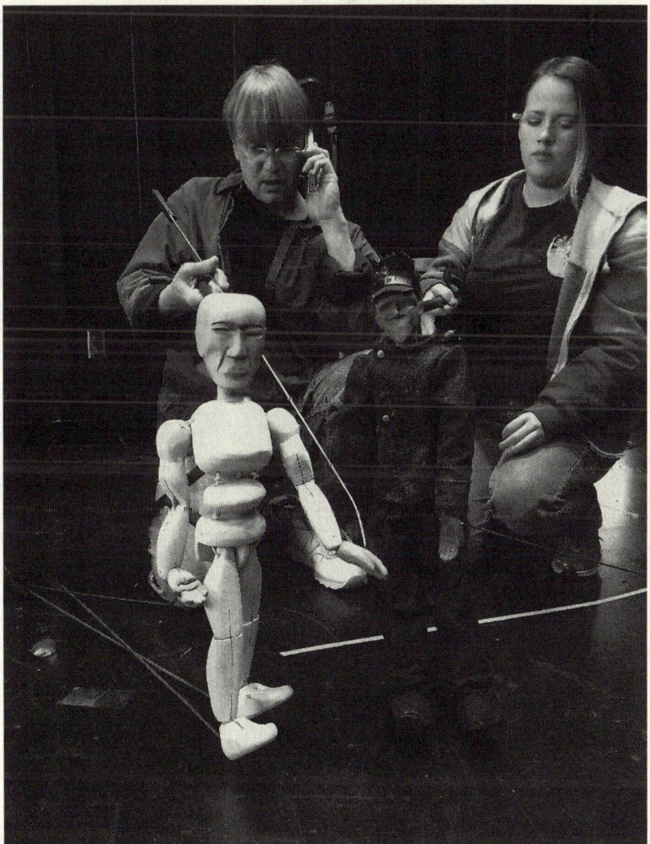

Fig. 7.3. Bryan Mercer and Jillian Jernigan with puppets designed by Tanner Slick for Auburn University's 2015 production of *Red Badge of Courage*, created by Michael Haverty and Jane Barnette. *Photograph by Parker Stripling.*

The simultaneous presence of the puppeteer and the puppet brings attention to the theatricality of the action in *Red Badge*, heightening the visual metanarrative onstage. By virtue of having a puppet onstage, before even considering the role the puppet plays in the adaptation, the audience is encouraged to consider the "spirit of the source," insofar as "a puppet is by its very nature dead, whereas an actor is by her very nature alive. The puppet's work then . . . is to strive towards life."[21] Our adaptation, both in script and staging, further emphasizes this ür-narrative, adding to it the quality of striving toward heightened consciousness.

The puppet appears four times in our stage adaptation: first, during a dreamlike memory and premonition sequence at the top of the play; then, when he encounters the corpse in the "chapel of trees"; again, when the Youth is injured accidentally; and at the end of the play, when the puppet carries a folded flag. While the initial and final appearance of the puppet function primarily as framing devices to establish the disconnect between the Youth's imagination or visions and his reality, the middle two appearances are tied directly to the puppet as a visible object that stands in for the concept of the Youth's enlightened self, as well as his very survival.

By directing the puppeteers to make the *Red Badge* puppet float in midair, we further emphasized the numinous quality of the puppet. This aspect, in addition to the fact that only the Youth interacts with the puppet, helps spectators recognize that the puppet is a figment of the Youth's imagination, or that the puppet can be seen only by the sixth sense, as a ghost or spirit of sorts.

In the first of these midpoint instances, the Youth has just run away from battle for the first time. In fear for his life, he does what he has been contemplating doing for some time: he escapes the carnage to protect himself, and in so doing abandons his fellow soldiers. He justifies this cowardly act by telling himself (and the audience) that "I done good saving myself, just a little piece of the army. . . . If none of the little pieces were smart enough to save themselves, why, where would the army be then?"[22] Although his words appear to justify the actions, inside he remains torn ("*his brain in a tumult of agony and despair*") and he retreats further into a forest, which Crane describes as featuring a "religious half-light," and containing a "chapel of trees." This experience is meant to be numinous, and offers the Youth an opportunity for redemption through an encounter with his own mortality when he finds the corpse in short order. To guide him along this extraordinary path, the puppet appears and hovers over the Youth's shoulder. Within the forest, represented on stage by two actors embodying trees, the Youth happens upon the corpse of a fallen soldier.[23] This dead man, in Crane's words (used as stage directions in our script),

> *is dressed in a uniform that had once been blue, but is now faded to a melancholy shade of green. The eyes, staring at the Youth, are the dull hue to be seen on the side of a dead fish. The mouth is open. Its red has changed to an appalling yellow. Over the gray skin of the face run little ants.*[24]

The puppet reaches out to the Youth and turns his head to face the corpse, at which sight he nearly faints, falling to the ground in shock. Once more the puppet approaches the Youth, with the intention of having him look death courageously in the face. The Youth cannot stomach the sight, and pushes the puppet away, keeping his gaze shielded from the corpse. In defeat, the puppet exits, and the encounter is incomplete—the opportunity for numinous wisdom is thwarted.

In this scene, there are two puppets—the corpse and the primary puppet—but only the latter moves.[25] Still, the design of the corpse puppet matters here, as it stems from our adaptation vision, or what we interpreted as "the spirit of the source." Without question, we intended for the corpse puppet to evoke shock, to make spectators feel some of the same push-pull energy that the Youth feels upon seeing this dead man. To achieve this, in both productions the designers created puppets that were uncanny in their likeness to a skeletal human figure, with ample decomposition of the "flesh" made apparent by the black light that we used to illuminate the portal in which the corpse sat. By using ultraviolet paint on the corpse-puppet, the designers could draw attention to the figure immediately, as it was dark elsewhere on stage, and this was the only instance of black light used, emphasizing how unique this encounter was.

The next time the puppet appears is when the Youth sustains his concussion, and falls dizzily to the ground. Helping him to his feet, the puppet checks on the Youth with concern, but when the Youth reaches out to grab the puppet, hoping to cradle him in his arms, the puppet dodges him, maintaining a close distance. As the Youth stumbles across the stage, the puppet gently guides him upstage toward the portal/gun barrel, and nudges him to enter it. He crawls through the hole and the lights fade out; when they come back up, we see the Youth's silhouette on the projection screen, staggering about.

Throughout both of these middle puppet sequences, because the puppet appears when the Youth is alone and in need, the audience associates the puppet with the Youth, even if spectators remain uncertain as to the exact nature of the puppet's being (is he real or imagined?) or the purpose of his visits. While they may have different ways of describing it, most spectators also recognize that the puppet represents a numinous creature, in part because of the uncanny nature of puppets as animated dolls, though here this is further emphasized by the times the puppet appears onstage as well as its specific design—to resemble the Youth in small scale, but without a mouth or fully designed face.

By animating the more enlightened part of the Youth's consciousness as a puppet, this adaptation uses primarily the visual language of the stage to articulate what we saw as the "spirit of the source." The spectacle of puppetry, combined with the projected animations, original music, and live silhouette work, give breath to both the Youth's inner mental state and the disquieting irony of war that we understood as Crane's vision in *Red Badge*. The frame of the adaptation—a brief opening and closing chorus of sorts—shows where we took the most liberty in departing from the familiar novel's dialogue, in service to our overall vision.

The Role of the Ending

In particular, the ending to our *Red Badge of Courage* demonstrates the merging of new play and production dramaturgy that is adapturgy in two distinct but related ways. First, our closing choral scene refracted our opening one, by including key lines from the script, but assigning them to different characters. For example, while the Youth originally says "Yeh ain't at all like yeh was" to Loud, in the last choral section, it is the Sarcastic Soldier who says this line to him, as he leaves the stage. Perhaps the most noticeable bookend is the repetition of the haunting victory song that occurs at the top of the show, in this final choral moment, and in the middle, just before Tattered's scene with Youth:

> Sing a song of Victory
> Pocket full of bullets
> Five and Twenty dead men
> Baked in a pie.
> When the pie was opened
> The dead began to sing
> Wasn't that a dainty dish
> To set before the King.

The repetition of these lines along with their placement highlight how adapturgy shaped our directing concept for staging *Red Badge*—the recognition that war warps the way soldiers perceive reality.

Thus, rather than ending on a hopeful note (as the published novel does), Michael and I chose to honor the ambiguity and irony that we most admired in Crane's voice. As part of the process of creating the script (that is, within the framework of new play dramaturgy), I researched the publication history of *The Red Badge of Courage.* Serendipitously, the version of the novel I first encountered included chapters and sections that were not in the book as it is commonly known.[26] Several pages from his original manuscript, including the entirety of chapter 12, never made it into the Appleton publication of 1895, probably because they could be perceived as blasphemous.[27] According to Henry Binder, who made the reestablishment of the missing text his personal academic mission, the omission of these pages makes the final chapter of the published book "erratic and confusing [as it] terminates on an inappropriate note."[28] In the deleted sections, especially in the original chapter 12, the Youth positions himself above nature, as a "prophet" who philosophizes a "new world modeled by the pain of life."[29] Michael and I decided to reclaim several passages from this lost chapter, adding them to the finale, so that the Youth's last words are: "I am entirely different from other men. I am the prophet of a *new* world. The laws of life are useless. I abandon the world!"[30]

As he spoke these lines to the audience, the actor playing the Youth climbed up on top of the gun barrel with the flag he captured, waving it aloft as he opened his eyes abnormally wide.[31] The image was one of a man who has lost his grip on reality, a man who is hallucinating and who, in his passionate commitment to these visions, is terrifying in his egomaniacal power. Directly following this proclamation, the puppet begins to march slowly through the portal, holding a folded flag. The final image is of the faceless puppet looking up into the audience, as the lights dim.

If we return to the model of spectator-based adapturgy introduced in chapter 3, we can chart the differences between where an adaptation with this ending might be located within it versus those that retain the Appleton publication's final lines. From our conversations with several veterans of war during the rehearsal processes in both the Atlanta and the Auburn productions, it became apparent that their perception of combat made them exceptionally wary of war stories featuring poetic justice. Their experience made it clear that there was no reward for the "good" and punishment for "evil" anymore than there was an absolute category for heroes and villains. Thus, to end the play in a way that captured the spirit of the Appleton ending (which includes the notion that the Youth "had rid himself of the red sickness of battle")[32] would likely make the play less recognizable to veterans, placing it in the "there" category. But to end the play as we did, with the Youth claiming to abandon the world, after the ecstatic rush of his "black rage" sequence, might locate the experience closer to home for veterans, somewhere on the "here" side of the axis. For those of us who have not been in combat, this perception of familiarity might be reversed, such that we associate the Appleton ending as closer to what we (want to) think war is like: a necessary horror that can be left on the battlefield.

The result of these adapturgy interventions was an adaptation that fully utilized the possibilities of live performance, by focusing on spectacle and unmooring the tidy resolution that poetic justice offers in the published novel. Our use of the portal, projections, and the puppet to articulate visually the daydreams, terror, and dissociation that Crane describes with the written word honored the spirit of the source without spoken narration. In so doing we highlighted the numinous possibilities of stage adaptation, creating a *Red Badge* that was uncanny for spectators with either experience with war or with Crane's novel. For those audience members especially, watching our adaptation was simultaneously familiar and strange, nostalgic and horrible.

8. WORKING WITH THE PRODUCTION

Production dramaturgs are generally involved in part or all of the production process, which can include early conversations with the director and creative team, casting, rehearsals, and audience outreach. As such, and as its name suggests, production dramaturgy deals more with product than process, and the work of adapturgy in this arena can range from work the audience never sees to the most public of "products"—websites available and searchable to anyone with Internet access. Not only are websites temporary, depending on domains and servers usually beyond the dramaturg's control, but most of the time, these so-called products exist to document the *process* of adaptation. There are probably as many variations of how to work with a production as there are dramaturgical (and directorial) personalities.[1] Dramaturgs will want to choose what works best for them and their specific team, with crucial attention to their audience. Of all the chapters thus far, this one contends most directly with the ways adaptation dramaturgs can interact with audiences.

In the last decade, I have worked as a production dramaturg for ten different adaptations, nearly half of which were for the same adapter/director (John Gentile), and most of which were produced during my tenure as resident dramaturg at Kennesaw State University. As this chapter aims to exemplify how an adaptation dramaturg can "practice theory," I will refer to examples from several of these ten productions, but the majority of my practical illustrations will be drawn from the adaptation with which I was (and remain) most intimately involved, *Red Badge of Courage*.[2]

Based on my experience, this chapter outlines seven specific areas where dramaturgical intervention can influence the production and encourage or solicit audience feedback: conscientious casting, cast/crew wikis, embodied experiences, websites and study guides, lobby displays, program notes, and audience conversations (whether held before or after the performances). Some of these areas include process-oriented dramaturgy (conscientious casting, cast/crew wikis, embodied experiences), while others feature products (websites and study guides, lobby displays, and program notes) or are reflective (audience conversations). That dramaturgy includes process, product, and reflection supports the conviction I share with many colleagues: to be a dramaturg is to be both a scholar *and* an artist. Readers will likely notice that the first area, conscientious casting, receives the most attention here. This admitted imbalance stems from my recognition that these questions of representation and inclusion are at the forefront of many artists' concerns, especially when approaching adaptation. As we consider each of these seven options, I will reference both primary and secondary evidence—that is, examples from my personal experience as well as from published sources.

Conscientious Casting

As discussed in chapter 1, the question of representation, especially with regard to casting, is one of the ways that theatrical adaptation can either reify or challenge societal norms and representations of history. In late 2015, the conversation regarding casting decisions reached a fevered pitch, in the wake of Clarion University's cancelled production of *Jesus in India* by Lloyd Suh. In addition to the extraordinary legal blunder of not obtaining the rights to produce this play, the director cast it with non-Indian actors in roles meant to be played by South Asian actors. Marilouise Michel, the director, had taken the cast through virtually the entire rehearsal process in the meantime and had contacted Suh to request a Skype conversation with her actors. Since the playwright was surprised to hear that a production of his play was taking place, he researched further and discovered images of the cast in costume on social media. At that point he and his agent Beth Blickers (the president of LMDA from 2014 to 2015) requested that the university recast the play with Asian actors. Unable to do so, the university was forced to cancel the show, less than a week before opening night.[3]

One of the outcomes of this controversy has been a groundswell of playwrights and dramaturgs (among other creative theatricals) who are outspoken proponents of color-conscious casting. "Color-conscious casting intentionally considers the race and ethnicity of actors and the characters they play in order to oppose racism, honor and respect cultures, foster stronger productions, and contribute to a more equitable world."[4] As seen with

Hamilton on Broadway, making these color-conscious casting choices can reframe the way spectators (and especially fans) see history itself. However, these casting decisions should align with the adaptation and the adapter's vision, and dramaturgs play a vital role in protecting those preferences whenever possible.

Because theatre is always already an adaptation of sorts, the question of casting can easily get misaligned between intention and reception within a discussion of stage adaptation. For example, a reader might imagine ways that certain auteur productions of plays (or even adaptations) fit into this conversation. When director Jude Kelly cast the white actor Patrick Stewart in the role of Othello, for example, we might consider that decision a case of "adapting through directing." The other roles of Washington's Shakespeare Theatre were filled by actors of color, highlighting the degree to which casting alone can have a transformational effect on a production. Similarly, when Sarah Bernhardt played the role of Hamlet in her infamous 1899 production, she was in fact adapting Shakespeare via casting. While casting a traditional play carries with it the potential for adaptation, casting a work adapted from literature brings special challenges.

Some of those challenges under consideration here include race, but others include gender and age (especially within the context of university productions). This only scratches the surface of this complex and critical topic. There is also room for discussion of body image, ethnicity, different physical abilities, and sexuality.[5] It is my hope that this section will begin a larger conversation about the role of adapturgy within conscientious casting that is unfortunately outside the parameters of this study.[6] In addition, as might be expected with the primary case studies under consideration (canonical literature written by white men), often the challenge of conscientious casting is a question of bringing attention to an *absence* of multiplicity; other times, it is an obstacle of transposing language and culture from what might be considered a racist, sexist, and/or ageist source to (what one hopes is) a more progressive audience that therefore may be offended by the dated and problematic original language and culture.

For our adaptation of Stephen Crane's *The Red Badge of Courage,* for example, Haverty and I made the controversial choice of casting three female actors in a cast of five, in an attempt to heighten awareness of the performance of masculinity that is central to war. It is worth noting that Mama is the only female character who speaks in the book; there is a brief reference to two other women from the Youth's hometown, but otherwise women are conspicuously absent from the novel.[7] More egregiously, Crane avoids any discussion of race or slavery in a book about the Civil War, though there is one memorable moment on the first page. "A negro teamster who had been dancing upon a cracker box with the hilarious encouragement of two-score soldiers was deserted. He sat mournfully down."[8] This lone mention of race carries with it a scenario of minstrelsy, which in another context about the nineteenth century might not be unusual. But, as other scholars have noted, the fact that these are Union soldiers in the midst of the Civil War makes its lack of any further commentary about slavery or race relations curious, if not downright troubling.[9]

The controversy over our cross-gender casting choice stemmed from what Rebecca Schneider has called "a drive to an authenticity that *should have been,* according to [Civil War] reenactors' reinterpretations, not necessarily the authenticity that was." And what was this yearned-for "authenticity"? A war that reflected white masculine traits, such as toughness and strength. Thus, while there is convincing evidence that women cross-dressed so they could fight in the 1860s, the myth of the War of Northern Aggression for many Southerners overrides all else, since (as Schneider puts it), "Reenactment communities often want a history sanitized of troublesome 'error,' *even if those errors were fact.*"[10] It is this same discomfort (among other discomforts) that led theatre critic Bert Osborne of the *Atlanta-Journal Constitution* to claim, in a review of *Red Badge,* that while the "age-appropriate casting of comparatively inexperienced college kids as the innocent soldiers in the story makes perfect sense," what did not "frankly, is casting the other three of those roles with actresses in drag." To clarify, while Haverty and I certainly encouraged our entire cast to reflect the displays of masculinity that Crane highlights (especially when the regiment experiences a victory), to call their portrayal "drag" belies a fundamental misunderstanding of what that word means within the drag community. However misplaced his verbiage may have been, Osborne's perspective does remind adaptation dramaturgs of the derogatory effects of the Janus effect discussed in chapter 5, the understanding of two-faced as an unfaithful servant of (the observer's interpretation of) the source.

More to the point of our interpretation of *Red Badge,* by applauding the youth while critiquing the gender of the cast, Osborne (dis)misses a crucial element of our dramaturgy: that by casting women we could highlight the performance of gender, especially as it functions within military culture. This insight factored into our early conversations and collaborative process for writing the adaptation (as discussed in the previous chapter).

Perhaps this casting choice added too much complexity to an adaptation as spectacle-based as ours was. To test that theory, when I directed *Red Badge* the following year at Auburn University, I cast four men and one woman (to play Mama as well as Tattered). Spectators who saw both the Atlanta and Auburn productions reported that they enjoyed the Auburn production more because the casting was more realistic. There was no resistance to casting Tattered with a woman in either production, however, perhaps because she also plays the role of Mama; perhaps because Tattered is a feminine role, who is said to speak with a voice as "gentle as a girl's voice" in Crane's novel.[11] Overall, our dramaturgical experiment with *Red Badge* cross-gender casting reaffirms that fidelity bias is still difficult to overcome with adaptations of well-known literature.

As difficult as fidelity bias may be to overcome, the production by Elevator Repair Service (ERS) of *The Sound and the Fury* nevertheless troubles it with the casting concept that is central to their adaptation. Questions of textual fidelity rarely arise for ERS, since they tend to leave the adapted literature intact, exactly as it was written. Instead, as discussed in chapter 4, company founder John Collins prefers to intervene with the language of the stage as his methodology for adaptation. In the case of *The Sound and the Fury*, this meant that every time the "idiot" brother Benjy's flashbacks change in historical context, the performers would take on different characters to play. Often this meant that men would play female characters, and white actors would play black characters, and vice versa. That said, ERS had far fewer instances of women playing male roles, with the notable exception of the lead role, Benjy, being played primarily by Susie Sokol.

The cross-racial casting of this adaptation was not without critique from within the cast, however. As company member Kaneza Schaal noted, one of the differences between the remount in 2015 for The Public and the previous run at NYTW in 2008 was about conscientious casting. As she put it:

> The big dramaturgical change at The Public is that Kate [Scelsa, a white actor] used to be the first person to play Dilsey [a black male role]. . . . At the top of the play, and there was always a little [concern], I think Kate . . . raised it the most. . . . And this round, Daphne [a black actor] is taking that role, because there was always something in that moment, where you're like 'ooh, wow—that's where we're gonna go? Right out of the gate? Okay, okay, here we go.' And I don't know, for me, it's all Faulkner's construct of race, so the fact that we're dealing with [race] as a material I think is brilliant.[12]

The notion of using race "as a material," like one of the found objects that influences ERS's scenic design or choreography, is one approach to how adapturgy can influence casting decisions. Crucially, ERS also understood that they "need[ed] black people to *make* [the show]," a recognition absolutely central to any adaptation that wants to grapple with race in meaningful, constructive ways.[13]

In the 2011–12 academic year, Kennesaw State University produced and subsequently toured *Splittin' the Raft,* Scott Kaiser's adaptation of Mark Twain's 1885 book *Adventures of Huckleberry Finn.* Directed by Harrison Long, this production was supported by the NEA's Arts Education in American Communities grant. Kaiser's adaptation, which began in the late '90s as a performance workshop to explore Twain's novel, was originally designed for traveling to schools in the region of the Oregon Shakespeare Festival, in and around Ashland. Soon thereafter, Kaiser "added his masterstroke: casting orator, ex-slave and abolitionist, Frederick Douglass as narrator."[14] This role, meant to be played by the same actor who plays escaped slave Jim in *Huckleberry Finn,* provides vital critique and context for the proslavery perspective represented by Huck (whom Kaiser notes should be cast with a female actor).[15] Like the members of ERS, Kaiser recognized that without the perspective of Douglass, the play would only tell the story of race from the point of view of "the people who believed themselves to be white" (Kaiser is white).[16] Instead, as director Long realized, "By placing Twain's language next to the words of Frederick Douglass, we are able to understand both texts more fully. In one scene, Kaiser splices the narrator's lofty rhetoric with one of Pap's racist diatribes. The juxtaposition clarifies and magnifies both speeches."[17] Because this production was meant to be educational and to be presented at schools in North Georgia, the dramaturgy for *Splittin' the Raft* was extensive and digital, as will be discussed in a later section. One of the immediate challenges for the dramaturg under my supervision (Melissa Harvey, then a TPS major at KSU) was the language of Twain's book (and Kaiser's adaptation), which includes copious utterances of the N-word.[18]

That same year, 2011, *Adventures of Huckleberry Finn* was published in a new version edited by Randall Williams of NewSouth Books, wherein he "substituted the word 'slave' for the word 'nigger'" throughout the text.[19] The essential question for all dramaturgs—"why this play now?"—was not difficult to answer for Harvey, but that was precisely because *Splittin' the Raft* spoke so directly to this ongoing controversy, and the stakes were perceived to be so high for southerners.

Harvey's solution embraced three of the seven categories of adapturgy under consideration here: she wrote program notes, built a study guide and website, and encouraged a plan Long already had in place to have audience conversation as a part of every performance. In her essay for the program (also accessible on the website), she explains Kaiser's conscientious casting specifications. "Kaiser's goal is to confront societal acceptance of what are considered normative identity traits. This is (partly) why he imagines a female actress playing the part of Huck, who is a young boy, and why Aunt Sally, who is a white slave owner in Twain's novel, is portrayed by a black woman in Kaiser's play."[20] The final member of the cast in *Splittin' the Raft* at KSU was a white man, Robert Hadaway, who was one of our major's nontraditional students, meaning he was several years older than the rest of the cast. This final question of age within casting for adapturgy can be seen in fuller clarity with another adaptation staged at KSU, *Everything That Rises Must Converge* by Karin Coonrod.

The ensemble for Coonrod's adaptation of Flannery O'Connor's two short stories ("A View of the Woods" and "Everything That Rises Must Converge") includes ten actors, half of whom must be black and the other half white. Two of the white characters, Julian's mother and Mr. Fortune, are older adults, while one white actor plays the child named Mary Fortune and one black actor plays the child named Carver. For this 2009 production, we were able to cast both older adults with nontraditional students—that is, actors who were close to the age of the characters. While this particular casting choice may not carry the weight of controversy that race and gender can, within the scope of adaptation for the stage, the age of the actors does matter. In part, this stems from fidelity concerns (do the actors represent the characters as the source author wrote them?), but it also has to do with the central concern of theatricality. Adapters, directors, and dramaturgs must ask themselves *what kind of theatricality does this adaptation bring to this stage at this moment in time?* A variation on the classic question of "why this play now?" this adaptation-based query zeroes in on the heart of the matter—that is, what bringing the source to the stage accomplishes that the original mode of reception (e.g., reading) does not.

In the case of *Everything That Rises Must Converge,* an adaptation that honors every word of O'Connor's short stories, including narrative attributions and description, the theatricality was already evident. As Coonrod explains, "The way O'Connor writes the narration—it's so tightly connected to the featured characters and so carnivalesque and sort of dialogic, it begs to be played out on stage by a company."[21] In a context like this, where the language is already evocative, even "carnivalesque," it would be less effective to use stage makeup and movement to create age. The language provides ample opportunity for laughter, as well as resistance.[22] Instead, having Mr. Fortune played by a student in his late sixties and Julian's mother played by a student in her mid-fifties grounded the otherwise grotesque comedy with a kind of gravitas. Far from a caricature, Mary Wolfson's performance as Julian's mother was singled out by a Kennedy Center American College Theater Festival respondent, who noted that hers was a "sensitive comic portrayal that was well-integrated with the production and recognizably human."[23] While it will typically be professional productions that offer this kind of flexibility with differently aged actors, it is nevertheless a consideration of adapturgy.

As I trust readers have anticipated, the differences in casting choices in each of the cases we have just reviewed would likewise shift the perspective on the z-axis ("here" or "there") within the spectator-based adapturgy model. For college students in their late teens and early twenties, the casting of nontraditional students for the older adult roles may have made the adaptation more familiar, insofar as the characters were believable and not portrayed by actors who were actually their peers, age-wise. More to the point, though, is how conscientious casting affects familiarity with regard to race and ethnicity. In the extreme (yet all too common) case of whitewashing casts for scripts that call for non-Anglo races, producers run the risk of alienating the very communities they have chosen to put on stage.[24] To be color conscious in one's casting process requires that the directors empathize with the different perspectives made possible by a culturally diverse audience. In a climate where it is necessary to defend how and why "Black Lives Matter," the stakes for dramaturgically sound representation could hardly be higher.[25]

That said, casting is rarely part of adaptation dramaturgs' purview—unless they work directly with the adapter, in which case they can offer suggestions for how the adapter can (or should) specify expectations of actor profiles for roles. For many (if not most) adaptation dramaturgs, the main opportunity for impact occurs in the next phases of production: rehearsal and performances. Ideally, we are given an opportunity to work well in advance of the first rehearsal, so that we can establish a packet for the cast and creative team. Sometimes called a "protocol," the dramaturgical packet is provided to the cast in the first week of rehearsal—as these packets can be unwieldy (and especially since actors at KSU often commuted to/from

Atlanta), I began offering the information contained within them digitally, via private wiki spaces dedicated to the production.

Cast and Crew Wikis

The use of a private wiki can be especially productive (if there is such time) in the weeks between casting and the first rehearsal.[26] For *Red Badge of Courage,* every production benefited from having the wiki as a resource—starting with the KSU premiere, extending to the edits and new material that Haverty and I added for the 7 Stages production, and (perhaps most of all) in the months between casting the Auburn production and my guest residency there. Not only does a wiki provide cloud space for shared materials relevant to the creative team (such as new drafts of the adaptation, inspirational images or text for the creative team, renderings of the design, and so on), but it is also a collaborative site that tracks contributions automatically. For the restaging of *Red Badge* at Auburn, then, this meant that the new cast could both review and contribute to the wiki that the Atlanta creative team built. Thus, David Tourtellotte, the Auburn student actor who played the Youth, could cross reference his own interpretations of the Youth's monologues with Josh Brook, the Atlanta actor (and KSU student) who originated the role.

Wiki spaces work best when directors embrace them fully as part of their process with the cast. For example, I typically build a separate wiki page for each actor, and then encourage directors who assign actors homework to require that the cast members post their work to their wiki page. I also include pages for each designer and for the director, and encourage the stage manager to use the notification pane for announcements, so that the cast and creative team can accustom themselves to checking the wiki daily, rather than email. The flexibility of what can be posted (usually embedded) on these sites is what first attracted me to using them as an educational tool. Users can embed YouTube videos and digital images, making wikis cater to a wider variety of reception than the paper-based dramaturgical packets. Moreover, they are mobile-friendly—users can check and post to the wiki from their smart phones or tablets. For ensemble work, wikis provide a platform where multiple users can edit documents or pages, allowing for collaboration to continue outside of the rehearsal room whenever inspiration strikes. Perhaps best of all, for PBWorks the editing pane closely resembles the formatting palette (or ruler bar) in Microsoft Word, making it extremely easy to learn, even for technophobes.

Embodied Experiences

Although it may at first sound counterintuitive, private wikis also support the embodied experiences that adapturgy can facilitate in rehearsals. For example, in the early phase of rehearsals for *Red Badge,* Haverty and I planned two excursions with the cast, and our dramaturg Robert Hadaway planned a third. First, we visited the site of Cheatham Hill, a Civil War memorial site for a battle that took place during the Atlanta campaign of 1864. We had the actors race each other up the hill, so that they could see how physically taxing such runs would be for the soldiers. Second, with Hadaway's assistance, we took a guided tour of the Civil War museum that commemorates the Battle of Kennesaw Mountain, which included several artifacts from the war, including a tent that ultimately inspired part of our opening set design. Finally, we met with two Civil War re-enactors, one of whom had an authentically reproduced musket from the era. These men patiently showed all five actors (as well as Haverty and me) the detailed (and taxing) steps of loading the weapon, and then we all got a chance to fire it. The embodied experience of each of these outings helped our actors make more believable choices onstage, and brought the dramaturgy of history fully into their senses. In addition, I recorded each of these field trips on video and posted those videos to our wiki, so that the actors could consult them as they wished whenever they wanted to refresh their memories. Because the wiki was private and accessible by invitation, these videos didn't require the kind of internal review for human subjects research that they would have if we had posted them on a public website. This concern over privacy was heightened even more with our other aspect of embodied experience for *Red Badge:* the visits made by veterans.

In light of the interpretation that Haverty and I shared about Crane's *Red Badge*—that it is a story about the experience of war, not (just) about the Civil War—we wanted to expand our dramaturgical research beyond the scope of the nineteenth century. With Hadaway's assistance, we located veterans from the Korean, Vietnam, Iraq, and Afghanistan wars. We scheduled each veteran to visit (either in person or via Skype) the rehearsal, so that each vet could share their story with the cast.[27] If they were able to visit in person, we would typically arrange the chairs in a circle and invite the vet to join us, and we encouraged the actors to take notes in their journals, rather than digitally recording these encounters. For most of the vets, talking to us was *the first time* they had shared these stories with civilians (including their family members). Needless to say, we recognized how privileged we were to hear these firsthand accounts of battle. Meeting these vets gave our actors a glimpse into the human face (and price) of military practice, and inspired us all to do justice to the production.

The location of the production—not just the place where it will be performed but the larger region of the place—often creates opportunities for embodied experience. Dramaturgs can typically assess this with simple research, but it's also important to discuss with directors how important place was to their decision to adapt this source. As discussed in chapter 6, the space will usually have great impact on the original adaptation staging, but even if the adapted work is not premiering at your theatre, there is frequently a local connection to be made. When Karen Robinson directed *Everything That Rises Must Converge*, it was several years after Coonrod's adaptation had been developed at the University of Iowa, but it was the first time this rare adaptation of O'Connor's work had the opportunity to be produced in her home state of Georgia. Therefore, one of the draws for the creative team was the opportunity to include a field trip to Andalusia Farm, the O'Connor estate located four miles northwest of Milledgeville.

Those in attendance for this embodied experience included the student set designer, James Maloof, as well as Robinson and her cast. Maloof noted how vital this encounter with O'Connor's family home and land was to his design process.

> In Andalusia, I tried to find . . . what about this place made it definitely Flannery O'Connor's home. . . . I went out to the front yard and sat and just watched. And really it's the wind, more than anything else. A kind of live energy of that, coming up? The stillness of that? And yet it's so active, and if you think about it, you know the wind is coming from miles and miles away, and it's blowing in, and there's so much life and energy in something that feels so still. And that was probably the most influential aspect of it, as far as the actual place goes.[28]

This observation, combined with the vision that Robinson had to foreground the language and keep the setting as "an abstract canvas of sorts," resulted in the decision Maloof made to "eliminate the horizon" in his design.[29] Highest on the up-left part of the stage and lowest on the down-right, his constructed landscape sloped abstractly, but was given believable texture and color (to resemble the red clay earth common in Georgia) and supported by a full cyclorama upstage. With the slant and surface of this memorable set, Maloof managed to capture the combination of stillness and wind energy that he described experiencing during his visit to Andalusia. Moreover, his design gave Robinson the ability to separate characters from narrators on the sloped surface, which helped spectators process O'Connor's evocative language and symbolism.

Websites and Study Guides

Of course, in the time it takes to take in a performance, it can be difficult to catch all the nuances of an adaptation. Moreover, depending on their privilege, spectators may need assistance in orienting themselves and empathizing with other perspectives when attending a performance. This is why the dramaturg's supplemental material can be so crucial to an audience member's potential to fully appreciate the palimpsest of adapturgy that led to the production. In the last few decades, theatre companies are more likely to have a robust Internet presence, certainly via their websites, but also through the use of social media. For the 2015 production of Catalin's adaptation of *Moby-Dick* for the Lookingglass Theatre Company, for instance, marketing employees (or interns) used the hashtag "#FindtheWhiteWhale" to accompany pictures on Facebook and Twitter of a large inflated whale inserted into iconic Chicago spaces.

For the adaptations in which I have participated as dramaturg or co-creator, we have primarily used public websites to serve as educational supplements as well as sites to host video clips and rehearsal or design photos that might interest the general spectator. Because the assistant director for *Splittin' the Raft* made a documentary about the creative process, for example, we embedded that YouTube video on our public website. This documentary showed snippets of rehearsal and performance, as well as interviews with the cast and director. As previously mentioned, *Splittin' the Raft* was designed for touring to schools, so the website for it also included a study guide, information about the set and costume design, and several external links to contextual information about Mark Twain, Scott Kaiser, and Frederick Douglass. Perhaps the most important link included on this site was that of Pearl Cleage's 2011 keynote address at the Southeastern Theatre Conference, "The Nigger Speech." As a black playwright and doyenne of Atlanta-area theatre, Cleage's speech was vital to share with potential spectators, especially educators and their students. "The other thing that makes me nervous," affirms Cleage,

> is the ongoing discussion of this particular word in a way that implies that the word itself is so lethal that we can't even spell it out or speak it out loud, but must content ourselves with using only the first letter, assuming the listener or the reader will surmise the word we would have said except that its awful, negative energy would have exploded in our mouths like a roadside bomb, or the very sight of it on paper would have struck us dumb and dumber.[30]

Even with this robust website, however, community and school administrators were gun-shy. In his reflection on directing this production, Long muses that although this was "the first production of *Splittin' the Raft* to be staged in the Deep South," after multiple venues cancelled plans to host it he realized just how controversial this show was perceived to be.[31] Eventually, he was able to capitalize on his family's reputation in North Georgia to reassure the local community that the production did not reify racist language as they feared.

Productions with less controversial (but perhaps difficult or obscure) language also benefit from public websites. In the multiple adaptations for which I served as dramaturg that were adapted and codirected by John Gentile, we found the websites crucial to giving spectators better access to the source as well as the staging concept.[32] These sites were especially helpful for the adaptations Gentile staged of poetry. Although W. B. Yeats was a relatively familiar author for our audiences, in 2009 he adapted the poetry of Katharyn Howd Machan, whose reputation is not as far-reaching. For both of these websites, samples of the poetry were essential to include, so that visitors might familiarize themselves with the language each poet used. Gentile's adaptation of Yeats's poetry and prose stories was crafted to tell the story of Red Hanrahan, a figure in Irish folklore who might otherwise be less well known. Because Yeats's fascination with magic and the influences of Japanese Noh drama were central to Gentile's production concept, the website allowed us to unpeel the palimpsest undergirding the various references to Hanrahan throughout his oeuvre. Thus, spectators intrigued by the *Sidhe* (the fairies, often referred to as "the others") could visit the website to learn more about fairy folk and the lore surrounding them. Those intrigued by the scenic design—a modification of the typical Noh backdrop of three pine trees to a Celtic-knot depiction of white hawthorn—could learn that the hawthorn was considered sacred for many Irish, and that Yeats knew the fairy thorns to be indicative of where "the others" lived.[33] In short, such dramaturgical websites support the potential for stage adaptations to trigger the palimpsestuous pleasures discussed in chapter 4, as well as offering background about the place and space inspirations discussed in chapter 6.

Lobby Displays

This recognition of spatial dynamics is central to how adaptation dramaturgs approach a lobby display, especially if they are given the opportunity to work in three dimensions. With material-based lobby displays, dramaturgs can work with texture and dimension in ways that help set expectations for the performance itself. As mentioned in chapter 6, the lobby display for the KSU production of Gentile's adaptation of *Moby-Dick* used fabric that closely resembled the fabric used onstage. This fabric—white and supple, so that it billowed and flowed—was key to scenic designer Jamie Bullins's abstract approach, and was variously used to represent water, sails, and the spermaceti obtained from whaling. By using this fabric to frame the bulletin board, not only did we draw attention from the way the fabric moved with the breeze of passersby, but because it mirrored the scenic design, the lobby display was more obviously a part of the production (and not part of the other uses of the building).

Even without three-dimensionality, however, lobby displays can supplement the stage adaptation. When the bulletin board was replaced with a flat-screen monitor at KSU, we began using high-resolution digital images on a loop to facilitate the adapturgy. For Gentile's 2011 adaptation of stories from the Brothers Grimm, *Dark Forest,* this digital presentation became the primary visual platform for exploring the one aspect of his adaptation that wasn't in the Grimm canon: his addition of the Green Man. Used as a trickster narrator, the Green Man character had the potential of seeming odd or out of place, without some dramaturgical explanation. The colorful images of this character's costume design, as well as those of the history and inspiration behind him, helped spectators contextualize what might have otherwise been an unfamiliar figure onstage.

Program Notes

For *Dark Forest,* as with all productions (especially of adaptations), the program notes added further clarity to the director's (and/or adapter's) concept. As Felicia Hardison Londré has ably demonstrated, the art of dramaturgical notes is both difficult to master and inexorably linked to the needs of the particular show and expectations of the venue and audience.[34] My notes for

KSU productions, for example, were meant to model scholar-artistry for our Theatre and Performance Studies majors. Thus, they included multiple citations, attempting to strike a balance between telling a story and joining the academic conversation relevant to the particular show, its author, or (in the case of adaptations in particular) its source. When I have contributed program materials for other productions, they rarely take the form of an essay—instead, I often submit tables, timelines, and images for professional programs. Generally speaking, when writing program contributions for a stage adaptation, dramaturgs must consider the source—the level to which that source (or its author) becomes the focus of the essay (or other material) depends on the director's concept as well as any intervention the dramaturg wants (or needs) to make.

The word "intervention" may at first glance appear to be at odds with other advice given to dramaturgs—namely, the perception of dramaturg as assistant to or in service of the director and creative team. While I agree that dramaturgs should not interfere with the protocol of the theatre with which they are working, to suggest that we do not form our own vision of the production demonstrates a gross misunderstanding of the dramaturgical sensibility. Thus, while I would never offer notes directly to an actor (protocol dictates that only directors give notes to actors, with a few exceptions for stage managers), I often disagree with the approach or concept of a director.[35] My responsibility is to balance my interpretation with unquestionable respect for the choices made for this particular production, so that my dramaturgy is both supportive and creative.

Audience Conversations

One of the few ways that audience members typically meet dramaturgs is through our work facilitating audience conversations. This is one reason why such opportunities should be considered for every stage adaptation, and why it matters when dramaturgs organize or help lead these conversations.[36] Usually the conversations take place as preshow or postshow discussions, with either experts, the cast, the director, the author/adapter, or some combination of these participants. Depending on the subject matter of the adaptation, the chance to interact with experts (whether from the community or the academic field in question) might be a vital part of the experience of seeing the production. For example, we offered talkbacks after every performance of *Red Badge* at Auburn University for several reasons. First and foremost, we wanted any audience members who were veterans or family members of veterans to have an opportunity to ask questions and give feedback. For the Atlanta professional run of *Red Badge,* we had one performance reserved for veterans and their families, in the hopes that more members of the military would participate. However, most of the patrons who stayed for these conversations were young adults who were intrigued by the fast-paced production and who had questions about the puppetry and animation we used.

In the *Routledge Companion to Dramaturgy,* Martine Kei Green-Rogers offers sage advice about the diplomatic role that dramaturgs play in such conversations, especially when they follow (or precede) performances with controversial or diverse subject matter.[37] Often, the experts invited to the table for these adapturgy-focused events are scholars who specialize in a field related to the source material. For example, for ERS's remount of *The Sound and the Fury,* the guests featured in such conversations were Faulkner scholars, or academics who specialized in the history of the American South.

The numerous examples in this chapter demonstrate the robust role that dramaturgy plays in the phase where the adaptation moves from page to stage. From concept discussions to casting considerations at the outset, to the rehearsals and performances themselves, there are multiple ways for adapturgy to contribute to the production. Not every performance or creative team will embrace all of these options, nor will every dramaturg find each of them equally useful for every project. But with these models as guides, I suspect that emerging and established dramaturgs will continue to develop the possibilities to help shape and nourish the process and product of stage adaptation.

9. POSTMORTEM ADAPTURGY

Every institutional production of live theatre goes through some kind of postmortem process, whether formally recognized as such or not. A postmortem is metacognitive and metacreative—it is the final production meeting, during which the creative team has an opportunity to reflect on how it solved problems and made art. It is *meta*cognitive and *meta*creative because the postmortem requires that we contemplate our rationales and imagine how we could invent different ways of creating theatre. If theatre is being made as part of an institution—as a company or within an academic department, for example—the postmortem is an essential step in keeping the "machine" of production well oiled and improving or altering the methods used by the company or department. As such, postmortems typically require the attendance of (the persons functioning as) the production manager, the artistic director, and the director of the production under consideration as well as all designers and technicians involved (especially the technical director). If they are musical productions, the musical director and choreographer might also sit at this table. For out-of-the-box plays—that is, plays that have been produced elsewhere or are otherwise part of the canon—there is usually no expectation that the dramaturg would attend a postmortem, much less a playwright.

However, for theatrical adaptations, it is vital that the dramaturg and adapter/s attend and contribute to the postmortem, whenever possible.[1] The reason for this goes back to a point articulated in previous chapters: whereas for typical dramaturgy the ur-question is "why this play now?" for adapturgy the question shifts a bit. The adaptation dramaturg and the rest of the creative team have a vested interest in answering the question "*why this source as theatre now?*" In other words, for adaptation the question of the medium (theatre) is up for grabs in a way it is not for established plays. Whereas, with nonadapted texts, we assess how the workflow from concept to production functioned, with adaptations there is another level to consider: *whether the medium was used to its full potential.* In addition to the other people mentioned above, then, having the dramaturg (and, if possible, the adapter/s) at the postmortem table matters.

This chapter addresses the kinds of questions that adaptation dramaturgs should ask after a production closes, in part by reflecting on the changes that were made to remounts of our primary case studies (*Red Badge of Courage, Moby-Dick*, and *The Sound and the Fury*). While in this chapter we will not go into extensive detail about the production workflow portion of a postmortem, this omission should not be taken as an oversight. Rather, such analysis belongs in a book about theatre technique, design, and directing—subjects that are vital, but beyond the scope of the present study. The meta nature of the postmortem encourages self-evaluation—thus, in this chapter we will also reflect on the overall impact of adaptation for the stage as well as that of adapturgy, offering suggestions for future interventions and involvement.

Why This Source?

For the adaptation postmortem, the primary question can be broken into parts to assist in the reflective process, beginning with the first section: "Why This Source?" Certainly, adapters and dramaturgs will be accustomed to this question by the end of the production run, since it tends to be a frequent question for publicity purposes as well as audience conversation. What is most useful for the postmortem, however, is the consideration of how the answer to this question might have changed in the process or during the run of the show. For example, early in the process of creating *Red Badge of Courage*, my answer to this question might have focused on the power of Crane's language and imagery, as well as the practical admission that the work was in the public domain. After transforming the book into live performance, however, I would say that the latter of those observations (the imagery) was much more informative to the adaptation than the language.

Following the KSU production, Haverty and I decided to add a second scene featuring the General, to provide additional motivation for the Youth to explode into his "black rage," during which he loses touch with reality and begins shooting compulsively. As mentioned in chapter 7, we recovered lines from *Red Badge*'s original chapter 12 in Crane's unpublished manuscript that ultimately were used as some of the Youth's final lines in the play. Because this section had originally held the Janus spot of being the central chapter of the novel, rather than part of the conclusion to the book, the insertion of these lines for our Youth's epiphany became a major point of assessment for Haverty and me. Did this work? Could it work better? We decided that including the additional scene with the General, where he refers to the regiment as "mule-drivers," would accomplish our goal of showing more buildup to the Youth's transformation, without sacrificing our nonrealistic style or what we considered to be the necessary brevity of the script.

Similarly, when given the opportunity to revise *Moby-Dick* for production in the Lifecycle Building for SAÏAH's production, John Gentile reviewed the entire script in light of the source, with particular focus on the unusual space as well as his main innovation: the character of The Whiteness of the Whale. While the basic conceit remained the same (indeed, she would be played by the same actor), Gentile changed the way she interacted with the rest of the cast, having her remain on the periphery of the action for longer periods of time than she had with the KSU production five years prior. This accomplished two goals: it increased the omnipotence of the Whiteness character, while further demarcating her from the other characters. Because Gentile wanted her appearance to be numinous or otherworldly, the previous placement of her entrances from the top of the raked stage, framed by the proscenium, needed to be replaced with a more formal, less potentially realistic entry.

Thus, the postmortem provides a useful opportunity for adapters to reconnect with their initial reasons for wanting to transform the source (here, literature—but of course the source could be from virtually any medium) into live performance. Ideally, they can reconnect to the passion they first felt encountering that source. "The book I have just read—this book whose scenes have banged off the walls of my ribcage—must be told again to my world, my age."[2] In reconnecting with that zeal, adapters may decide to edit their scripts so that the story is better told. As is likely already apparent, in the postmortem stage especially, it is difficult to separate the "script" from the performance of it, since the postmortem follows the run of the production. This is to be expected. Even so, parsing the larger question into sections can still make a difference to the thought process.

Why This Source *as Theatre*?

Throughout this study, we have returned to one crucial tenet: when transposing, interpreting, and engaging with a source, we must be steadfast in recognizing the value and strengths (as well as weaknesses) of the medium into which the source is to be adapted.[3] These are not idle decisions. One should not adapt a source into theatre for the sole reason that it is the medium of which one is most fond. Adapters must understand the language of their chosen medium. In the case of theatre, we must recognize what *theatricality* can accomplish that other media (film or dance, say) cannot. In addition to reconsidering those other media options, adapters can take the postmortem as a welcome opportunity to remind themselves what the live performance of their chosen source(s) can bring about that the original medium could not. This is not to suggest that theatricality belongs to the realm of theatre alone. There are multiple ways that other media (such as opera and dance, for example) rely upon theatricality as well. "Rather, theatricality is the result of a perceptual dynamics linking the onlooker with something that is looked at."[4] It is the vibrancy of representation that either solicits or is solicited by the gaze of spectatorship.

In this book, we have purposely limited our focus to the transformation of canonical literature for the (nonmusical) stage. In addition to being practical, this restriction has kept the focus on the kinds of questions and concerns that arise with interpreting narrative prose from the mode of reading to that of watching theatre. In the postmortem phase, however, adapters and dramaturgs should remain open to the possibility that perhaps a different mode of reception would suit their adaptation better. Upon reflection, for example, they might decide to hire a composer for the next draft, because straight (that is, nonmusical) theatre "is not adequate to supply the visions that the book has projected on [their] mindscreen."[5] Modifications of this magnitude are rare, to be sure, but adapters and, in particular, dramaturgs benefit from thinking flexibly about the medium of adaptation, especially in retrospect (with 20/20 hindsight). This is another way of engaging with the dramaturgical question introduced in chapter 3: that of the road not taken. How else might this story be told?

More frequently, this question addresses a matter of degree—that is, does the level of theatricality in any given scene need to be altered so that the story can be communicated more effectively? Often, these are concerns with practical and technical limitations that either could not be solved with the initial production or were not yet realized. For example, in our initial production of *Red Badge*, Haverty and I were disappointed with the level of fog that could be achieved in the Onyx Theatre at KSU. The limit on fogginess was not just an aesthetic problem but a practical and technical one: the fog machine only fit backstage in one configuration, aiming the fog directly toward an air duct. Thus, most of the fog was swept into the duct rather than hanging in the air. We knew that this would not be a problem at 7 Stages, but it was still a valuable realization to discuss how much fog we ideally wanted, and where we would like it to linger. For the second production of *Red Badge*, we were able to direct the machine in such a way that the fog filled not only the theatre space but also the walkway to it, which was exactly the effect we wanted, until we realized that holding that much fog in the house meant that spectators could barely see the puppet at all in the first scene. By the end of the 7 Stages run we struck a compromise between the two options, and I sought the same kind of balance for the Auburn University production the following year.

The question of why to do this source as theatre often defaults to questions of design and technician improvements, but it can also highlight reconsiderations of blocking, casting, and movement. As discussed in chapter 6, the space in which the adaptation is staged has the potential to both limit and inspire how the adaptation is (or could be) embodied. Although the next opportunity for producing their adaptation might not be known yet, adapters and dramaturgs will get more out of this step if they embrace "what if." While there was no way of predicting the future opportunity to stage *Moby-Dick* in the Lifecycle Building, for instance, Gentile and I nevertheless recognized during the postmortem that his vision might be better served in a different theatre. Part of this recognition had to do with institutional constraints—by producing *Moby-Dick* in a university setting, we had to operate as part of a larger unit (the College of the Arts), the administrators of which ultimately controlled the way the space could be used. But other constraints were practical—there was only so much vertical space the Stillwell Theater could offer, and only so many possible configurations for the audience space. Imagining how *Moby-Dick* might play in a different space, without such limitations, kept the embers of Gentile's passion for the project aglow.

In chapters 4 and 8, we reviewed the changes in casting for *The Sound and the Fury* that came about because of both practical and aesthetic decisions. With regard to feasibility, three of the actors from the original production were no longer available for the remount at the Public, so they had to be replaced. But in the process of working through these changes, the company realized they had an opportunity to address a lingering concern raised by Kate Scelsa, a white actor who was the first to perform the role of Dilsey, a black character, in the 2008 production. By reassigning that first representation of Dilsey to Daphne Gaines, a black actor, ERS arguably made their overall conceit of character switching both more recognizable and more palatable for audiences in 2015. Once again, we are reminded that the parts of the adapturgy question are interrelated and difficult to untangle—for surely this decision had as much to do with theatricality as it did with the zeitgeist.

Why This Source as Theatre *Now*?

This question of timing—so essential to any dramaturg—is particularly instructive for adapters and their dramaturgs. With regard to the adaptation that has just closed its run, they might review any outreach strategies that were involved with the production, making note of any missed opportunities for communication or collaboration. If any feedback was received from members of the community outside of the typical audience base, those opinions should have significant impact on this section of the postmortem. For example, although we received encouraging feedback from the veterans who visited our *Red Badge* cast during rehearsal, we were less satisfied with the attendance of veterans at performances, in large part because there was no way to recognize that a spectator was also a veteran unless they chose to self-identify. Thus, when we moved the production from KSU to 7 Stages, we advertised a discount for any patron with military identification, so that we might better assess the impact and appeal of our adaptation. In addition, we dedicated one night of the 7 Stages run as "veterans night," although (as previously mentioned) only one veteran stayed for the talkback following that performance. In retrospect, it is possible that the location of 7 Stages in Atlanta—it occupies a central spot in Little 5 Points, an eccentric neighborhood with a punk rock vibe—detracted from our potential to appeal to military audiences.[6]

When *Red Badge of Courage* was remounted for Auburn University, there were several advantages that made the attendance of veterans and military family members more likely: first, the campus culture is conservative—while outliers certainly exist, most of the students appeared to be more likely to join a young Republican club than an antiwar protest. Second, one of the veterans who came into rehearsals to speak with our cast was the president of the Auburn Veterans Organization. Not only did he encourage attendance to the members of this student organization, but he did so with enthusiasm because, as he shared with us during his visit, before he joined the army, he had been active in theatre in high school. In addition, our assistant stage manager was an ROTC student whose father served in the air force, and he also encouraged his ROTC peers to attend. Finally, Auburn students have the distinct advantage of being able to attend all university theatre productions free of charge. While we do not have records to verify how many spectators were vets, during the talkbacks, several spectators self-identified as having served in the military and the box office reported that most of the guests who shared their stories with our cast made reservations to see the show.

So far, while discussing the "now" portion of this question, we have been considering the present with regard to space—as in "here and now." While local outreach is frequently a necessary and productive component of adapturgy, the primary meaning of now refers to the occasion for staging this adaptation in the current moment. Recalling the Janus effect from chapter 5, although the question will be asked during a postmortem, it also requires the practitioners to consider both past and future at once, as well as reconsidering how effective their augury was. Opinion editorials can help dramaturgs take "the pulse" of that point in time, although they are more effective when we can have face-to-face conversations with local citizens and regular patrons of the company or theatre for the adaptation in question as well.[7] Beyond these traditional research methods there is an instinct or energy that dramaturgs (like other creative artists) develop—a way that the problem and solution line up together that just seems to click. Following this sensibility alone can be problematic, because (like other creative artists) we should remain open to learning more about what matters to others around us, through interpersonal interactions as well as secondary research. But overlooking instinct can also be myopic for adaptation dramaturgs, because of the Janus effect of adapturgy.

Postmorteming the Postmortem

Overall, the practice of conducting a postmortem with the creative team remains an essential part of producing any kind of theatre within a healthy organization. For new works, however, the postmortem phase is even more crucial, so that the playwright or creators can continue to develop the new piece. As others before me have argued, premieres of adaptations should be considered new works, with the added layer of reflection about the source/s upon which they were based.[8] In the same way that playwrights might invite dramaturgs into the postmortem process, adapters should consider the benefits of having dramaturgs participate in this assessment and reflection phase.

It appears that we have come full circle, returning to some of the basic arguments of this study. Because this book both theorizes practice and practices theory, it is only appropriate that we should turn these same techniques and questions on the previous sections herein. Instead of WSTN (why this source as theatre now?), though, we might ask *why adaptation dramaturgy now?* As before, we can consider this question in sections, beginning with "why adaptation?" At the root of this question is often a misplaced or mistaken comparison of adaptation with so-called original works, and a not-so-hidden bias against (what some consider to be) "derivative" works. Why adapt when you could create something new?—is often the subtext of this question. Of course, setting the two (originals and adaptations) against each other is a false binary. As we discussed in the first chapter, adaptations *are* creative (and new) works. In addition, most of what might be considered "original" was inspired by something or some things. Instead, here when we ask this question, we are better served to consider the benefits of explicitly adapting and thus transforming or otherwise engaging with a source. The assumed medium for the adaptation here is also the nonmusical stage, although in several of the case studies discussed there has been live or recorded music composed for these productions.[9]

What do we gain by adapting a source for live performance? Like the Janus effect, the advantages can be seen in both directions—that of the source and of the stage. After seeing Gentile's adaptation of *Moby-Dick*, for example, spectators shared with me their renewed (and in some cases, newly ignited) interest in reading Melville's book. There were also spectators whose viewing of *Red Badge of Courage* was among their first (if not *the* first) viewing of live performance. For many, it was their first opportunity to see experimental theatre of its ilk. Several of these audience members—many of whom were young adults or teenagers—reported that seeing *Red Badge* made them want to create theatre, when it previously did not appeal to them. These are anecdotal reports, but there is truth in them. The palimpsestuous pleasures of adaptation encourage spectators to see both the source and the medium into which it has been adapted differently; it stokes their desire.

These pleasures are experienced not just by the audiences of stage adaptations, however. The creative team—including actors and designers as well as technicians—is likely to feel a renewed respect for or interest in both the source and the medium. This is especially true for the adapters themselves. There is perhaps no greater way to engage with a source than to adapt it. Adapting requires a level of awareness and contemplation that simply reading a novel cannot match. With regard to the adapters' target medium—in this case live performance—in the process of imagining the source for the stage, adapters must connect to and define what they consider theatrical. In so doing they must also consider their potential audience members, engaging with the questions enabled by the spectator-based adapturgy model. This concentrated attention to the languages of the stage has the potential to sharpen the adapters' commitment to the art of theatre, invigorating their creative process.

From a materialist point of view, adaptations are also profitable ventures. Their recognizable sources draw audiences with what we might assume to be relatively little effort from public relations or marketing departments. "However," Simone Murray cautions, "new-wave adaptations scholars, like their traditional counterparts, fatally overvalue bestselling works' pre-sold nature, naively assuming the property's almost talismanic cultural power is in itself sufficient to lure readers (or those who've merely heard of the text) into [theaters]."[10] In other words, the audiences for books and performance are not likely the same population, nor are they likely to respond to the same kind of advertisements. Even so, a new adaptation of a known entity (such as a work of canonical literature) is more likely to sell tickets than a new play, especially if the playwright is unknown to the general public (as most emerging playwrights are). Whereas the adaptation industry for theatre is less powerful and far-reaching than that for film production, it most certainly exists. Adaptation dramaturgs, much as we might prefer to define ourselves by aesthetics and scholarship alone, are—or at least, can be—crucial parts of that industry.

Here we shift to the second part of this metapostmortem, Why adaptation dramaturgy? How can having a dramaturg onboard for the process of a stage adaptation be most beneficial? Likewise, how can integrating adaptation into dramaturgical training and practice improve the experience and potential effects of dramaturgy overall?

Why Adaptation Dramaturgy?

Not only is adaptation a creative practice, it is necessarily an intellectual one as well. Certainly this observation can be made of theatre writ large, but with theatrical adaptation, the pendulum swings further in the direction of generative research. Whereas dramaturgs working on Shakespearean productions, for example, will certainly steep themselves in research about the language, culture, and socioeconomic history of these plays, and their research will ideally affect choices made in rehearsal, in publicity, and in audience interactions, none of these choices will change the architecture of the script itself (unless the creative team has decided to work with an adaptation). In other words, while there are irrefutably plays (like those by Shakespeare, Brecht, Samuel Beckett, Sarah Kane, Maria Irene Fornés, and many others) that provide substantial and deeply satisfying opportunities for dramaturgical research, adapturgy is necessarily more inventive because the script flexes to meet the demands of production.

On the other hand, if the play is new and the playwright is in residence, dramaturgs who have the opportunity to work with that playwright will ideally have an impact on the development of the script, but while that feedback involves research, the production itself is typically more focused on the playwright's voice and the emerging themes or arc of the play, such that the level of production dramaturgy that occurs is minimal. There are exceptions to this observation, I am sure, but in most instances the dramaturgical focus for producing the premiere of a new play is quite properly placed on the playwright rather than the director and production concept.

As we have seen throughout this book, adapturgy combines the skills and expectations of new play with production dramaturgy. Therefore, when given the opportunity to mentor or train emerging dramaturgs, working with adapted scripts provides a more holistic approach to their education. This is true whether the script is already completed or currently in process, due to the desire, with adaptations, to discover their full theatrical potential.

The very nature of adaptation is its flexibility. What better opportunity for dramaturgs to hone their abilities to adapt to creative needs than in collaboration with an adaptation for the stage? From another perspective, we might also ask: how better to demonstrate dramaturgical litheness than through adapturgy? As discussed in chapter 5, both the adapter and the dramaturg can be (and often are) subjected to intense scrutiny by practitioners, spectators, and critics of theatre. The skepticism often arises from a notion of both roles that is unrealistically static or myopic. Of both roles, any expectation of fidelity assures disappointment, and this is often at the root of the negative assumptions about dramaturgy as well as adaptation.[11] Dramaturgs can help assuage these concerns for audiences of stage adaptations, and in turn, (re)affirm their integral role in the making of theatre overall.

In the United States, the time is ripe for increased dramaturgical diplomacy.[12] As Michele Volansky eloquently stated at the 2015 LMDA conference in New York, "Dramaturgs can be agents of empathy, compassion, and honesty in a world that wants it, needs it, yearns for it."[13] As our country becomes more diverse and the conflicts between clashing beliefs grow more acute, representation onstage must also adapt to reflect and refract the complexity of what it means to be human.

Why Adaptation Dramaturgy Now?

If we accept as a premise that adaptations of stories function like memes, as Hutcheon argues (adapting Dawkins's hypothesis), then we might also embrace the notion that dramaturgy can facilitate (and intervene in) the transmission of culture and ideas. Adaptation dramaturgs are uniquely positioned to recognize the "infective power" of some stories over others, and to encourage those stories that best speak to what our audiences need to hear.[14] As "agents of empathy," as Janus-like augurs, we have a responsibility to help locate and create art that responds with compassion to the changing cultural environment.

Far from passive recipients of entertainment, audiences of contemporary theatre—especially theatres of encounter, in which spectators participate in the unfolding event with differing levels of engagement—experience performances and interactions that ignite their imaginations. As the previous chapters have articulated, the avenues for dramaturgs to participate in the process and product of adaptations are plentiful and pleasurable. As the practice and theory of adaptation continue to proliferate, so too does dramaturgy have the opportunity to thrive and—dare I say it?—evolve. After all, the twenty-first century promises to be the century of the dramaturg.[15] As we take on that challenge, let us do so by embracing the reflective and generative power and pleasure of adapturgy.

APPENDIXES

NOTES

BIBLIOGRAPHY

INDEX

APPENDIX 1: INTERVIEWS

During the course of my research for this book, I had the opportunity to interview several artists who create adaptations for the stage. In this first appendix, I include six of those interviews—the first three are about the adaptation process of Elevator Repair Service (ERS), with primary attention to the company members' stage version of William Faulkner's *The Sound and the Fury*. The second set of interviews concentrates on three adapters' versions of Herman Melville's *Moby-Dick*. Each group of interviews invites comparative analysis: the first, featuring three members of the same company, provides insight into how different artists interpret and remember the decision-making process within a collaboration. The second allows a glimpse into the pivotal questions any adapter must face about how to transform the page for the stage—in this case, how to extract the essence of the American epic *Moby-Dick*. While every source has challenges for adapturgy, the theatrical difficulties of adapting Melville's tome—the language and length of the text, the setting, and the whale—are the focus in these interviews.

Every one of these artists references the soul or spirit of the source. For all, their passion for the process of adaptation stems from their desire to translate that spirit using the language of theatre. While in some cases this passion might become reverence for the author and their writing (both subject matter and methodology), not one of the artists herein loses sight of the dramaturgical reality that most spectators will see the performance only once, and many of them may have only a passing familiarity with the source. Thus, each artist emphasizes the significance of discovering and communicating the spirit of the source, of conjuring the energy found in reading the novel and transforming it for live performance.

John Collins

New York City, 22 April 2015

John Collins founded Elevator Repair Service in 1991. Since then, he has directed or codirected all of the company's productions. John is the recipient of the 2014 Doris Duke Performing Artist Award, a 2010 Guggenheim Fellowship in Drama and Performance Art and a 2011 United States Artists Donnelley Fellowship. John received the Lucille Lortel Award for Outstanding Director and the Elliot Norton Award for Outstanding Director for ERS's production of Gatz. Other notable ERS projects include The Sound and the Fury, Arguendo, The Select (The Sun Also Rises), *and* Fondly, Collette Richland *(a new play by Sibyl Kempson). His writing about theatre and sound design can be found in the books* Theatre Noise: The Sound of Performance *(2011) and* Encountering Ensemble *(2013).*

John Collins: Sound is very relevant to *The Sound and the Fury.*

Jane Barnette: [*Laughter*]

No, it really is. You know, we developed an approach to the show that started with trying to understand what exactly [William] Faulkner was describing.

Because we knew we wanted to do the book exactly as it was written. We didn't want to make an adaptation that told the same story but shied away from his incredibly complicated *way* of telling the story. We were actually most interested in the incredibly complicated way. And a big breakthrough we had was discovering a hypertext version of the book online. Someone had actually broken it down into, "here are the twenty different things that are happening in the Benjy chapter. For example: this is a short paragraph that takes place on the day that Roscus died; and this is a short paragraph that happened on the day that they went to visit the cemetery." So, we *used* that and our own digging into the book to understand what was happening. We were in the process of developing this very complicated thing, with a different casting configuration for each of the twenty different episodes the chapter depicts. We would switch the casting configuration every time the book switched to a different episode. As you can imagine, like the book itself, it was kind of blurry.

And when we first brought sound to it, that was the first time our approach started to make sense to me. For a couple of reasons: one, a sound score gave it a kind of a smoother texture. There's something disjointed about all the bouncing back and forth—these are Benjy's memories. And it can be hard to imagine that they're really coming from one place.

But the sound helped sew everything together. We could make the sound transitions gradual or make changes on a button. So that was the first thing that it did. It created this kind of *glue* that held all these disparate elements together and helped remind you that this was more like listening to music than it was like listening to a narrative being told. . . .

So. It helped a *lot* that way, right off the bat. The palette of sounds our designer, Matt Tierney, came up with *really* transformed things, right away. But then when he really started digging in and working on it, he created different aural signatures for each of the different episodes. So, for example, you always get an aural signal that you're at the funeral for the grandmother, when they're all children. That scene always has what we call the funeral music, a sad, sort of religious sounding organ piece.

There are other scenes that are much more activated and a wild banjo music comes in. . . . The sound changes became a way of marking all the temporal change. I think the way we go about this show is, we try to bring some kind of clarity through layering on rather than by simplifying,

We embrace the complexity of the book and its multiple layers, rather than pick and choose among them. Because we feel that the soul of the book, and the soul of this chapter, lies in Benjy's perspective and you can't tell it from somebody else's perspective. This part of the book has to be told from Benjy's perspective. If you're going to use Benjy's perspective, you gotta go there. [*Laughs*]

So the music helped illuminate that soul, that consciousness—

Because Benjy is—for lack of a better word, I mean, he is mentally—I mean, disabled.

Yeah.

And he has—

Well he can't distinguish between the present and the past. And his associations and his memories, rather than a linear narrative, form the engine of the book.

Right.

There's a linear narrative in there somewhere, and it can be discerned. One of the things we did as an experiment was to put the various memories into proper order. We could do that with the hypertext version of the book. Using that tool, you can click a button and it rearranges all the text into the correct chronological order.

Wow.

Yeah, which is crazy! And amazing that they were able to do that!

That's amazing that that was out there.

Yeah, but the interesting thing was, doing that made it a less compelling narrative. Seeing it that way, you really understand that it has to be presented as Faulkner wrote it, or it loses its soul, I mean it's just not *The Sound and the Fury* anymore. It's not Benjy anymore.

What I am especially intrigued by is the fact that this is the chapter people talk about with *The Sound and the Fury,* but it's also the one that sometimes people stop—they don't even finish reading the novel. They'll start there, and they'll be like, "I can't deal!"

Yes. [*Laughter*] I mean, I think something that happens all the time with adaptations is that problems are sidestepped. On the assumption that incorporating the problem of the different form is going to amount to an unsatisfying failure. And I feel the opposite about it—starting with *The Great Gatsby,* when we said, we're going to do the whole thing.

That was one where the problem was pretty straightforward: there was just too much of it. But with the way that book is written, if you start taking away, if you start paring it down, if you start saying, "oh: this is important, but this isn't"—then, you are writing a new book. And it's not going to be a better book. [*Laughs*] You know?

I like a problem. I like a *bad* problem, and I think that when it's the integrity of the other form that gives you the problem, then I think it's worthwhile to take it on.

So part of what attracted you was precisely the thing that people flip tables for—

Sure, I mean this seemed like a great challenge. My medium is language, but it's the language of *theatre.* So it's the language of movement, it's the language of sound, it's the language of all of those things being coordinated together in time. Faulkner gave us the verbal language already—it's there. I want problems as a director, because *then* I solve them with my own theatrical language. Which is moving, and figuring out how it sounds, how it looks, making it into an experience. So I'm happy for verbal language to give me a problem that way.

I want to pick up on something that you said earlier about how the first time you ran the sound it transformed what you'd been working on. I wanted to see if you could unpack that a bit.

I can go back further than that. When we looked at it on the page (I had read it before), it seems frustrating, it looks like a puzzle.

It's got the italics.

Yeah, it looks like it's trying to hide something from you.

Yes!

But the first important sound that we heard, was the sound of it being read aloud. That was when we decided to do it, when we heard the actors reading it. That's when I heard the humor in it. It jumped off the page then, that's when I heard the musicality, the rhythm of it, that's when I understood in a different way, the way it flowed from one memory to another. Just *hearing it.* Recognizing that musicality, that aural quality, suggested to me that sound was going to be key to unlocking it.

So literally the actors sit around with the novel itself and just read the first chapter?

That's how we started, just sitting around a table. We tried it a million different ways. We had made decisions about changing the casting, and knew that that was going to add a layer of complexity, but it was going to feel like an honest layer of complexity, and one that reflected the complexity of the novel and not one that smoothed it over.

Like I say, the sound has a way of indicating some underlying fluidity and consistency. It's a subtle way of telling you as you listen to it that you don't have to track it sentence to sentence to sentence.

But that there is a kind of music to it. Also the sound has a way of reinforcing a kind of altered reality. It just has a way of telling your ear that it all belongs together. . . .

So, you started off as a sound designer?

Well, not really. I mean, I did sound design work concurrent with my directing work. I started directing in college. Then I came to New York, and started ERS, and while I was doing that, I started to get work as a sound designer. So sound was always a very important part of my work.

The first sound design work that I got was because of a directing job that I did, that had sound in it, so I was already directing. I had done some performing before, and sound to me was a way of performing. As a sound designer I got to be involved in some productions, and I always ran the sound when I designed it—I almost never designed sound and gave it to somebody else to run.

Because that was part of it.

Yeah, it was like playing a musical instrument. I mean that was what I wanted to do. It was like I was a musician who was just writing some music to play. But it was as though what I wanted to be was a musician, not just a composer! . . . With sound, one thing that sets it apart in theatre is that sound can be anything. It's really in this class by itself.

There can be sounds coming from offstage that suggest things that aren't true at all but which your brain tends to believe in the absence of visual evidence. Sound becomes a kind of escape hatch from a visual reality that is beautifully limiting. Sound, though, is beautifully unlimited. Sound presents opportunities to seamlessly manipulate reality while our sets tend to come from limitations of physical space that we find. . . .

But it's all the cast and the creative team—there's not necessarily a separate person who is called the dramaturg in y'all's work?

In ERS's early days, there was just me and four actors, or maybe five? No, four. And I did everything *I* could—I designed the lights, I designed the sound. We didn't use a set—we just put some chairs out in a room. We made costume decisions as a group. And you know, as things got more complicated I realized I really needed to be working with designers and not doing this myself anymore, and we need a company manager. But I don't think we ever felt the need for a dramaturg because I think we were all content to continue doing that ourselves, collectively. Doing that as an ensemble.

So, it was a while before I really appreciated that that's what we were doing. But the more I learned about dramaturgy the more I understood that's more or less what we all do. That's what we're doing when we take two years to make a show. We always start with dramaturgy, rather than starting with a play. We get a performance out of a bunch of dramaturgy and research.

Although the next thing we do will be with a playwright. We didn't start that with a play, either. We just started with the playwright and a bunch of pages of text, and she'd try some things out. She'd throw—that's her rehearsing next door, actually.

Oh—that's Sibyl [Kempson]?

Yeah.

That's fascinating to me, because I think adaptation dramaturgy is a way of looking at dramaturgy more holistically.

Yeah, well you could say that we make new plays using production dramaturgy. [*Laughs*]

Exactly!

Or, adaptation dramaturgy, because, on some level, whatever text we're using is a found object. Something that has its own form, has its own integrity, and is going to have to find a way to live through these actors on some stage, in some room, with a bunch of *stuff*. And the difference with working with Sibyl is that, because a new play was being written, a lot of the decisions got folded right into the play itself. They got written down and became a part of the play. And one of the first things I was attracted to in her writing was her amazing stage directions. I didn't want to not *hear* that. So, we made Mike [Iveson] into a character that spoke them all.

And in *The Sound and the Fury* do y'all have someone who speaks the narration as well, I mean—

Oh yeah. Yeah yeah yeah. We did it differently when we did *Gatz*. There we always had Scott Shepherd do the narration because he was Nick, the narrator of the book. But here, here it's a little different. The wonderful problem with the Benjy chapter is that Benjy's narrating it but Benjy can't speak!

So, Susie, we hear from her—twice. At the very beginning, she reads the first few lines, but then the other characters just treat the sound that she's making as incomprehensible moaning.

Such a Southern thing, by the way. [*Laughter*]

And then later on, when everyone's passed out, then we hear from her again. And what we otherwise did was to make it a matter of people reading to her. It's like Benjy's having his own thoughts read to him. . . .

But how does the casting begin to have an intervention in that?

The cast itself is a kind of found object for me. I mean, insofar as we begin with the cast, and then we find the thing we're going to make. And there's some back and forth with that. With both *The Sound and the Fury* and *Gatz*, the cast needed to grow for various reasons. We begin with, in the case of this show, with about seven people. We just decided to take on the text with what we had and see what resulted with that clash.

It was important that the image of the character changed, to help us see that we were moving to a very different place in time. And I just embraced the problem of exaggerating that rather than smoothing it over, so if there'd been one actor who played the same character at different ages, you might not realize that Benjy's remembering something from 1898, and then from 1920, and then from 1905.

I let the sudden changes in casting exaggerate that. And it goes to some extremes in that, we have actors who are of different races and different genders, and yet we don't even tether them to their own race or gender. And that was partly a way of taking something that was present in the book and running with it. Benjy doesn't ever identify characters by race.

That gave us a certain license to make those leaps. We're crawling inside [Benjy's] consciousness and looking at things in this absurdly innocent way.

His innocence was an inspiration to Faulkner. He wanted an extreme innocence in this character. So we apply that and take a certain political risk in that commitment. We let Benjy see white Ben Williams in the character of Luster, and we let Greig Sargeant play Mother in one scene—a black man playing a white woman.

And it creates a kind of parallel, another mosaic of ours that reflects what the book presents. I guess that's a way of thinking about it—as a mosaic. You know, if you look at it really closely, you see things that don't make sense. But when you allow yourself to see the entire picture of the thing, then something begins to form, and you begin to understand Benjy, in a way.

How do you make the decision about the actors who are going to play the role onstage versus in rehearsal?

It's a sensitive process. We start by just trying things. And sometimes there's just something about certain actors that immediately connects to a character. But still, we try it in lots of different configurations, and then we see—it's intuitive, you know, where it just feels right. And sometimes it'll feel right for obvious reasons. Other times, it's less intuitive, but, I mean, Susie made a good Benjy because she's a very physical performer. You know?

Do you have auditions?

I would prefer that whatever the person brings is something that will *change* the role, not *suit* the role, but I knew, for example, that when I lost April Matthis to another show, that I needed another black actress to play her part. Because we had very carefully calibrated the way the characters would switch and the different races they would play, and that's a delicate subject. And so I couldn't be too casual about that. But in the early phases, it's not about changing it so much as it is, finding out what is the crazy filter that we're going to put the text through.

It's particularly difficult with dated Southern texts that embody racism—how to adapt them for today's audiences, without being teach-y.

Well, we have to make decisions about that. For example, in the early workshop of this, we only had white actors, and I found that, you know, after talking about it among the cast and getting reactions from people who saw the early version, what finally struck me was that we were trying to exaggerate some complexity and we had actually smoothed over some of it.

So it suddenly became very important to have a cast of both black and white actors—it was an uncomfortable thing to do, because like I said, I don't ever want to go to somebody and say, I'm thinking about putting you in this show, because of your *race.* [*Laughs*]

Yeah—"can I get a black actor?"

Yeah, something feels weird about that. I'd had actors of color in shows before but they were there because they were part of our ensemble and community, not because they were being typecast. But anyway, it needed to happen, for this one. And fortunately, as often happens, for whatever reason an actor comes into the company, they tend to stay for the next one.

This was one of the most difficult shows to make, in many ways. It required the biggest leap of faith. It was much more difficult to make than *Gatz,* where we just made a singular decision to not cut the text. This was a lot more challenging that way, but also in some ways more engaging. We really had a lot more to confront with the disconnect between what the book was and where we were. But I'm pleased with where it arrived.

Ben Williams

New York City, 23 April 2015

Ben Williams is an actor and sound designer in New York City. He grew up in Culleoka, Tennessee, attended the University of Tennessee at Chattanooga, and got turned on to experimental theater while studying in the Czech Republic. In 2003, he moved to New York and began an internship with The Wooster Group. Shortly thereafter he began working with Elevator Repair Service. He would go on to perform in all of their shows for the next twelve years, touring across five continents, and winning several awards for sound design (Obie, Lortel, Los Angeles Drama Critics Circle). Ben is also a founding member of minor theatre with Julia Jarcho and has collaborated with many other downtown artists, including Christina Masciotti, Sibyl Kempson, Suzanne Bocanegra, Richard Maxwell and the NYCPlayers, Big Dance Theater, Kate Benson, Lee Sunday Evans, and Lily Whitsitt. In a successful effort to stay one step ahead of a day job, Ben has embraced various technical aspects of theatre, freelancing as a technical director, production manager, engineer, and master carpenter. Occasionally, he works as a voice-over artist (theater, film, audiobooks). Building on his collaborations with playwrights, he serves as editor of Performance Texts for BODY, *an online literary journal, and he has also worked freelance as a ghostwriter. Recently, he has begun developing his own multimedia work. www.benwilliamsdotcom.com.*

Jane Barnette: We were talking about sound, and how the sound designer gets more notes than anyone else.

Ben Williams. Well it seems that way from the perspective of the sound designer. I don't know anyone else who works that way. I mean John [Collins] has no problem telling you exactly what he wants and how you should build it. There's no other director I know who works like that. Similarly, Liz [LeCompte] is a visual artist, a painter, so she directs in terms of visual compositions. Doesn't matter what you say—stand over there, wear this. John doesn't even think about costumes until the last possible second. But yeah, the sound designer has to be there. For every rehearsal. In the room.

That's very unusual.

Yeah, before we even know what the show *is*. We're just sitting there talking about the show, what we're interested in. The sound designer—

Is part of that process. So it sounds to me like sound is like a crucial part of that dramaturgy.

Yeah, designers are in there from the very beginning. Part of it is also because I'm an actor.

Kate [Scelsa] was telling me about the process of bringing things into the rehearsal. And she mentioned that you had brought some kind of Appalachian dance—

Uh-huh.

and that you're like the YouTube king?

For this show, knowing how to start is always the hardest thing. Because you know you're going to rehearse for a year and a half.

And this is kind of true of the ERS's MO, the notion that if everything's feeling too comfortable, it's a sign that we should go in a different direction.

And so we had this meeting, at the office, and we were like, "What is the thing that ERS would never do?" And in the past, that's led to poetry and Tennessee Williams, or [whatever]. And Steve Bodow—who was around still then, as kind of an assistant other directorial mind—he said, "The thing we would never do is the thing we just did." He [*laughs*] was right. That is a thing we would never do. So what if we did another book? So then it became a quest. If *The Great Gatsby* is a relatively easy thing to pick up and read, then what's the hardest thing to read; what's the most problematic book?

Well, let me back up. Before that, it was like, well, what books would you be interested in, more generally. And a bunch of us are from the South. Scott's from Georgia, John's from Georgia, I'm from Tennessee, Vin's from Louisiana. So, we started thinking of . . . I mean, Flannery O'Connor came up immediately.

Talk about a difficult estate to deal with.

And that was the thing, after *Gatz,* we didn't want to go down that road, even though we wanted to work with a female author.

So we started poking around, and more or less, by the fall, we ended up with Faulkner, and we started [reading]. I hadn't read much Faulkner. I wasn't really into it. I didn't read it in college. And then I read them all.

You just sat down and—

Yeah. As I started, I realized his writing is kind of mythology, and they're all connected. They all reference each other.

But with *The Sound and the Fury* the first chapter is the one that stands out as the one where you read it out loud and it completely changes. The experience of hearing it aloud is different from the experience of reading it on the page. And so, by the time we settled on that, it was weeks and weeks of these meetings. And we also—you know, there was other stuff we were bringing in. It wasn't just the book, it was music, and some video. Everyone's looking for some inspiration. Even if you don't know if it relates *at all.* But if it's interesting to someone, you kind of keep it in the air. Stick it in your pocket. And that's true for all the shows—whatever comes up, we kind of see it, watch it collectively and try not to pass judgment on it (or do pass a lot of judgment on it) and then maybe there's a point where it can inform something later on.

And so one of the things I brought in early on was *The Dancing Outlaw,* which is a PBS documentary from 1991 in West Virginia about this guy named Jesco White who was this redneck glue-sniffing flatfoot dancer up in West Virginia.

And the documentary is kind of exploitative, I mean, it doesn't really make him or his family look very good. But his father was this kind of legendary flatfoot dancer who was shot down by his neighbor.

What? [*Laughter*]

There's some archival footage in there from a Smithsonian documentary from back in the '80s and that's the really fascinating stuff. This guy is this lanky, skinny guy who would just, like, dance on a piece of plywood out in the yard, you know—it was just something simple and fascinating about the way he moves. So, that stuck. And then, through researching that, I found the original, the Smithsonian documentary, which was called *Talking Feet,* by Mike Seeger. And in that there's Appalachia in the 1980s so there's all these people. One of the guys is this guy Stanley Hicks who is this local storyteller up in the corner of North Carolina, who my friends in Tennessee actually knew, who made a banjo for them out of a possum hide.

[*Laughter*]

Really small world. So then that became this whole trove of stuff. The music from that is all in the show. Sounds of like whenever Benjy runs you hear tapping feet and breathing? That's from the Smithsonian thing. The hand-clapping stuff is also from the Smithsonian. A lot of the banjo music is from that documentary. The laughing is all Stanley Hicks.

The other dance—a bunch of the, I would say like 90 percent of the choreography for the entire show comes from that documentary, which includes the sections from *The Dancing Outlaw.*

So then, looking at how ERS translates dance is a totally different bag. It's not just about the dancers but the camera cuts to someone talking and gestures; it includes the hand gestures his mother is using when she's telling a story and that kind of stuff.

So, it's a totally different way of looking at dance. And then there's another thing that came up around that time—we saw on YouTube this video of these fainting goats. It was like some local news story about, you know, goats that get excited and—play possum, and so that's in the show. A guy selling a belt-buckle knife, that's in the show.

It seems random.

Totally random—but it's really—jokes, you know.

We're rehearsing Faulkner, so it's heavy, heavy, heavy—relentless, terrible stuff. So and this is a company that is mostly, that works on a sense of humor, so you know. It wasn't like we were deliberately saying, like there was a deliberate choice, you know—[*mock scholarly voice*] "this stupid redneck video will be a perfect counterpoint to Faulkner's sense of inevitability," it was just like, oh this is around, and it's funny. Maybe we can use it.

But you have a year and a half—you can just relax and let things inform each other, because there's not the pressure to force it to work.
That's much more of a European style than what we typically see. It sounds like there's stuff in the air, that you guys have these conversations, you go back to your houses and because of that, it's in your brain. So when you're looking on YouTube, there's some element—
Susie brought in a ton of stuff from her kids. Like, the kids would tell a story—she steals from the kids all the time. Hands down the pants, etc., so that's her big source of inspiration for her. She's also really been into traditional Indian dance, so that's in the show. The moaning that you hear from Benjy? That's more from a Kathakali traditional Indian dance. I'm sure if someone from that specific part of India heard that, they'd be like, why are we going to that specific epic or whatever.

And so anybody can bring in anything. There's no—
Hierarchy—
No, there's no hierarchy.
One of the other things I keep coming back to is the concept of space and the concept of time.
Mmm hmmm.
And the time for gestation and just sort of reflection?
Um, it's never a year and half straight. It's always like six weeks here, and then time away from it, then come back to it. John does that very deliberately so that he and everyone else has time to, like, sit on it, you know.
Absorb.
Absorb, and see it from a different perspective. That's true of all the shows. And we do work in progress shows along the way, so that we'll be forced to deal with a deadline, get it up on its feet, see what an audience . . . and then go away from it, and come back.
So that audience feedback, is it informal? Do you just talk to the people who were there? Or is it a formal process, where you have talkbacks?
No. And a lot of the time it's—sometimes, I mean, it's good to hear from people, but a lot of times you *know.* Just performing, you know what works and what doesn't work. And if we don't know, John knows.
Because he's out there—
Suffering in the back row—
[*Laughter*] When they fall asleep.
Yeah, but that's the crucial thing.
I was reading one of the reviews, I think it was of *The Sound and the Fury,* but it might have been about *Gatz.* Talking about—I think it was Ben Brantley—about how happy he was that some people left at intermission, or something?
Yeah.

And how, basically, that there was a way, that you guys basically created a piece that self-filtered the right kind of audience? [*Laughter*]

When we did this show in New York, the circumstances were such that it was our off-Broadway debut. So not many in the New York Theatre Workshop's subscription audience, especially then, knew who we were. None of their audience had really seen *Gatz*—I mean, we'd only done it at the Performing Garage by then.

Not the same crowd.

Not the same crowd—I mean, they probably knew who The Wooster Group was, but the reality is that these people were subscribers, and they had tickets but had no idea what it was. So, of course, they didn't like it. We lost about a third of the house every night.

So I think it's not quite as simple as just oh, Faulkner is filtering the crowd. A lot of people stayed and totally loved it! The people who stayed really loved it, you know. And others were surprised that they stayed. People felt like they wanted to leave. But now, this show is sold out a month away. So, like, people know, they know *Gatz,* they've seen other shows, they know that this will be something else.

I wanted to ask you a little about the dance, or the dances in *The Sound and the Fury.* I left last night before the dance rehearsal, but I've read about the disconnect between the feet, the hands, and the face.

Well, some of it goes back to what John is interested in, in making theatre, which is putting stuff onstage that doesn't necessarily belong onstage. Stuff that's not easily translatable, something that's not designed to be translated to the stage.

So, if you see a video of a flatfoot dancer dancing on the stage—that seems pretty straightforward, right?

But if the camera suddenly cuts to someone talking about that person while the music's going on in the background and then cuts back to them, John and Kathy [Profeta] might respond to that—they're still gesturing on counts to the music—but it's there, you know? What happens if you put some kind of rigor in everything that you see? And this goes back a little bit to The Wooster Group thing, because they're always using the source videos—the camera pans back, the actors move upstage, or—you respond to everything that you're seeing in some way or another.

So, a little bit of, you know, the mechanics of it aren't necessarily unique to ERS but John has this really almost perverse interest in seeing what happens when, you know, what kind of awkward and perhaps interesting things come up when these things clash together.

Like what happens when you put a book onstage. You know, what does it force people to do, hearing it—everything. It creates all these awkward, problematic things, and John really likes to solve problems.

Going back to the dance thing, how you translate the dance from a video for the show. Seeing this video of a flatfoot dancer, it seems easy. But also, we're not flatfoot dancers, at all!

But—and this is true of Wooster Group too, taking something like flatfoot dancing, some kind of highly advanced specialized art form or thing that would take a lifetime to master, which we don't have time or the ability really to do . . . so, and knowing that we're a company of people who aren't dancers.

And this is true for other shows too, like, *The Select*, when we're doing this crumping stuff. . . . That's another thing that came from a YouTube video. Like, knowing we could never do it as well as they do it, so, you know, what does—how does it mean, how do you do it—and then it becomes, well, identifying things that you can do, and all the things that would be interesting to do.

Do you bring in a choreographer?

Well for the *beginning* of this, Kathy wasn't around. Usually the way we do it—because it's not really feasible for Kathy to hang around and watch us rehearse, when we're not always going to be learning some dance stuff. So, a lot of—it's about finding out who's gonna do it. Who's in the room. And for this, it was me and Mike, just kind of, "yeah we can do this." And we went to the next room, and—

So, with a mirror, or—

We just like put it on video and got it on counts, made a grid, and said, okay well we can't do his feet. But as he's dancing, he has this stiff upper-body stuff, like these jerky moves and the head and shoulders . . . and that's easy, and honest, because it's happening after the downbeat, and it comes in on these weird counts, so we started with that. And made a dance out of that. And so once we got that in some kind of shape, after John was like, "Yeah this has potential," and we kept working on it for a couple of days. Kathy would come in and say, okay this is what you can do to make this work. Both of you have to agree on what these moves are, whether it matches on the video or not, just decide—shape it up. It was Kathy—she used to perform with the company and now she's like this—

The fixer?

Very specific, yeah. The Fixer, yes the dance fixer.

She's like the Olivia Pope of dance. [*Laughter*]

She shows up, gets it done, really specifically, and—

And then she leaves.

Yeah, and then she gets out.

I was fascinated last night at rehearsal because Susie kept wanting to see the video, and yet she's done it before! I mean, she's got this really—meticulous eye for detail. She kept asking in the scene in front of the fire, "Do my legs go this way or that way?" and I thought, "Why does it matter?" Except for a dancer. That's when it matters, is when it's choreography. But it's odd to think about it that way for theatre—

John's also that way. John thinks about everything all the time.

I noticed that with the set, he kept saying, "Let's move this that way" and—

And that goes back to how decisions get made at the very beginning. John's genius is for working with what's in the room right in front of his face.

What you saw last night is us working with a bunch of stand-ins, so everyone's like, oh, well we only have a fraction of what we need to do the show. We're working with a compressed set so that changes everything. And that's because John doesn't know how to say, "Just do this for now," which can be really frustrating for everybody.

Especially for the newcomers, I would think.

For the newcomers and, I mean, I've been here for twelve years, so, like, as a sound designer, when we were working on Sibyl's show at the Walker in Minneapolis, we had this big three hundred seat house and a massive sound system with, like, twenty speakers, and now we go back and we have, like, two speakers. And the show is built to run on twenty. But now we have to work on two. *This* show is built to work on twenty speakers. But we're working on four. It's built differently, but we also rehearsed differently than we did with Sibyl's show. There are things that, you know, running of the sound for the show is more like playing a musical instrument, right? There's a lot of engineering involved, but it's mostly a guy at a keyboard playing effects.

It's not like Q-lab or anything.

It's not like Q-lab. With Sibyl's show, I'm designing it but I'm also in it, so I had to build it so that Gavin could run it having only two weeks to learn it. And it's also a much more complicated thing, much more running around.

It's such a different way of working.

Most directors don't have sound come in until tech.

What keeps you coming back?

One big thing is that we kept touring the same shows. I never had a day job—I was always freelancing. So, touring was a chance to sublet my apartment and make a stipend and not have to rehearse. And doing *Gatz*—I got tired doing it, after nine years—but it was always a great show. The show itself never felt tired. And that has a lot to do with John.

Kaneza Schaal

New York City, 23 April 2015

Kaneza Schaal is a New York City-based theatre artist. She received a 2016 Creative Capital Award to develop her next work Jack and Jill, *a multimedia comedy of errors that draws on social codes and trainings: from prison re-entry programs to debutante balls. Schaal's piece* Go Forth *premiered with Performance Space 122 and was presented at the Genocide Memorial Amphitheater in Kigali, Rwanda. Her work has been supported by Baryshnikov Arts Center, Performance Space 122, Lower Manhattan Cultural Council, Nathan Cummings Foundation, Foundation for Contemporary Arts, Theater Communications Group, Princess Grace George C. Wolfe Award, Bogliasco Fellowship, and Kara Walker's 68 Months Project Space.*

Schaal's work with Elevator Repair Service, The Wooster Group, Richard Maxwell/New York City Players, Claude Wampler, Jay Scheib, and New York City Opera has brought her to venues including Centre Pompidou, Royal Lyceum Theater Edinburgh, The Whitney Museum, Brooklyn Academy of Music, and MoMA. She is an Arts-in-Education advocate and works in New York City public schools with recent immigrants, and with refugee communities internationally to address migration and storytelling.

Kaneza Schaal: The sound is this tapestry.

Jane Barnette: Vin and John both talked about sound helping audience. But no one talked about it with regard to the actors.

We had this amazing annotated script with time period—dramaturgically, that was key.

Even last night [at rehearsal], Daphne [Gaines] was asking, "Who am I here?"

I do not envy having to step into the show. Dramaturgy is a funny word—maybe I should know more about what it means in your context. The theatrical dramaturgy, not the literary dramaturgy—the performance logics that we've built to get us ready to step into it, as an actor not having built those logics and stepping into this world. I think that's a really big task.

So would you say then at the New York Theatre Workshop when you and Greg and April joined the group, did y'all feel like you got to help create some of it as well?

Oh yeah, they'd only gotten through the first twenty pages or something at that point. Yeah.

Well that's great. When it first started, and this is an awful metaphor, I thought it was more like, "Oh we've got this lovely cookie batter, and now we need some—"

[*Together*] *Chocolate chips.*

And I was like, really? You're just going to fold those in there?

No I think the understanding was, we need black people to *make* it. In order to make the show. I think Dartmouth was that very initial work period, and then—

Well that makes a big difference, then. This remount is—

Those logics we've created—

They don't have any sense memory for that—

Or even that sound triggers that memory, or the structure. And because it happens over time and through experimentation, because it is a long development period, the complexities of how everything works off each other is much thicker than a four-week rehearsal process in a traditional setting, where the structures have to be so . . . they don't have time to iterate and transform.

It was so interesting to see the video—to keep going back to the video, and then back to the real life, and back again to the video. At first it didn't make sense to me. Those decisions are what, three years in the making?

Yeah. And you pull a straw out of that, and you don't know what starts to unravel.

It's wild. Even those of us who are stepping back into it—I was reminded of that last night, we were starting an overlap three lines later than we started it on the video, and we'd rehearse like that for two days, and something wasn't quite lining up, which then changes somebody else's entrance. And I was like, "Huh, huh—well I guess we just haven't gotten it yet," but nope, the overlap starts three lines after this and it starts there for a reason. [*Laughs*]

What I love about that is that it sort of echoes the ensemble aesthetic itself—the decisions you make in the enactment, it really creates solid ensemble. Whereas a lot of ensembles—you could change decisions and have a fully logical play. But it sounds like these decisions got solidified through legitimate cooperation and conversation.

Mmm hmmm—yeah. The biggest dramaturgical change that's happened, which relates to this untangible [*sic*] what do you call it, intuition, or I don't know . . . I wonder what John would say. But—I'm going to go backwards and then go forwards. In picking a text, it's largely about how the language sits on the people, right? So when something works, like, what is that moment of recognition? What is that dramaturgical choice? "It's working," you know what I mean? That's the thing you can't really name. You can talk to people—you can engender trust and everything, but I think Sibyl would talk about it in terms of intuition. I'd be curious what John would say about when something works. And so, one of the materials that gets passed around is race, right? I mean, we all play these different characters—there's a lot of balance in what is tolerable, and what is intolerable in Faulkner's depiction, and in our performances? And to whom. And there's this scene where Vin's on the floor and gets kicked. Like, I don't think any of us are gonna want to watch Greig on the floor and get kicked by

Vin. Do you know what I mean? [*Laughs*] All of those delicacies, and like *that* dramaturgy—that unnamed logic or sensitivity or, um, set of values that we're working with. I'm curious about how you can talk about that in a concrete way, or a tools type way, because it really is about what you can tolerate or put up with . . . so . . . and on the other side of this is the question of whether we have "sanitized" the text, a text is racially violent, and in which the word "nigger" is used hundreds of times. These "logic systems" at play in the room, these "values" are not neutral. Big questions.

The big dramaturgical change at The Public is that Kate used to be the first person to play Dilsey. Kate Scelsa. At the top of the play, and there was always a little, I think Kate had a "aarrghh"—I think she's the one who raised it the most, but everyone was like, "no, it's good." And this round, Daphne is taking that role, because there was always something in that moment, where you're like, "ooh, wow—that's where we're gonna go? Right out of the gate? Okay, okay, here we go." And I don't know, for me, it's all Faulkner's construct of race, so the fact that we're dealing with it as a material I think is brilliant. . . . And I don't know, I was probably thinking about other things when those decisions got made. It's the play that happens in the room, it's what people gravitate toward, it's this complex matrix of all these people doing all these things. I don't think at any point there's a decision being made about "let's have the guy step in as the Mother." I think it's like when Vin does Mother it's amazing! When Greig does Mother it's amazing! When Mike does Mother it's amazing! You want to see that, you know.

And I think, but I think John privileges that—you know, kind of theatrical, over some kind of literary-historical logic, like what works on the stage. *What works on the playfulness* [of the source], what makes it fun, what makes it work theatrically? What is the successful dramaturgy of the theatrical moment above the—whatever? And again, it's not neutral, right? Those decision-making processes. Whatever is fun about watching the guys do Mother. This isn't neutral.

Historically relevant or even source-text authentic. There's this whole longstanding issue of adaptation having some kind of fidelity issue, like what would the author want?

And I really believe that, with this piece, the final product produces something that relates to the experience of reading the book.

Yeah.

In a way that trying to write a play out of *The Sound and the Fury* could never give you, so—the people I have spoken to, like friends and people I've spoken to after the shows, over the years, people talk about, like "what is this story?" and "I'm frustrated," and eventually giving over to the fact that they're there and they have to be there, or that they paid to be there. [*Laughs*] And so they're going to stay.

And when you give over, that's when something starts to happen, that's what happened to me, was 100 percent the experience of reading the book, which was *so frustrating* at the beginning, and then you're, like, "Okay, forget it, I give up." And THEN it starts to happen, in that "I give up" moment.

Well, that's interesting though, because—there's *The Great Gatsby* where, I don't know anyone who is, like, "Oh I tried to read *Gatsby* but I couldn't finish it." It's not like that; you can't put it down.

Yeah, but I mean, *Gatz*—you gotta sit with *Gatz.* John makes you earn it. You gotta be present. For a while there, Scott's reading to you, and I feel like sometimes you zone out, and then, "Wait, I'm back."

There's a way that the role of the stage—so, Mo [Maurina Lioce] is quite new, and Sarah Hughes who was hired just after I was hired—the role of the stage manager is very dramaturgical, in terms of checks and balances and communication with people.

And that makes sense. Because—it's not all about calling the cues.

And then also that company model of like Ariana [Smart Truman] is the producer, so she's dealing with—one thought-question, about the piece I'm making? So I have a dramaturg that I'm working with, and his role in the room is very much about process. About thinking about how I'm working on things, how performers are relating to the material. It's the whole machine—it's dramaturging the work, but also dramaturging the process, and ways of building. And did Ben talk about the movement stuff in the piece?

Yeah, that got me really excited about being free and encouraged to go off and do research and come back and say, "Look what I found!" Some folks call it *devising.*

I hate that word.

Coming back to the music? It has almost a meditative quality to it? Contemplative?

I agree. I find that in the sound score too—that's where a touch of the divine is. I really do think the piece is in conversation with Faulkner and *The Sound and the Fury* as he wrote it. And that contact, and that pursuit? That's where the divine lives. And the humor—all the transgressions and jokes, there is something very earnest in the task of taking something that was not made for the stage and putting it on the stage and doing that honestly, solving that problem.

John Gentile, Adapter of *Moby-Dick*

Via Phone, 25 January 22016

John S. Gentile's credits in stage adaptation include major works of literary and folk narrative: Over Nine Waves: Myths of Ancient Ireland, Jack of Beech Mountain: Folktales from Southern Appalachia, *Nathaniel Hawthorne's* Twice-Told Tales, The Bell Witch and Other Legends, American Gothic: Stories by American Masters of the Macabre, Ovid's Metamorphoses, Redwing: Voices from 1888, Dark Forest: Tales and Poems from the Brothers Grimm, The Scarlet Letter, The Hero's Journey: Mythic Stories of the Heroic Quest *(featured as a plenary session at the international Mythic Journeys conference), and* Red Hanrahan *(which toured to the Edinburgh Fringe Festival). His adaptation of Herman Melville's* Moby-Dick *was presented at the Casablanca Theatre Festival in 2009, where it was named best performance.* Moby-Dick *was restaged for an experimental immersion production by SAÏAH Arts International in Atlanta in 2013 and was named best play by* Creative Loafing. *His most recent adaptation,* A Christmas Carol *by Charles Dickens, was directed by Patrick Sutton and produced at Smock Alley Theatre in Dublin, Ireland, where it enjoyed a sold-out run in 2016. He is currently working on a new version of* Moby-Dick *for Smock Alley Theatre's 2017 season. Additionally, Gentile is the author of* Cast of One: One-Person Shows from the Chautauqua Platform to the Broadway Stage. *His essays have appeared in* Text and Performance Quarterly, Studies in Popular Culture, On the Culture of the American South, The Future of Performance Studies, Storytelling, Self, Society, Queers in American Popular Culture, *and* Eighteenth-Century British and American Rhetorics and Rhetoricians. *His latest essay, "Meeting with Great January: An Archetypal Interpretation of the Slovak Fairytale 'The Twelve Months'" is forthcoming in* Text and Performance Quarterly. *Gentile holds an MA and PhD in performance studies from Northwestern University and an MA in mythological studies with an emphasis in depth psychology from Pacifica Graduate Institute.*

Jane Barnette: You've had several different scripts [of *Moby-Dick*], and I've been looking at the difference between the SAÏAH and the Kennesaw script. And I just wanted to hear from your perspective what the major changes were that you made.

John Gentile: When one of my adaptations is staged for a new production, whether I'm the director or I'm simply serving as the adapter, I go back and adapt it afresh. That has been the pattern. So, every time I'm adapting a work, it is production specific. I consider my adaptations open. I want to be the one doing the adapting, of course, but if somebody is interested in staging one of my adaptations, I am totally open to reconsidering the adaptation. It's not a closed script in my mind.

Those productions of *Moby-Dick*—and now this new one for Smock Alley Theatre—have had very different space-specific limitations and restrictions placed on them and I have to work within those parameters. I have the expectations of a specific production, and then I have my own sensibility. My preferred length for a theatre experience is ninety minutes, and I try to aim for that, and I have a good sense of that. However, there are some works that are resistant to that level of compression.

I have found part of it is simply my own learning curve with the adaptation itself. After a staged reading, and again after the initial fully staged production—I cut, and cut, and cut. After I stage the script the first time, I have almost an internal understanding of what I have to do to tighten this. Now I would have a much easier time, let's say, of cutting *The Scarlet Letter,* than I had prior to actually going through the staging.

And I think professional productions, let's say of a new musical, have time for revision on the road through previews. And I've never had that luxury, so in a sense I have had it moving from production to production of an adaptation. Also, I work very closely with the director—if I'm not the director—or even if I'm the codirector, I have someone else's feedback, responses, desires. So, it's the limitations of a given production situation, plus the requests of the directors, for what they are wanting. And sometimes it can be very impactful. You know, they want certain scenes. That kind of thing—they've seen the initial adaptation, and they request a certain way for it to be revised. And I'm open to working with all of those limitations. At other times, I am given a wider range.

For all those reasons, I like to readapt the work in a sense, or rather *revise* my adaptation, given the circumstances of a specific production and a specific director.

For your production in particular, I wanted to think about how you had to reconsider *Moby-Dick* in the huge Lifecycle building versus the Stillwell stage.
Right. Well, the Kennesaw Stillwell is a proscenium, traditional theatre. It allows the full range of technical components available in a well-equipped theatre. And the situation was such that it made sense for that initial adaptation to be a full—two acts—theatrical experience. I recognized that, even though it comes much earlier than halfway through the book, "The Quarter-Deck" chapter is simply a perfect ending for the first act. It's just made for it, theatrically. So I really wanted to explore a two-act structure for that production.

The next production, the one in Morocco, was going to be on a proscenium stage, but it had to travel, and it had a certain limited amount of playing time, and we needed to include segments in Arabic and segments in French. All of those realities drove the revision—and plus I had to reduce it down for a much smaller company. So those are all considerations that were handed to me. And then I was working with a director who had been my codirector [Henry Scott], who knew the script inside and out, and had very specific ideas about what he wanted included. And that's the way the Morocco version of *Moby-Dick* came into being.

When *Moby-Dick* was reimagined again, for the Lifecycle building, I was given more time, that ninety-minute mark, and I literally walked through the space with the director, and she [Marium Khalid] told me, "This scene is going to occur here, and that scene is going to occur there." And so I knew the geography of the spaces for that "immersion performance"—that's the style of site-specific theatre SAÏAH creates—I knew where each of the scenes would take place, such as the loading dock of the warehouse serving as the docks of Nantucket. And so how could it not take place at this location? And, so, that scene has to be included. That kind of thing. When you have such a perfect physical environment to enact a certain scene, then, of course, you're going to include it. And by then I had learned from the previous incarnations of my adaptation which scenes were expendable.

In the earliest version, I wanted to include some scenes of comic relief, those scenes with Mrs. Hussey. I learned we didn't need those scenes, ultimately.

It's a big book [*laughter*]. But it's also—it's a big concept, it's happening in a vast expansive ocean. There's so much space.

Mmm hmm—

I can't remember exactly which production it was in, but I have this vivid memory of Briana being up high as The Whiteness of the Whale.

Raked stage. We used a raked stage that gave her height for the ending scene. And, then, the moment when—I mean, there were several really powerful visual moments in the SAÏAH production—but I love that long walk The Whiteness of Whale took of the length of the warehouse with that huge bright light behind her. You were literally blinded by the whiteness. I thought that was—out of anything out of that entire production—it was that moment, that image that was the most impressive visually.

But I did want to ask you about the difference between when you have worked with a dramaturg versus when you have not, in terms of what it means for your adaptation?

Well, one of the things that I really liked about *Moby-Dick* was having the conversations and the process. I remember one time Paula Bowen [assistant dramaturg] made the comment about the whale ships and rowing in them, and how we tried to accommodate that, at least in the main stage production that we did, though Henry made a different choice in the Morocco production.

But I found that helpful. And being able to discuss the script in that kind of way. When you're working with a dramaturg, you have somebody who is script oriented and research oriented, and not just production oriented. Most people that are working on a production are just production oriented.

Usually, production considerations drive the artistic choices, as opposed to things that are text based and source based. I think the two of us work very well together. I would have to say that the dramaturgs I've worked with have been more or less effective because I do so much of my research myself. It may feel like there's no space to enter into the process.

Because dramaturgy is not just a role, it's also a function and a process, and many people take it on, including designers and of course adapters and directors.

Right. Right.

And, of all the people I've worked with, you take it on probably the most! [*Laughter*]

Well, I really enjoy that part, Jane. I have to say, the creation of the script—and, especially, the background research leading into the creation of the script—I think that may be my favorite part of the process. I thoroughly enjoyed the research for *The Scarlet Letter.*

Some of that was also primary, in terms of you going to the places—

Yes—visiting Salem, Massachusetts, and Concord was very inspiring—certain elements went directly into the scenic design.

Can you give me an example?

I call the aesthetic we worked with for *The Scarlet Letter* poetic realism. I wanted the architecture of first period New England to inform the set design in a poetic way. So I visited many of those buildings that are in existence in Salem. I photographed them, both exterior and interior, and I brought in a lot of research, and I gave it to Ming [Ming Chen, scenic designer]. Now, she's a strong artist. She listened to my comments and my research; she heard what Henry and I wanted. Henry was very helpful in discussing the scenic design, and, then, she's able to come up with something of her own, which is what she did. That set was remarkable and fulfilled our vision beautifully.

We described the feeling we wanted from that set—that sense of the oppression, of the society pressing down on the characters. We filled that proscenium arch with those terrific wall units Ming designed for *Scarlet Letter.* And that was the intention: to fill the vertical space. I would have liked it to be even more impressive—higher, but we literally couldn't do it in that theatre space. I wanted something that looked operatic.

So that the human beings were that much smaller, in the face of it.

Right, yes.

That reminds me a little bit of when James Maloof did the design for *Everything That Rises Must Converge,* and he went to Andalusia, Flannery O'Connor's estate, and just sat there, and took it in, and that, of course, became such a beautiful design.

Yes, I did like that design very much. But the conversations with Henry are very helpful. The most helpful, of course, is getting the script onstage, to rehearse the entire thing with a cast, to then go through the tech week, and the production week, when it meets an audience—that's a huge learning curve for me as an adapter. I know my script *better* after all that. How it works and what can be tightened up.

I mean, there is the text snob in me; the text is the filet mignon on the plate, and these other elements—the spectacle and music—are the desserts or the sides, you know—you want more steak, don't you? [*Laughter*] So, I had a really hard time trimming the main course down to accommodate the sides, to continue with this metaphor. But now that I've gone through it, I could force myself to cut twenty minutes from that script somehow. And it would be painful cutting. Killing a favorite author's darlings. But sometimes it takes me an initial production to get that, and to really understand it.

You've been doing adaptation for several years, you've studied it, and I just wondered if you could give me any insight as to what you've learned over the years. What are some of the takeaways that you have as one who both enjoys doing adaptations and loves the literature from which they come.

I was thinking of this today, knowing we were going to have this interview. And I remembered that the very first production that I was in and that convinced me that I wanted to go into theatre was an adaptation of *A Christmas Carol* that I was in in sixth grade.

So, my very first theatre experience that gave me the direction of my life was a literary adaptation. And it was a work that stayed with me for the rest of my career, actually, because it was an important text for me in graduate school, both as a performer and also in researching Charles Dickens's readings, and then all these years later, lo and behold, I'm adapting it for a production in Dublin. *A Christmas Carol* was my first theatre experience. . . . So, for me the interest was ingrained very early and it was an exciting form of theatre for me. And then, of course, studying with Robert Breen and Frank Galati and Paul Edwards—I just became extremely dedicated as an artist to literary adaptation. I find it extremely rewarding, and I feel like I'm facilitating the original author's work and bringing it to a new audience that may have never encountered the work in a full way. Audience members may have resisted reading a work of literature during their educations, and so for me there's almost a sense of public service, to revitalize people's interest in literature. And that is, in a sense, where the passion for this work comes from. I'm someone very interested in the question of, "How can I put this work onstage that is both theatrically compelling and responsible to the source text?" And I realize in thinking about this question that it really is a reworking of Wallace Bacon's idea of the dangerous shores between text and performance.

You know, it's *still* the same question, just reimagined specifically for adaptation. He nails it—that sense of navigating. He uses the metaphor of navigating the waters between those two shores, and it's a really fine way to think about the challenge of making literary language theatrically compelling. It is a creative challenge. It is rewarding work, really, and you see that getting to work with Henry, because he comes to the work with such a different sensibility. I come with such a high regard for the literature, the word, and he immediately is interested in a sense of movement and music.

I think that's a really complementary combination. And so, I still find the work of adaptation very interesting, still find it compelling. And when I have, in the few times that I have directed a play script—someone else's creation—I have found it very hampering, I felt like I was in a straightjacket, because I had to have each one of these words said, that's the agreement that you signed.

And it's just not for me. There are many other directors who thrive with that, who are not interested in adaptation, but I like the malleability of working with an adaptation that I can make whole sections come or go. So you're working in a sense as—I do recognize that you are working in service to the author. Since I have such a high regard for them as artists, I am fine serving in that capacity.

If I am serving Yeats or Melville or Hawthorne or Dickens—to have his work on the stage and to be enjoyed again, then I think I'm doing well by the author. One of my faculty colleagues, Jan Wikstrom, has said to me: "Performing literature is one of the reasons you were put on this Earth." I get that. It is my passion, my bliss.

That's a long answer, Jane. [*Laughter*]

No, I love it—I think that's very helpful! One of the things that I keep coming back to is that the field itself—adaptation studies—you know, it's fought long and hard with this question of fidelity, which I think is a false question, really. Because you can't ever really be exactly faithful, because it's a different medium.

Right—that is correct.

What makes you want to adapt a work?

Let's see. It's probably a work that I've known for many years and it's been percolating in the back of my head. That's usually the case. Many times the works I choose are ones that I have very positive memories of. As you know, I tend to be interested in works that posit a numinous realm, and the intersection between this world and that extraordinary world, however it's imagined, is of interest to me. I think that is inherently theatrical, in and of itself, working with the idea of two levels of reality onstage. And finding ways of suggesting that with power. It is an interesting challenge to me. And that's an intersection of where Henry and I and our sensibilities meet.

That's very much how both of us see the world: works that posit a numinous realm. I'm drawn to such works, and I do tend to gravitate toward works of the nineteenth century; that has been "my century"—for all of my career, actually. I started working on Dickens very early in graduate school; that's part of the influence of Dickens for me. And my fascination with that period has since only deepened. Also, the production of *Chautauqua!!* by Patti McKenny directed by Lee Roloff was another important influence. Productions have often pointed the way for my future research and creative work.

I have one follow-up, because in the process of writing this book, I have had these weird serendipitous moments where several different people in different contexts have asked me if there is something that is connected between adaptation and the uncanny.

Well, I guess in the sense of taking a work of literature that people have thought of as something that exists only on the page and putting it on the stage. That whole transformation that the source text goes through—an extraordinary experience to extract its essence and completely reimagine it with bodies on the stage. And, yes, I think there is this sense of being the conjurer, of being the Prospero. It could be thought of that way, certainly. I am now working on a conference paper for the Hawthorne Society Meeting. I will be speaking about my work adapting *The Scarlet Letter* for the stage and I am working with the idea of the adapter as alchemist, which is another way of considering the act of adaptation as magical transformation. And, for me, I have a strong sense of *the author* while I'm adapting his or her work for the stage.

So—you mean, you feel like you're connected to them?

I do, and as if they're watching what I'm doing.

When I'm doing adaptation I imagine that the original author is going to see it. Particularly while I was working on *Red Hanrahan,* which is a magical story to begin with, and then you're dealing with [William Butler] Yeats, who went to séances and believed in reliving one's life in the afterlife. Right? So, you're not only feeling that yourself—you're also working with an author who believes it. So, if anyone's going to come back from the dead to see a production of my adaptation of his stories, it's going to be Yeats. [*Laughter*]

I even remember saying to James Pethica that I imagined Yeats would come to see this production, and he said, "Oh, I'm sure he would." [*Laughter*]

And so I said, "What do you think he'd think of it?" And he said, "Oh, I think he'd love it!" There's this whole conversation in my mind imagining how Yeats would respond when he comes to see it. [*Laughter*]

We've had this conversation about *Doctor Faustus* as well, right? There are certain texts that when you speak them into the air, it feels a lot like conjuring.

Yes. There it is!

It feels like something very magical is happening!

Yes.

And that was absolutely true of your *Red Hanrahan*. I remember sitting in on some of your rehearsals and just being transported, and the cast as well! Talking about having these experiences with the Other Ones.

Right. That sense of the Other World, of Faeryland. While we were working on *Red Hanrahan,* I remember Henry telling me that Yeats's poems are spells. His language entrances the performer as well as the listener.

And, then, you have his images and what they are doing to you. Yeats was activating, as he would say, the Great Memory and the Great Mind. You're working with an author who has that intention.

Same with Marlowe, of course, I mean absolutely—

That's a beautiful example of conjuring, and what can happen.

Blair Thomas, Founder of Blair Thomas and Company

Chicago, 11 August 2016

Blair Thomas started his first puppet company The Palace Puppeteers when he was ten years old and for three years toured churches and schools in his hometown of Jacksonville, Alabama. The second company he started was Redmoon in 1989, where he served as the artistic director and co-artistic director until 1998, during which time he led the creation of all its productions, parades, and pageants. He returned to puppet theatre with the founding of his current company Blair Thomas and Company in 2002. Thomas's theatrical adaptations include: The Hard Headed Heart, *a collection of solo puppet performances based on the writings of Federico García Lorca and Wallace Stevens, as well as a traditional New Orleans blues song;* The Selfish Giant, *adapted from an Oscar Wilde short story; and* The Vinegar Works, *a toy-theatre adaptation of Edward Gorey's "three volumes of moral instruction,"* The Gashlycrumb Tinies, The Insect God, *and* The West Wing. *His* Moby-Dick or The Brotherhood of the Monastic Order of Ancient Mariners Purges the Ills of Society through a Reading of the Tales of Moby-Dick *was directed and coadapted by Greg Allen with songs by Michael Smith and live sound by Michael Zerang.*

Among Thomas's many honors are two UNIMA (Union Internationale de la Marionnette) awards for excellence in the art of puppetry and two Illinois Arts Council fellowships. He was the first artist to fill the Jim Henson artist-in-residence position at the University of Maryland and his work has been presented in countless venues including: the Museum of Contemporary Art, Chicago; Steppenwolf Theater; Blacksheep Puppet Festival, Center for Puppetry Arts; PS 122; and the Slovenia Puppet Festival. He is currently adjunct associate professor of performance and sculpture at the Art Institute of Chicago.

Jane Barnette: So I guess my first question for you is—why this piece? What drew you to *Moby-Dick* in the first place? What made you want to do it for the stage?

Blair Thomas: Right. This question is always asked, and I *truthfully* have no answer for that question, although I have lots of answers that I have given. And this is not the first time I adapted the book.

So, I had a big period of adapting it from '92 to '95. And then I put it down for a while, and then I started to work on it again, and I was a different artist, and I was drawn to the novel in different ways. The first time I adapted it without having ever read it, I just liked the idea of creating a performance that would happen on the beach here at Lake Michigan. I thought, I mean, wouldn't you go see a performance of *Moby-Dick* on the beach?

I would.

So, I mean, it was just purely spectacle, you know, I was 28—whatever. And then I read the book, with the purpose to do that adaptation, and I was like, wow! This is a really good book.

And it's got a lot more in it, and so then we made another adaptation for indoor theatre, and this was at Redmoon in the 1990s, and so we did several workshops. And during that time I was just really interested in the story. I was interested in the relationships between Queequeg and Ishmael, particularly. And I liked—even then, I would describe it as the unstageable parts of the book, which is not really accurate, but whatever. The things that are not dialogue and action—more of the meditative ruminations of Ishmael, I really found very compelling. And also the sense of wonder at the natural world, as an example of the spiritual quest.

I always wanted to just take Father Mapple's sermon, and I have this image of Father Mapple walking out, and a big devil opening the Bible, and out of the Bible pops a toy theatre stage, and he delivers the sermon as a toy-theatre puppet show. And so I made this show, this little one-man show—I distilled the monologue down to only twenty minutes. That chapter, if you just read it, it's almost fifty minutes long. Just that one chapter! Just the sermon.

And in '92 I was in Buenos Aires, and I heard Javier Villafañe speak, and he talked about that. And the thing that I remember from his talk was that he [said], "The puppet theatre cannot exist without the devil." And that simple phrase is one that's always stuck with me, and so when I look at a piece like *Moby-Dick*, which draws from a Judeo-Christian America in the nineteenth century, while the devil is not in *Moby-Dick*, the devil is in the theology. Good and evil [are] in that theology, and that's a theology that we inherit here in the twenty-first century. So, I was aware of that, and I performed that for a while, and I was like, "I'm trying to work on *Moby-Dick!*" And I was really interested in the text as this found object.

I was like, "I'm going to say every single word that Melville says in that sentence, and it's a paragraph long, so how do you perform it?" And it's something else. It's another thing. And I was interested in this gnarliness just being on the stage, and people just having to wrestle with it. And what I learned from that—oh my god, I've got a lot to say!

It's okay.

Okay, I'll just keep going. What I learned from that was that the density of the text was so demanding to the audience that the other images had to be even *more* distilled. So, it meant that if I'm delivering that mode of text, I've got to cut down the puppet images. I've got to really pare them down. And speak really slowly.

[*Laughter*] Yep, really articulate it.

Yeah. It's always compared to Shakespeare, but this is different, because Shakespeare is written for the stage, and this is not, this is written to be read, and so—

I understand.

But at the same time, that doesn't mean it can't be delivered onstage; it's just a different beast. But I feel like I captured some energy [of the devil], I was interested in this idea of the fallen angel, in this idea of Mephistopheles, in the Milton idea of this revolutionary who is trying to do good for the cause, but it turned out that he was full of hubris and needed to be excommunicated. So that became really interesting to me because, on some level, our entire country is built on these kinds of people. We're full of iconoclasts—the ones who are successful are the ones who we build monuments for, and the other ones we don't. But we constantly propagate them, you know, like Donald Trump is one of these men who are their own man, and doing it their own way, and when they're successful they're Thomas Jefferson or Abraham Lincoln, and when they're not, they're—

Forgotten.

Forgotten, right. But that notion is heavily tied to "Being a Light to the World." This Christian idea of American exceptionalism that we inherited, that's part of our fabric. And so, on the second return to the text, I was more interested in the relationship between Melville's text and the American religious experience. That was the thing that to me felt most relevant because it's something that today is still resonant for many people in a very real, immediate, and believable way. So much so that everyone else has to deal with it as well, whether we believe or not.

And so, it's tied into political and philosophical ideas that are taken for granted in a way that they become assumptions—they're not reexamined or questioned. And so, in [*Leviathan*] there was an article proposing that *Moby-Dick* was a third testament, and I just thought that was a really brash thing to say. The author [Zachary Hutchins] was saying how the characters, many of them carry Old or New Testament names, and walk into the story of *Moby-Dick* with the history of their characters' experience in the Old and New Testament, and so it's like playing out again—Ahab *is* cursed, and he has a history. Ishmael *is* the outcast. All these men are revisited in a new context—part of which is this capitalist venture, the business of whaling, and the other is dominating the world, literally, by being able to own the oceans, and then to defeat the leviathan. So it gets back to this powerful image of destruction that comes from the Old Testament that carries this apocalyptic power. It escalates the demands or tensions of the situation by the confrontation with the ultimate form of destruction. And Ahab is using all of his skills and faculties to ultimately do good for the world. He wants to defeat this source of suffering for the world—he doesn't want the world to suffer the way he did.

He wants to free them, so he sees himself as a righteous man. And the righteous man is an icon in our culture, and revered. So he's willing to go against the tide and the ideas, because he knows that he's right. This inner conviction is this driving force, so [he has] this notion of this thing that needs to be defeated and that he has to do whatever it takes. If that means usurping the power of God himself in the universe, then he will take that task on. And so that ultimate hubris is like an extreme version *of the self-reliance, ambitious, "light-unto-the-world" vision of being American.* That's why he continues—I mean, how many *New Yorker* cartoons each year are devoted to *Moby-Dick*? [*Laughter*]

Still!

Still! I mean, that vision of a monomaniacal leader who is confronting something that clearly is going to destroy him. And there's tons of stuff between Melville and the Bible that the contemporary reader just doesn't get. No one carries around the context of the Bible in such detail, but we carry around the burden of it all the same. So I was trying to get after something with that—these are the things that inspire me. I literally sat down and pulled all the text I liked—I'm like, "What do I like?"

"I like this passage, I like that passage." I just pulled it and copied it, put it in a book, and called that my script.

[*Laughter*] No strategy!

Yeah, it's sort of *not* a script. But I had this dilemma, because if you just deliver the dialogue or monologues of the book on the stage, it just somehow, it's *missing* something. Something to me that's really significant.

So, what I couldn't see was having somebody stand there and presume to be any of the characters of the book and say the lines. Between the heightened strata in which the whole epic story is being told and the pedestrian world of human beings standing there with their feet on the stage, it's just too great of a distance, and I don't believe it!

And worse, it's hokey, right?

Yeah.

I don't look to some performer or some puppet to embody that in a way that will carry it through the evening. And so that means that I need to have a *context*—a larger frame in which all the stories are told. So there's basically a bunch of storytellers up there telling stories, and they pick up something that's going to represent the character, and it's not burdened with that level of believability. It just needs to temporarily fill in that place.

Because the story is living somewhere else, it's not living in the relationship with the characters, in what I was choosing to adapt. . . .

And [eventually] the idea of the Monastic Order of Ancient Mariners came up. And our founder was Ishmael, and he started a religious sect that was carrying the torch for all the religious men who perished in the Pequod, and the vision for the world that they had.

So that idea became the world that we built our show around. And so, that means that we can do whatever we want to do! Michael Smith makes folk music, so that's how he contributes, and Michael Zerang makes these weird noises, and Monte and I are puppeteers—and we're the four remaining members of the Monastic Order, and we're kind of moving forward into the future, but we're also drawing from some weird, ambiguous monastic past. So our robes look like they're from Andrei Rublev, you know, and so we were interested in that idea. And there's this whole interesting relationship between sailors and religious sects in that way, and so that's where that idea, and thus the long title. And literally that's what it is.

And so around this time, Greg Allen becomes the director. We were like, "We need a director; we need a captain of our ship." Because we're all on the stage, we can't see what we're making. And so we asked Greg. And when we did the version of *Moby-Dick* with Redmoon on the beach, Greg played Ahab.

And Greg is a playwright guy, so he's like, "Can I see the script?" And I show him this pile of stuff, and he's like, "This is not a script."

[***Laughter***]

So, the adaptation that you saw was finalized by Greg and I [*sic*]. So, we share credit on that adaptation. [He] really functioned as a true friend and collaborator and sat down and said, "What are you trying to say with this story?" Rather than saying, "Here's what I want to say with this story."

And so, he's mining the text as much as he was mining my instincts and where my impulses were. I mean, the whole way. I remember the day before the first performance, I was standing on the stage, and I said, "Hold on, Greg—wait, wait, we gotta stop. We have to rearrange these sections; the thing we just did we have to move forward," and he just stopped all the tech crew and listened to me, and said, "Okay, let's do it!"

I mean, he listens within reason—sometimes I would propose things that don't work, but he had faith that I had a lot of instincts that were sending us in the right direction. Greg is also very skillful—he was doing a lot of dramaturgical and continuity work for this show, and focus.

So, the piece became focused. It was just a mash of impressions and ideas, and he shaped it. And he shaped it from—he didn't go back to the text and scour the text. He took what I got him and said, "What is this?" And the one disadvantage to that is that Greg is the real theatre guy in the room. We're all fine with twenty minutes going by and no one saying anything. So, we had to say, "Greg, can we cut some of the text, so we can just have some moments?" So there was a balance with that, but I had a lot of faith in his ability to know how to cut and what to cut. That whole, to understand the audience experience of material—this is a central dramaturgy question.

To understand how much can you take in, and not get lost, but not be bored. So that balance is a thing that we're striving for, and in many ways, the puppetry is really simple. There's not a lot of fancy manipulation—there's a lot of shadow puppetry, and every time it's done it's a little bit different. The light, the scale—all that stuff is a language. Because then you [ask], what do I really need in this puppet of Ahab as he does this scene with Pip? What does that puppet need to look like? What becomes a distraction that takes us away from what you're saying? And what is actually taking us into something that you're not saying that's in the language, right?

What does the whale look like? What is the ocean like?

So, we made a whale puppet that was kind of cool—it was fourteen feet long, with a single operator, and it had a way of moving that was kind of interesting. It was a little Handspring-esque in its design, and it could swim around the stage and open its mouth and use its tail to hit a boat, but after thirty seconds, it was, "So, okay, so there's the whale puppet." So that was not resonant—it was just representational.

So, my thought is, "We're not putting the [whole] whale onstage," but instead, when we came up with the image of the [whale's] head, and we were thinking about it as a head, but then we saw that it looks like a threat. There's this notion of a big sphere, a nondescript sphere that's hanging in the space, like it's just hanging there. "Is it going to fall? What's it going to do?" And it had a little bit of movement, so it wasn't rigid, but it looks incredibly light. And it's massively large, that it dominates—

Yes, and it glows!

It glows—it has all these qualities to it. So then I started to realize, "Oh! It's unnameable, and that becomes what Melville has Ishmael say—this is not an allegory. This is a real fish swimming around in the sea." And you know, that's a red herring. Because it is and it isn't. But what it is, is—clearly the whale is many different things. And also that structurally, he arrives at the end of the story. In the book—

You're waiting!

You're waiting, waiting, and then this thing that is clearly massive appears.

And you can't see the whole thing—

Yeah, yeah, all that.

Can't possibly take it in.

Yeah—the whole notion that you could never see it, the notion that if it's in the water you can't see it, if it's out of the water, it's no longer what it was. It's impossible to really fully know it.

We only discovered that the sphere was something that we reveal at the end when we got to the MCA. Before, we weren't thinking that—actually, you saw it when you came in, and then we covered it up, and brought it back in. But it's great that there's this thing—there's this confrontation that's talked about and talked about and then finally we see this thing that is played out, there's a metaphorical fight that's played out. It does move, and it does destroy, and it has power, and it has presence.

I was really interested in how can the puppet theatre actualize things that the actors' theatre cannot? The actors' theatre can actualize certain things, but other things—all they can do is talk about them. All they can do is describe things. But the puppet theatre can actualize it.

And so, I was really happy with that actualization of the whale.

There are clear moments when I myself as a performer make the puppet have life, but that's something that can be dropped or tossed to the side at a given moment. I'm interested in that—that energy that obviously objects do have.

I'm interested in when it starts to *startle.* I'm interested in the puppet theatre having the ability to startle people awake, and move them away from the pedestrian. So, the puppet theatre, when you talk about numinous, you're talking about it being up here, and it's true—it does exist up here, in the nonpedestrian level. But it's also, the puppet has two roles that it can play: it's either going to be sacred or it's going to be profane.

And those are its strengths. And when it's profane, it doesn't have that same kind of preciousness, but it still has incredible vitality of life, right? And that's where parody exists. Almost every—all the work of the Muppets and *Sesame Street* is based on parody, and that kind of profane, even though they're not profane at all, but they are profane.

And then there's something that's more sacred, that's used in a religious practice, or spiritual practice, where now we're asked to believe that this puppet is the spirit of someone who is deceased, or this puppet reminds us of grief, and we're not asking you to now think this is the deceased person, but it elevates this above, because it's able to move in a way that's otherworldly. And so those two things exist. I guess on some level, that would be—when you were saying numinous, that would be the sacred type of puppetry. Whereas the other one is more mercurial and trickster, in that kind of vein. And puppets themselves can switch in and out of that, you know.

They're both interesting, because . . . the puppet doesn't exist in the human experience. When the puppet interacts with a human, the puppet has to talk down or talk up—they can't be at the same level as the puppet. Even if the puppet is literally at the same level, they're not at the same level, and [what's] funny about the interaction is that there's this shocking—"that's a human talking to a thing that doesn't exist, that's not alive, but they're acting as if it's alive." As if they're talking to another human being who has agency. But then all that disassociation is jarring and funny and pulls you in with engagement. It's just when the anatomical puppet is skillfully manipulated, the audience is immediately awakened with the recognition of reference to the self and to the human experience. It's the, "Oh, that looks exactly like a human being. But it's not a human being, but it looks like—it is; it's not; it is; it's not." It's that back and forth thing, right? Like a human being is just not interesting in that way, because we're constantly alive.

Right.

Where the puppet is dead, alive, dead, alive, dead, alive, dead, alive.

The puppet needs to be well built, and it doesn't need to be fancily built, because this is the skill of the puppet design, the execution of how you create something that creates that illusion in a very economical way. Because if it's too mechanical then you start to go down that uncanny valley, the more it starts to become imitative, and that's just a different track. And it actually needs to veer away from the uncanny valley, so that the human does the work, right?

Right.

Which is like, "I thought those eyes moved on that puppet—I'm sure that [they did]!"And why did I think that? They don't move, I know. The puppet's eyes don't move, but they look like they move. "What's happening? I don't know what's happening." That was my unconscious.

So what appeals to me is that the puppet has the possibility to speak directly to the audience's unconscious. And make them respond bypassing their own discursive mind.

And to me, I think that's one of the great strengths of the puppet. And yeah, someone could miss it, or not be able to see it, or not be open to seeing it, or whatever you want to say, but that's one of the strengths of the puppet—it can do that.

Lookingglass Theatre Company

Via phone, 16 August 2016

David Catlin is a founding ensemble member of the Lookingglass Theatre Company, the recipient of the 2011 Tony Award for Outstanding Regional Theatre. He served as the company's first coartistic director (with David Kersnar) and more recently served as artistic director. Other leadership positions with Lookingglass include managing director, interim executive director, and director of artistic development. His adaptation of Moby-Dick, *which he also directed, was produced by Lookingglass in association with the Actors Gymnasium in 2015 and won the Joseph Jefferson Award for production of a play—large, among numerous honors and accolades.*

A theatre maker who acts, writes, directs, and teaches, Catlin's aesthetic is ensemble based, storycentric, and utilizes physical, visual, and aural storytelling in collaboration with a traditional emphasis on character and text. His work has appeared in Chicago, New York, Los Angeles, Philadelphia, Atlanta, Syracuse, Louisville, and Princeton, New Jersey.

Catlin has appeared in, directed, or written and directed over thirty-three productions for Lookingglass, including Arabian Nights, *directed by Mary Zimmerman, and* Our Town, *directed by Anna Shapiro and Jessica Thebus. In addition to* Moby Dick, *his adaptation and directing credits include* Icarus *and* Lookingglass Alice. *Catlin also helped found Dark Harbor Stories, a film development company. He was a producer for (and appeared in) the independent film* Humanoid. *David can also be seen in* Since You've Been Gone *(Miramax/Film Colony/Lookingglass). He is a lecturer in theatre at Northwestern University.*

Jane Barnette: Why this particular text for the stage at this time in life?
David Catlin: Yes. Well I'll try, but like the novel I might diverge a little bit here and there. I initially, I read the book in college when I was a student at Northwestern, and I put it off. I was supposed to read it as a part of a class, and I didn't read it until the week right before finals in a kind of overly caffeinated haze. I plowed through it and consumed it and loved it—and in some respects it was kind of a blur, but it was an exciting thing even with the divergent chapters that go off and talk about cetology and the importance of a good rope.

Even with all that, it might have been the caffeine and it might have been the lack of sleep, but I just loved it, and I kicked myself by not going through it with the aid or mentorship of a good professor. So, nonetheless, fast forward twenty-some years, a colleague up here named Blair Thomas, who [does] large-scale puppetry that is both for kids and also for adults. And Blair has had a long fascination with the book and created several adaptations. He had convinced somebody from the Boeing corporation to fund a three-company collaboration. So, there was Blair Thomas and Company, the idea that Lookingglass would be one of them, and then House Theatre of Chicago.

So, it wasn't necessarily—I wasn't burning to tell the story; it kind of came from Blair's energy saying, "Let's do this."

And Lookingglass, we've often been for some reason attracted to seafaring novels. We had done *Argonomica, The Odyssey*—a lot of Mary Zimmerman's work is kind of in and around, based on the sea. And there's something about that that I think is just a little bit impossible—the notion of creating a sea-feeling environment feels in some respects impossible. There's something about standing above a body of water, where you just feel the vastness of the water around you. Whether it is an ocean or even Lake Michigan—that's one of the reasons I chose to be in Chicago, was that massive body of water.

There is something about that [water] that is simultaneously calming but also a little unsettling, not knowing what mysteries lurk beneath the silvery surface. Right? Not knowing what kind of monsters swim under there—that's thrilling to us, I think, as human beings. And even just knowing that this massive body has this literal gravitational pull, perhaps imperceptible gravitational pull on us, right? I mean we know that the gravity of the oceans exerts a force on the moon that causes it to wobble ever so slightly. So certainly on little us, it's going to have some power that draws us to it. So even that simplicity of the story of an ocean—and Ishmael in that opening chapter talks about glooming, he talks about when he's feeling grim about the mouth and it's damp and drizzly.

November.

About his soul. When he just wants to walk into the street and he just wants to throw somebody's hat off or reach for it, so he's drawn to the water's edge. That's the place that he needs to get to in order to kind of calm himself and it is that sort of double—the simplicity of calming you but also churning up some psychological, emotional undercurrents. A kind of unknown that's both under there and out there. . . .

But, so, anyway, when Blair came and said, "Will you join this collaboration?" and Lookingglass got onboard, I felt really—all of those kind of elements became really interesting to me, and we had this great collaborative experience.

The unique thing about this particular collaboration—you know often with collaborations there are a group of artists bringing their talents together to create a single piece of art. But in this case, it was three companies and their designated artists coming together to collaborate, to inspire each other, to create three distinct pieces of art. We would get together at this, like, pie shop in Chicago and sit and eat pie and talk about the various chapters and Blair would say, "You gotta look at the 'Quarter Deck' chapter." And then he would talk about how the puppets were going to be [made of] chunks of pine and even burnished, as if they were burnt by a thunderbolt. And that began to inspire me in terms of thinking about some of the aesthetic. I kind of stole that from him a little bit—there's chunks of wood [onstage], as you recall. [The set] looks like it came from a piece of wreckage. There's even some shadow play at the top. I was also struck by—in the famous edition of the book, Rockwell Kent has those illustrations that I think are woodcut.

And so being inspired a little bit by that as well, but—[also] I think we as human beings at some point in our lives, you know—life is long and it's filled with ups and downs, and sometimes we just feel disconnected. We feel like we want to walk into the street and knock somebody's hat off, or we feel unmoored and rudderless, right? You know, not sure what to do next. I know that in between projects if I don't have something that I'm working on I feel kind of unmoored—I feel like an outcast a little bit.

So, I understood that, and I thought, well, lots of people have sort of had that feeling. So [Ishmael] sets out and he feels disconnected and then he meets this Other, this somebody that he's not supposed to have a connection with. A delinquent, [one of] the cannibals, the quote unquote savage who is terrifying and has this big murderous harpoon that is terrifying. So then he meets them, and instead of fear he finds this profound connection.

But he still doesn't quite have purpose yet. And so, they go to sea, they climb aboard the Pequod along with all of the other Isolotos, and—I love that invented word, that I believe Melville created—this word *Isolotos*, the sort of lonely souls, each one kind of an outcast. And they board the Pequod, looking for purpose and what greater purpose than to go and bring light into the world? You know? From our context, we understand that the slaughtering of whales and slaughtering of natural resources is not always a great thing. For them, the notion of going out on these ships past the horizon to where no land can be seen, where these monsters, these quote unquote monsters are looming and lurking ready to kind of snap them in half—and then they get into these tiny little whale boats, that barely fit five people. They go out and stick a pointy stick into the back of a whale, which is just sort of terrifying and brave, right? They're the sort of knights who are out to slay the dragon, so there's a kind of nobility to it, especially in that time. And they are literally bringing this precious oil that will light the world, that will allow people to feel safe at night, that will allow people to read and to better themselves. So it is this beautiful and noble task, but even still, the real purpose, the real volition comes with the entrance of Ahab.

You know, to him, in his kind of twisted mind, in his kind of monomaniacal mind, this one white whale, this Moby Dick, represents all of the evil in the world from Adam on down, right? That's a bad paraphrasing of it, but he wants to go and kill this one whale, and I feel like that's something else we can understand, that kind of consuming passion. We all *crave* that, we all want something, whether it's a job, we want to be consumed by it, right? It feels great when we're, even doing a puzzle—we want the world to disappear. Does that make sense?

Totally.

We want to be obsessed, whether it's being in love—but then we also know that, that is dangerous, right, and we lose sight of that. So, enter Starbuck, who is the voice of reason, who is hopefully going to provide some balance that brings us home safely. "Let's do the task we need to do, to kill whales for his living rather than be killed by them for theirs"—he wants to bring us home, back to Nantucket, back to our wives, and daughters, sons. Back to safety. And we have to sort of understand that as well—we have to understand that Ahab's kind of all-consuming passion—and his crew buys into it—everybody except Starbuck, of course.

And so to me—it's that understanding what it's like to be an outcast, and how we can get consumed by an obsession, and how *good* that feels. But, then, also Starbuck's balance, and the need to feel connected to another like Queequeg, the relationship that Ishmael and Queequeg have—those lines that connect us, are really important.

I also just love the journey that Ishmael goes on, where he starts, you know, we buy into this nobility of this quest and then as we move into what is our act 2, we begin to see the bloody slaughter of the whales and it culminates in a way. And there's even the swearing in of the crew to ratify their promise to go hunt Moby Dick, as this kind of secret sacrament, right?

[It's] kind of a beautiful moment, and then in act 2 we experience the slaughter of the whales and at first it's thrilling and then it becomes more and more bloody. There's this moment in the book that we tried to capture on stage—and I think we get at it a little bit—where they're going through the Straits of Sunda and because of the bottlenecks going through there are just whales all around, right? And I think it's called "The Grand Armada," is the name of the chapter.

It's like this—they get into slaughtering every whale they can, and catching those [things] which the whales dragged to slow them down so they could go back and harvest them later. And so, then they get into the *center* of this area of whales where it's calm and they're all just kind of exhausted and bloody, and Ishmael looks down into the water and there's this little infant whale looking up through the gully weed at him. And it's—with its umbilical cord still attached to its mother [it's] this sort of pietà moment, but also where that infant whale is like a human baby, and so suddenly there's a humanity in these heretofore monsters.

Ishmael recognizes that, I think, and so it begins to change a little bit, and then we get into the darkening of Ahab's soul and the sacrament of the devil with the forging of the sword. Using pagan blood, and calling on the devil. "I baptize thee not in the name of the father, but in the name of the devil" is the translation from Latin that they have there. So, in act 3, we get closer and closer. We have this moment where Ahab could relent, where he wants to return to his wife and son, and Starbuck sees that, and we almost are able to avert this impending, this looming doom, and it just doesn't happen.

And then, Ahab and Moby Dick meet, and for us, what occurs—one of the challenges, and part of the fun of theatre, is that it can do impossible things, and the audience, this community will say yes—if we do it right. But one of the challenges of this book, is how do you—you've spent most of the book setting up this massiveness, the ferocity, the scale of this whale—how do you bring something out that lives up to what the audiences have in their brains?

That one split second of the tail flip? I almost blinked and missed it, because I was watching it on DVD, and I was, like, "What? What!?'

Yeah—

And I went back, and it is *literally* a second. [*Laughter*]

Yeah, yeah. Yeah. It's very fast.

Amazing. I can't even imagine being in the audience and having that—how *visceral* that must have felt.

It was pretty startling. . . .

And it also occurred to me that if we had set up these stakes, and the ability for [actors] to play whales—if Ahab's fate *is* Moby Dick, then logically, they could then embody Moby Dick. In the sense that they become his fate.

So, that was what kind of made sense to us. And there's also something that feels like fate in that instance, because they—we have seen these women respond to, when they take, after the harvesting of the whale when the woman—is kind of hoisted up, and then—

That killed me.

And then the Fates come and take her away. There's kind of a very simple look that they have on their face, that then makes sense later why they have come back for Ahab.

Oh, I immediately registered it as, you know, "We'll be back." [*Laughter*]

Yeah, it has that absolute feel.

That scene is tremendously powerful, especially as a woman, watching it—

Yeah.

Because it is all too familiar. You said, how we make it human, but also how to understand the violence, both the physical and psychic violence. If you consider that whales are not just some kind of monster, but they actually have sentient ideas and feelings, that's just a very apt and terrifying way of showing that violence.

Yeah. And to go back to the gender issue, the dudes on a boat, when we think of—at least, when I—this may be a—I don't know if this is sexist of me or not, but when we think of ships, we think of feminine pronouns. And, when I think of the water, I think of that as a feminine, whether it's amniotic or, there's something feminine to me, about water. I associate it with a feminine pronoun, and even nature itself feels feminine. And even the whales, even though Moby Dick is a male bull whale, any whale, you know, anytime they see a spout, they say, "Thar she blows!"

So, there *is* something, and even just the very act of going out on a three-year whaling voyage is detrimental. There is a slow violence against the family structure. Where, in order for the—at least, as we traditionally, typically know it—the family unit cannot exist if men are going out for three years and [then another] three years.

At the very least reproduction—if what your goal is, is to *grow* a family—

Yeah. Right, exactly. The family can't survive if the men are all, always gone. So, it was intentional that these women played the whales, and that we see the men senselessly, or somewhat senselessly slaughtering them, and not understanding the—and, for me, Ishmael begins to understand that.

Yes. You could see it on the stage, that he kind of takes a step—he does sort of participate, but he also beholds it, and takes it in.

Yeah.

Which is effective—you know, one of the things that maybe you can help me with, because it was unclear to me, and right now I've only identified them as, you know, "one of the three fates," and it would be nice to be able to give their names? And so—

Yeah.

I'd like to know which woman was hoisted upside down. But also I'd love to talk to you about that final image with the huge billowing skirt that's the ocean, or—

Yes. So, the woman who was hoisted upside down was Emma Cadd. And then Kasey Foster played the woman in the billowing sea dress. And again, that's a way of feminizing the sea, and that image occurs twice—the first time, it's pulling Starbuck away from his wife, and that's actually one of the things I'm excited to have a chance to work on again. I've written in a couple new lines, to give a little bit more space for Starbuck, who we haven't really met yet, but the actor playing Starbuck is drawn away from his wife and son to the sea, and so there's this kind of fight between—not a fight, but—

A tug of rope?

Between the—competition for his heart, between the allure of the sea and the allure of family, and so, at that point, Kasey looks very attractive, and, for me, at times, the Fates wanted to have a kind of blank quality, but at times a kind of Siren-like quality, and other times like The Weird Sisters, sometimes haggish—to be all of that. And at that point, she is more alluring. And when we see her in the end, and this is partly kind of a practical thing, but it works really well, I think—she's still in the Victorian nightmare, [a] kind of hurdy-gurdy nightmare where her makeup is kind of melted away, or her hair is kind of more matted, and haggish. So the sea then is less seductive, much less seductive, but it's still pulling men in to kiss their fate and meet their doom. . . .

Did Mara [Blumenfeld] do those costumes?

No, this was a woman named Carolyn Ratke. She goes by Sully. Sully Ratke.

[The costumes] were tremendous, I loved them—especially that last image. [It] has just stuck with me ever since.

Yeah, it's pretty haunting. Part of it, it's a combination of light, sound, costume. But also—again, Kasey Foster is a trained dancer/choreographer as well, so she's just, she has this genius grace. It's kind of breathtaking. Her simple arm movements are just—I think it's part of what really sells that image.

Yes. And also that portal, with the sort of light—you know, there are several times where important—

Yeah. We actually, we were taking advantage of—part of that comes out of the fact that our theatre is not very large, and so that became . . . initially, it was just useful because we needed a crossover in the back. I'm very interested in a kind of—a lot of the plays that I work on have an open aesthetic, where you see the parts of the theatre as well, and you see the stage crew. And the other thing—right around that time period, the theatre, if men weren't working on boats, many of them would go into the theatre and work, and that's why it's bad luck to whistle in a theatre. It might be a sandbag might fall on your head because whistling on a boat means a certain thing, and so instinctively a sailor might lower the boom, which would not be good in the play. And even much of the nomenclature that we have—rigging, catwalks, crew, deck—all of those are sailing terms.

And so, for me, wanting to see the theatre and ship all in one was a little nod to that. And even the sailors, you know, since they were gone for three years, they had to mend their own clothes, and they had good needles, so they would come in and they would sew the main drape, they would work on some of the costumes. But even the kind of rigging is very similar to what you might have on a ship, with the ropes and the pulleys and the weights.

I'm sure you've drawn on this already, but in one of the chapters, [Melville] uses that dramatic language throughout, because the chapter headers will be "lights up on the Quarter Deck," or "Curtain rises on the Quarter Deck" or, "Enter Ahab."

And even "Call me Ishmael." You know, "call me" is storytelling.

Yeah.

It invokes from the beginning that this is a story to be told.

Yeah. And one of the really important—one of the reasons that the Fates exist in this version is, there's a line in there, I think it's in "Loomings": "These stage managers of fate have set down for the shabby part of a whaling voyage."

And, when we did it—we actually did a version previous to the Lookingglass production. I did a workshop production at Northwestern, and the Fates were even more decidedly stage managers. They started with headsets on; they were calling some of the cues, so we kind of played into that even more. In the end we pulled back a little bit because it was too much of a layer for audiences.

But it was that line—"these stage managers of fate"—that helped me think of them as characters, and not just something we refer to.

There's really no more vertical space than a traditional theatre, or is there?

Well, I think it has a little—no, I think you're right. A normal theatre might have twenty feet between the stage floor and the grid. And so we have the same vertical space, but it depends on how it's configured. It's totally flexible, so all of that stuff can come out and be a black box, and then you can put it in and set it up the way that you want to. And depending on whether a balcony is in—you feel the verticality when that's out. When it's empty, it feels much higher vertically. But, in comparison to another theatre, they're about the same. We're taking it to three theatres on the way, and there's really only a foot or two difference one way or the other.

But we use that—we like that [vertical space] as a way to build composition in the air, and with our relationship with Actor's Gym, we often exploit that. Not every time, but—

I don't know which crew member he played, but one of your actors climbed—I mean, I've never seen anybody climb like he can!

Yeah, he is a circus performer first. He's from Mongolia, but he came here when he was I think sixteen or seventeen. His American name is Javen [Ulambayar]. But when we wrote him in, because Javen can speak Mongolian, there is some Mongolian written into the text. If he wasn't able to do the tour—and in fact, he's not able to do the Lookingglass leg next summer—it's important to me that it's not played by a white actor. But that might be the case. If it's a white actor, that character will become Bulkington, he will be called Bulkington. Because we know Bulkington disappears early in the book. Or he might become Daggoo—another harpooner.

Is there anything else you'd like to add?

Well, the only other thing, when I think of challenge—is how you take that literary medium that doesn't need to be so compelling, that doesn't need to have that drive to it, the dramatic tension to pull you along? And I find it part of the—as you know, when you adapt something, when you're reading a book you can set it down, and go make a sandwich and then come back to it, or spend a couple of days and cogitate with it. With theatre, we have to find some way to make sure that that dramatic line is driving us along, and so that, I think, is also something that informs our choices as we move from a literary medium to a dramatic medium.

Yes. I would add to that, and I think it's connected, is this question of surgery—there's always, you can't possibly get it all, so you're compressing—

Yeah.

And you're trying to find the moments to expand, and which ones you can compress, and I think that's connected to what you're talking about.

Yeah. Yep, yep. We often, we'll talk about "killing babies," where, you have these scenes, these moments, these characters you *loved*, and that are great! But they don't serve that bigger idea, and so you have to let them go. So we, you know in our adaptation, I loved Bildad, and at the end we kind of collapsed them all into—or, specifically, Peleg and Stubb, into each other. And it was sad for me, but it actually helped it move along, and it helped the audience be able to track the different characters a little better.

But killing those babies, it's hard. [*Laughter*] And that's true, too, for companies like Lookingglass, where we use visual storytelling. So oftentimes we'll find that we're able to come up with an image that doesn't need words, that in a fifteen-second image, we're able to convey something that might be half a scene, or half a page of scenes.

That really resonates with what Blair [Thomas] said—how much it felt like killing babies for him, because he's had so many different explorations of this text.

Yeah, [in] the workshop that we all did together—our work culminated in a two-week residency and then a public sharing, and he kept so much of the narration intact, and I get it! I would love to see Blair's twenty-three-hour show. Because it's all great, you know? So I get how hard it is to let go.

APPENDIX 2: PROGRAM NOTES

During my tenure as resident dramaturg of Kennesaw State University's Department of Theatre and Performance Studies, I incorporated various means of communicating with our audiences—but the one method that remained constant in each instance was the inclusion of dramaturgical notes in every playbill. Because this was an academic environment, I was encouraged to model scholarship for the spectators, which meant that my notes would typically include extensive references and incorporate peer-reviewed journals, just as students are required to in their research projects. This expectation differed from my professional dramaturgical writing for programs, which tended to emphasize interviews or factual information relevant to the production. When I am invited to contribute program notes for productions outside of the academic environment, I consult scholarship, but I rarely cite it.

In this section, then, are four examples of essays that were written for theatrical adaptations produced by Kennesaw State University. Inspired in part by Felicia Londré's *Words at Play*, a book that charts her development writing dramaturgical notes over the course of more than two decades, this appendix provides examples of program notes that typify audience-based adapturgy. Like Londré, I do not present these as exemplary in the sense that they are meant to be models of perfection—quite the contrary! Rather, the essays summarize and reflect the process each adaptation has taken dramaturgically, as well as my own development as an adaptation dramaturg. As such, they are snapshots of my work with different production teams and adapters, each of which had distinct goals and challenges. It is my hope that they help round out readers' understanding of how adaptation dramaturgy might appear in the familiar format of program notes. *Moby-Dick* was produced by Kennesaw State University (Stillwell Theatre) in 2008, adapted by John Gentile, and directed by Henry Scott and Gentile.

Staging the Numinous

> Moby Dick is the supreme "*ur*-symbol" of our literature, whose Meaning —as Ishmael well knows—no meanings can encompass, nor any Ahab comprehend; he must be sought in little, not in large, and he is inexhaustible. —Martin Leonard Pops, *The Melville Archetype*

> The question to my mind that Melville keeps asking in *Moby-Dick*— and which informs this new stage adaptation—is, to use [Rudolf] Otto's term, "*What is humankind's proper relationship with the numinous?*"
> —John Gentile, Director's Notes, *The Moby-Dick Project,* December 2004

As a New York theatre critic recently noted, in reference to Orson Welles's *Moby Dick— Rehearsed,* "It takes a fool or perhaps a genius to adapt one of the greatest American novels for the stage" (Zinoman A19). John Gentile, chair of the Department of Theatre and Performance Studies at Kennesaw State University, has dared to tackle this leviathan work in a new stage adaptation developed over the past five years. First drawn to the book in his youth, Gentile began to see its theatrical potential in 1982, when he witnessed the Remains Theatre ensemble's "ground-breaking" adaptation of *Moby-Dick* at the Goodman's studio theatre in Chicago (McGavin). As a graduate student at Northwestern University, Gentile studied with Robert Breen, who had developed *chamber theatre,* a technique for staging prose fiction that "resists the temptation to delete narrative descriptions and rewrite summaries as dialogue" (Breen 4). During his years at Northwestern, Gentile also studied with Paul Edwards and Frank Galati, two of Breen's students, whose work with chamber theatre in the professional theatre world brought the form to audiences beyond the Northwestern campus.

Given the centrality of narration to Melville's masterpiece, the approach of chamber theatre allows the actor playing Ishmael to relate both "to the action of the story and to the audience" (Breen 39). Influenced by the revolutionary (yet oft-misunderstood) "epic theatre" of Bertolt Brecht and his director Erwin Piscator, Breen advocates the use of the "alienation effect" not just in rehearsal (as Brecht envisioned), but also in the performance itself. Counterintuitively, this technique has the potential of drawing audiences *into* the world of the play rather than alienating them, because the actors directly address spectators, eschewing the realist tradition of the fourth wall. "When the character addresses the audience," Breen explains, "the system of relationships opens up to include the audience and that is only possible if the audience now sees not only the character but the actor who is portraying them" (45). From the adapter's perspective, moving between narration and dialogue facilitates this duality, allowing the performance to simultaneously tell and show.

Collaboration is another common factor in devising chamber theatre productions. For Gentile, the process of creating *Moby-Dick* for the stage began as one of several units in a course (Adapting and Staging Literary Texts) in the spring semester of 2003. A little over a year later, he taught a senior seminar class with Robert Hill, professor emeritus (KSU Department of English) and Melville scholar, devoted to analyzing and performing scenes from *Moby-Dick*, which ultimately resulted in a staged reading of the first draft of the script you will see today. Throughout this process, Gentile solicited feedback from the students as well as the spectators and continued to fine-tune his adaptation. When the department's current season was announced in January 2007, he turned to the draft again, this time with an eye toward a fully mounted production.

The concept driving Gentile's vision can be summarized as an attempt to stage the numinous, that quality defined by Rudolf Otto as the paradoxical combination of fear and fascination experienced in the nonrational perception of the mysterious and sacred. Inspired by archetypal depth criticism, Gentile sees the quest for the great white whale as a "story of the soul's pilgrimage towards redemption" (3). Through the characters of Ishmael and Ahab in particular, spectators witness two different approaches (one successful, one not) to this journey of individuation. Captain Ahab, "the prototype of the heretic," represents those of us who refuse to acknowledge the power of the numinous (Edinger 54). He wants to conquer the unknown, to pierce the heart of the holy, as articulated most clearly in chapter 36, "The Quarter Deck":

> All visible objects are but as pasteboard masks. But in every living act . . . , still some reasoning thing hides behind that mask, that wall. If man will strike, strike through the mask! How can the prisoner reach outside except by thrusting through the wall? To me, the white whale is that wall, shoved near me. (164)

Of course, Ahab's hubris prevents him from penetrating the mask/wall. Instead, as Jung would have warned him, he reaps what he sows. If we consider Moby Dick to be that wall/mask, as Ahab did, "we know that the mask of the unconscious is not rigid—it reflects the face we turn towards it. Hostility lends it a threatening aspect, friendliness softens its features" (Jung 25). Instead of the *mysterium tremendum et fascinans* that Otto characterized the numinous as evoking, Ahab remains closed off to that possibility, admitting that the "path to [his] fixed purpose is laid with iron rails, whereon [his] soul is grooved to run" (Melville 169). Aligning himself with the machine rather than the garden, Ahab invites the fury of the numinous in his pompous disregard for the mysterious, terrifying, and tantalizing sperm whale.

In contrast, Ishmael (whose name means "listener" in Hebrew), enacts the entire "ritual pattern of separation, transition, and incorporation" that constitutes the spiritual rebirth of pilgrimages (Gentile 4). He begins with profound depression—the "damp, drizzly November in [his] soul"—and this "urgent psychic need" catapults him into a search for meaning, for Truth, ultimately for the numinous (Edinger 25). And what better to represent that manifestation of all we hold holy than an albino whale? Rarely seen above water, sperm whales prefer to avoid human contact—and those that do surface tend to be black with white spots, rather than solid white. Melville devotes an entire chapter to the significance of Moby Dick's whiteness (and Gentile, for his part, creates the narrative character Whiteness of the Whale from these pages), turning on its head the Western association of white with purity. Yes, white is pure to Melville, but in a terrifying way: it represents "the impersonal, infinite, external undefined vastness that lies behind the personal, particular, concrete and ordinary phenomena of everyday life" (Edinger 82). However horrible, it is this sacred encounter for which Ishmael yearns. At last, "the whale appears to Ahab and the crew as the very vision and embodiment of the god and goddess of wilderness nature and of the dreams of the subconscious mind, which the Puritans feared to release" (Slotkin 547). Because he allows this realization to surface, transcending the mundane remains of his ordinary existence, Ishmael's soul is reborn and his pilgrimage complete.

—Jane Barnette, Resident Dramaturg

Works Cited

Breen, Robert S. *Chamber Theatre.* Evanston, IL: Caxton, 1986.

Edinger, Edward F. *Melville's Moby-Dick: An American Nekyia.* Jungian Psychology by Jungian Analysts Series 69. Toronto: Inner City, 1995.

Gentile, John S. "The Pilgrim Soul: Herman Melville's *Moby-Dick* as Pilgrimage." Unpublished paper. 2008.

Jung, Carl Gustav. *The Collected Works of C. G. Jung.* Trans. R. F. C. Hull. Vol. 12. Bollingen Series 20. Princeton: Princeton UP, 1977.

McGavin, Patrick Z. "Ted Levine is Not a Bad Guy." *Chicago Reader Story Archive.* 1 March 1991. 9 March 2008. <http://www.chicagoreader.com>. Path: Archives; Search.

Melville, Herman. *Moby Dick; or, The Whale.* New York: Norton, 1967, 1976.

Pops, Martin Leonard. *The Melville Archetype.* Kent, OH: Kent State UP, 1970.

Slotkin, Richard. *Regeneration through Violence: The Mythology of the American Frontier, 1600–1860.* Middletown, CT: Wesleyan UP, 1975.

Zinoman, Jason. "That Great White Whale through a Wellesian Lens." Rev. of *Moby Dick—Rehearsed,* dir. Marc Siberschatz. *New York Times.* 10 March 2007: A19.

Everything That Rises Must Converge was produced by Kennesaw State University (Stillwell Theater) in 2009, adapted by Karin Coonrod, and directed by Karen Robinson.

Staging the Southern Epic Vision of Flannery O'Connor

> The white characters speak more than they know; the black characters know more than they speak. —Karin Coonrod, 2008

> But *essential* O'Connor is not about race at all, which is why it is so refreshing, coming, as it does, out of such a *racial* culture. If it can be said to be "about" anything, then it is "about" prophets and prophecy, "about" revelation, and "about" the impact of supernatural grace on human beings who don't have a chance of spiritual growth without it.
> —Alice Walker, 1975

Georgia native Flannery O'Connor is often misunderstood or even overlooked within the literary canon, in part because her razor-sharp language and grotesque imagery reveal a South that many readers might prefer to forget or deny altogether. But her stories persist in our imaginations long after we first encounter the power of her words—they reveal glimpses of human cruelty and vulnerabilities on an epic scale. A devout Catholic, O'Connor saw the South as "Christ-haunted" rather than Christ-centered and thus found it necessary to "draw large startling figures for the nearly blind," given that she believed her "subject in fiction is the action of grace in territory held largely by the devil" (34, 118). Tragically, she came to know on a corporeal level what the devil's territory felt like. At the age of twenty-five, she was diagnosed with the same disease—systemic lupus erythematosus—that had taken her father's life just a decade before. "Perhaps the most disturbing characteristic of lupus . . . is the fact that the body nonsensically destroys itself and, in O'Connor's case, with a constitution her father bequeathed her" (Gilbert 125). Although she lived much longer than physicians expected, the perverse unpredictability of the disease she endured for fourteen years is mirrored in the volatility of her characters.

It's not just the characters in her storytelling that are volatile—the narrative voices in O'Connor's fiction have been described by Bruce Gentry as reflective of "Mikhail Bakhtin's model of the novelistic literary text as a battleground, where rebellious characters fight for what they sense is the truth, in opposition to the standards supported weakly, most of the time, by the narrator's authoritarianism" (8). From this perspective, the polyphony of beliefs expressed by characters contradicts the narration, even O'Connor herself, marking a clear departure from the more traditional view of an "omniscient" narrator.

Such concerns became particularly influential to the challenging task of staging *Everything That Rises Must Converge*. This adaptation, devised by Karin Coonrod of Yale University in 1998, is the first and only dramatization authorized by O'Connor's estate, and as one of the conditions of that release, Coonrod kept every word of the short stories intact. It has been performed only twice before: first at the University of Iowa (where O'Connor received her MFA at the prestigious Writers' Workshop) and then again in 2001 at the New York Theatre Workshop.

Thus, Kennesaw State University's production marks the regional premiere of Coonrod's *Everything That Rises Must Converge*. Under the shrewd direction of Karen Robinson, the cast and crew have endeavored to capture the essence of O'Connor's startling and often wickedly funny vision through an ensemble approach that embraces the chamber theatre techniques familiar to many of our patrons who took in last year's original adaptation of Herman Melville's *Moby-Dick*. With performers playing multiple roles and often switching from the full embodiment of a character to the observational and often judgmental role of a narrator, this approach to making theatre reflects—indeed, gives life to—the aforementioned "battleground" interpretation of literature. In so doing, I would argue, it has the radical potential of awakening in spectators a lifelong respect for the uncanny wisdom of O'Connor's writing.

—*Jane Barnette, Resident Dramaturg*

Works Cited

Coonrod, Karin. Interview by Karen Robinson. 7 December 2008.

Gentry, Marshall Bruce. *Flannery O'Connor's Religion of the Grotesque*. Jackson: UP Mississippi, 1986. Print.

Gilbert, Susanna. "'Blood Don't Lie': The Diseased Family in Flannery O'Connor's *Everything That Rises Must Converge*." *Literature and Medicine* 18.1 (1999): 114–131. Print.

O'Connor, Flannery. *Mystery and Manners: Occasional Prose*. Eds. Sally and Robert Fitzgerald. New York: Farrar, 1969. Print.

Walker, Alice. "Beyond the Peacock: The Reconstruction of Flannery O'Connor." *In Search of Our Mothers' Gardens: Womanist Prose*. Orlando: Harcourt, 2004. Print.

Dark Forest: Tales and Poems from the Brothers Grimm was produced by Kennesaw State University (Stillwell Theater) in 2011, adapted by John Gentile, and directed by Henry Scott and Gentile.

The Allure and Peril of the Big Bad Forest

> The forest provides them with all they will need, if they know how to interpret the signs. —Zipes 89

> Isolation in the Grimms' tales, like silence, has a female face, and it is most frequently seen in the forest. —Bottigheimer 111

Poetic justice is a powerful tool. Our desire to see the wicked punished and the good rewarded is invariably satisfied by most fairy tales, especially those collected and edited by Jacob and Wilhelm Grimm in the early nineteenth century. In part because audiences typically assume that fairy tales are "just" for children, we rarely stop to ponder how the writer, adapter, or teller of these stories necessarily shapes the moral landscape of them. For scholars of fairy-tale literature, however, the interpretive possibilities of this genre are vast, ranging from psychological (with an emphasis on Freudian and Jungian theories) to Marxist to feminist and even ecocritical. Within this impressive scope, the sustained relevancy of the fairy-tale genre continues to build upon the scaffolding of poetic justice: namely, how the author and/or teller defines good and bad behavior.

In the case of the Brothers Grimm, who are commonly acknowledged "as pioneers in the field of folklore research," most of the tales attributed to them were shared by learned female peers who visited the Grimms' home to perform the stories for them (O'Neill 107). While these privileged women might be understood as the Grimms' research assistants, it was generally the peasant classes who "were predominately attracted to the tale and became its prime carriers." Thus, it is not surprising that "power and oppression [are] the key concerns of the folktales" within the oral tradition (Zipes, *Fairy* 7). As the brothers edited the anthology that would become their famous repository of this research (*Children's and Household Tales*, first published in 1812), they altered the rewards and punishments of poetic justice to favor the civilizing force of the patriarchal bourgeois class. To say so is not to "distort the basic facts," as Jungian scholar Marie-Louise von Franz claims "many current sociological and feminist theories" do, but rather to analyze the values that may have led to the changes Wilhelm made in the forty-five-year period during which their anthology underwent seven editions (20).[1] From her thorough analysis of transgression in the Grimms' tales, literary critic Ruth Bottigheimer isolates a pervasive "witch-burning notion of eradicating (general female) evil [that] coexists within an indulgent tolerance of (generally male) malefaction" (94). Connecting this value system biblically to Eve's original sin, Bottigheimer convincingly argues that the poetic justice meted out in Grimms' world punishes girls while forgiving boys, an observation all the more compelling with the recognition that in Germany the only book that surpasses the popularity of *Children's and Household Tales* is the Bible.

And yet, to suggest only worldly/material relevance would be to miss the forest for the trees—literally. As the title of this production indicates, adapter John Gentile selected and arranged these tales and poems for their relevance to the "energy, magic, mystery, beauty, and danger" that the forest symbolizes (Gentile). For the Grimms, the forests evoked (however paradoxically) both nostalgia and terror: a yearning for the unspoiled lush woodlands of Germany's heritage, along with the fear of getting lost or attacked within them. As ecocritic Nicole Thesz demonstrates, "The woods of nineteenth-century tales contain supernatural powers that reflect the unnamable dangers of a precarious life" (109). Carl Jung considered the forest representative of the unconscious itself. "The forest, dark and impenetrable to the eye, like deep water and the sea, is the container of the unknown and the mysterious" (194). Gentile's addition of the Green Man, a pre-Christian god of vegetation and plant life, highlights the numinous potential of the Grimms' forest and helps unify the "multiplicity of voices" in his unique script. As he shared in an interview for the production's dramaturgical website, "*Dark Forest* does not follow the typical dramatic structure of a play. Its structure is more like a musical composition with its use of counterpoint; the different stories create the script's forward movement and its emotional rhythm" (Gentile). As a kind of master of ceremonies, the Green Man (played by TPS alumnus and guest artist Andrew Crigler) welcomes us into the liminal arena of the forest—a place that "allows for enchantment and disenchantment, for it is the place where society's conventions no longer hold true" (Zipes *Brothers* 67). Therein, we might decide that we prefer civilization to the sort of poetic justice that abounds in Grimms' world. But for many of us, the terrifying freedom of the dark forest might be where we'd prefer to live, happily ever after.

—*Jane Barnette, Resident Dramaturg*

Note

1. After the initial publication of *Children's and Household Tales*, Jacob pursued other interests, while Wilhelm became the primary steward of the anthology; thus, most editorial decisions can be safely attributed to his hand alone. For more on this account, see Siegfried Neumann, "The Brothers Grimm as Collectors and Editors of German Folktales," in *The Reception of Grimms' Fairy Tales*, edited by Donald Haase (Detroit: Wayne State UP, 1993): 24–40.

Works Cited

Bottigheimer, Ruth B. *Grimms' Bad Girls and Bold Boys: The Moral and Social Vision of the Tales*. New Haven: Yale UP, 1987. Print.

Franz, Marie-Louise von. *The Interpretation of Fairy Tales*. Rev. ed. Boston: Shambhala, 1996. Print.

Gentile, John. "Entering the Dark Forest: On Adapting and Staging Tales and Poems from the Brothers Grimm." Interview by Jane Barnette. *Dark Forest Dramaturgical Website*. College of the Arts, Kennesaw State University. Web. 27 Sept. 2011.

Jung, C. G. *Alchemical Studies*. Trans. R. F. C. Hull. *The Collected Works of C. G. Jung*. Eds. Read, Fordham, Adler, et al. Vol. 13. Princeton, NJ: Princeton UP, 1983. Print.

O'Neill, Thomas. "Guardians of the Fairy Tale: The Brothers Grimm." *National Geographic* (Dec. 1999): 102–117. Print.

Tatar, Maria. *The Hard Facts of the Grimms' Fairy Tales*. Princeton, NJ: Princeton UP, 1987. Print.

Thesz, Nicole. "Nature Romanticism and the Grimms' Tales: An Ecocritical Approach to Gunter Grass's *The Flounder* and *The Rat*." *Marvels and Tales: Journal of Fairy-Tale Studies*. 25.1 (2011): 96–116. *Project MUSE*. Web. 26 Sept. 2011.

Zipes, Jack. *The Brothers Grimm: From Enchanted Forests to the Modern World*. 2nd ed. New York: Palgrave, 2002. Print.

———. *Fairy Tales and the Art of Subversion*. 2nd ed. New York: Routledge, 2006. Print.

"All the Dead Voices": Silence and Stillness—The Voice in Beckett was produced by Kennesaw State University in 2013 (Onyx Theater), and was adapted and directed by Patrick Sutton.

Negation and Resonance in Beckett Country

> *Noli timere* (Don't be afraid).
>
> —Seamus Heaney's last words, via text message, to his wife

The psychological landscape of Samuel Beckett (1906–1989), "replete with bicycles, dogs, dustbins, and destitutes in hats, greatcoats, and ill-fitting boots," is often called Beckett country by scholars (Ackerly and Gontarski 41). The reference owes much to Eoin O'Brien's photography book of the same name, which illustrates the Irish roots of place—especially the topography of Dublin—appearing throughout much of Beckett's poetry and prose. To locate Beckett is no easy task, however: even if we might be convinced of the physical scenery referenced in his writing, understanding the geography of meaning therein proves much more challenging.

To grasp Beckett's philosophy requires uprooting our Western concept of identity, so grounded in Cartesian logic ("I think therefore I am"), and relocating it to the very country our campus happens to be celebrating this year: Japan. At the core of his writing, Beckett questions and ultimately negates any stable sense of "I" that could think itself into being. Following the Japanese Zen tradition, the pathway to enlightenment is not thinking—but, rather, through the embodied practice of *zazen* (sitting meditation) and focused breathing, to embrace a kind of stillness that negates both thought and any sense of an "I" who is thinking. "It is not the goal of *zazen* to clear away all thoughts but instead neither to cling to nor reject them as if they were real," dramaturg Kyle Gillette reminds us. "*Zazen* provides the still point against which the activity of the mind appears conspicuously repetitive and unreal" (289). It is from this austere perspective that the riddles (or *koans*) created by Beckett begin to resonate: while his characters suffer the consequences of attachment, we need not.

The submission of will necessitated by Zen practice parallels a capitulation of the authority traditionally granted to Western production teams (director, designers, actors) when staging Samuel Beckett. Unlike many playwrights, whose work directors bring to life through a unique vision or "production concept," Beckett's plays specify exact choreography and design, which are protected by his estate. Critics often read this insistence on control as one that disempowers actors and directors, but these readings are based on "assumptions that full personhood is achieved primarily through subversion and resistance—never submission" (Preston 157). As dance history scholar Carrie Preston argues, we should instead read Beckett's theatrical tradition in light of Japanese *noh*, which requires "the *noh* student to submit to the authority of the teacher and pedagogical decorum" (172). Dramaturgically, Beckett's plays have remarkable affinity with *noh* drama, which "is closely connected with the ancient Japanese belief in the unpacified spirit of the dead" (Takahashi 100). While the exorcisms sought by most of Beckett's characters ultimately fail, his characters are nevertheless obsessed with memory, with ghosts, and "all the dead voices."

For this particular production, under the direction of guest artist Patrick Sutton (director of the Gaiety School of Acting–The National Theatre School of Ireland), highlights of plays, prose, and poetry create a unique opportunity to experience Beckett as he is rarely seen or heard: in adaptation. Throughout the two-week, intensive-rehearsal process, Sutton has urged the actors to "listen to the words; they'll do the work," while insisting on their absolute precision with movement, breath, and voice. While the scenes from plays are staples of the internationally esteemed acting program Sutton leads, this is his first opportunity to stage Beckett's nondramatic writing. The actors were invited to choose phrases from the three novels and from there Sutton guided them in creating minimal, yet evocative movement. The result, as you will see, demonstrates the uncanny echoes of negation that resonate throughout Beckett country: from Moran's report (in *Molloy*) that "it is midnight. The rain is beating on the windows. It was not midnight. It was not raining" to the opening interrogatory of *The Unnamable* ("Where now? Who now? When now?"), Beckett beckons us to find presence through stillness and silence.

—Jane Barnette, Resident Dramaturg

Works Cited

Ackerly, C. J., and S. E. Gontarski. *The Grove Companion to Samuel Beckett.* New York: Grove, 2004. Print.

Gillette, Kyle. "Zen and the Art of Self-Negation in Samuel Beckett's *Not I.*" *Comparative Drama* 46.3 (Fall 2012): 283–302. Print.

O'Brien, Eoin. *The Beckett Country: Samuel Beckett's Ireland.* New York: Arcade, 1993. Print.

Preston, Carrie. "Taking Direction from Beckett: Noh / No, *Footfalls / Pas.*" *Back to the Beckett Text.* Ed. Tomasz Wisniewski. Gdansk: U of Gdansk P, 2012. 155–78. Print.

Takahashi, Yasunari. "Qu'est-ce qui arrive? Some Structural Comparisons of Beckett's Plays and Noh." *Samuel Beckett: Humanistic Perspectives.* Ed. Morris Beja, S. E. Gontarski, and Pierre Astier. Columbus: Ohio State UP, 1983. 99–106. Print.

NOTES

Introduction

1. For more on the intersection between hip-hop and theatre, see Persley, "Hip-hop theater and performance," 85–98. Some examples of the proliferation of *Hamilton* in other media include their forthcoming annotated book of lyrics, a mixtape, a possible film, and—perhaps most intriguing—the company's innovation of "#Ham4Ham" performances for the many hopeful patrons who gather outside the theatre to try their luck at winning a lottery ticket. These sidewalk performances are free and can include meta-adaptations of the musical itself (such as when the women in the cast performed the male roles) or feature stars from other productions (e.g., *Fun Home*) rapping or singing *Hamilton* lyrics.

2. Linda Hutcheon credits the Scottish poet Michael Alexander with first using the term *palimpsestuous* in *A Theory of Adaptation* (6). The genealogy of this term will be discussed in greater detail in chapter 4.

3. Although there is one individual (Katherine Profeta) who is called a "movement dramaturg," from my conversations with company members in spring 2014, it was confirmed that Profeta consults with the company to set movement sequences but does not contribute dramaturgical research or adaptation material for the productions.

4. Geoff Proehl, "Foreword: The Roles We Play," in Trencsényi, *Dramaturgy in the Making*, xv. Proehl is the 2016 recipient of the Elliot Hayes award from the Literary Managers and Dramaturgs of the Americas association.

1. Adaptation for the Stage: A Dramaturgical Intervention

1. *Oxford English Dictionary*, s.v. "Adaptation."

2. Murray, *The Adaptation Industry*, 19. See also Bourdieu, *The Field of Cultural Production*.

3. Murray, *The Adaptation Industry*, 195 n26. *Adaptation*, a film "based on the book *The Orchid Thief* by Susan Orlean," is (like other Kaufman screenplays) highly

meta- in its treatment of the subject matter. As Orlean states in the introduction to the published shooting script, "hilariously, [Kaufman's] screenplay has ended up not being a literal adaptation of my book, but a spiritual one, something that has captured (and expanded on) the essential character of what the book, I hope, was about. . . . It is about orchids, about how they adapt to their environment, sometimes resulting in the strangest and most marvelous forms, proving that the answer to everything might indeed be adaptation." Kaufman and Kaufman, *Adaptation: The Shooting Script.*

4. Hutcheon, *A Theory of Adaptation*, 32.

5. Dawkins, *The Selfish Gene.*

6. Hutcheon, *A Theory of Adaptation*, 176.

7. *Oxford English Dictionary.* Emphasis in original.

8. Newell, "'We're Off to See the Wizard' (Again)," 79.

9. Ibid., 78.

10. Murray, *The Adaptation Industry*, 10. See also Stam and Raengo, eds., *Literature and Film: A Guide to the Theory and Practice of Adaptation*, 1–52.

11. Oregon Shakespeare Festival, "Play on! Further Reading."

12. Pollack-Pelzner, "Why We (Mostly) Stopped Messing with Shakespeare's Language."

13. In May 2017, for example, Portland-based director Michael Streeter reignited discussion about one of these sacrosanct plays when his proposal to cast a black actor in the role of Nick in Edward Albee's *Who's Afraid of Virginia Woolf?* was rejected by the playwright's estate. For more on this controversy, see Tran, "When a Writer's Rights Aren't Right," and Paulson. Adapturgical casting will be discussed in further detail in chapter 8.

14. See, for example, Bial, *Playing God*, and Wolf, *A Problem Like Maria.*

15. For more about the various incarnations and the history of Baum's Oz, see Swartz, *Oz before the Rainbow* and Burger, *The Wizard of Oz as American Myth.*

16. In the interest of disclosure, I should mention that I also attended Northwestern University as an undergraduate theatre major. My acting teacher was David Downs.

17. Bacon, "The Dangerous Shores—One Last Time," 356.

18. See Dieckmann, "Toward a Feminist Chamber Theatre Method"; Bowman, "'Novelizing' the Stage"; and Bell, "Performance Studies as Women's Work."

19. Breen, *Chamber Theatre*, 6. Emphasis mine.

20. Breen, *Chamber Theatre*, 114. Emphasis in original.

21. Breen, *Chamber Theatre*, 86.

22. Robert Bolt, preface to *A Man for All Seasons* (London: Heinemann, 1968): xvii. Quoted in Breen, *Chamber Theatre*, 45.

23. See Dieckmann, "Toward a Feminist Chamber Theatre Method"; Bowman, "'Novelizing' the Stage"; Bell, "Performance Studies as Women's Work."

24. The cast breakdown for *Wrath* is 18M 14W, though it states it can be done by an ensemble "between 20 and 25 actors." Galati, *John Steinbeck's The Grapes of Wrath*, 110.

25. According to an interview published in the spring of 2014, Galati's next Steppenwolf production will be a new adaptation of John Steinbeck's *East of Eden*. *Stay Thirsty Magazine*, "A Conversation with Frank Galati."

26. Galati, "Adapting *Kafka on the Shore*," 43.

27. Catlin, "Curiouser and Curiouser: Reflections from Twenty Years in the Lookingglass (Theatre)," 111.

28. Ibid.

29. Catlin, "Curiouser and Curiouser," 112.

30. Regarding these interventions, see Lavender, "Modal Transpositions toward Theatre of Encounter" and Wood, "Gentlemen Prefer Adaptations." Lavender's insightful analysis of what he calls "theatres of encounter," including immersive theatre as well as game-based performances, is especially noteworthy for bridging the gap between discussions of media intermultimodality (Elleström, 2010) and live performance. Wood's focus on adaptation's production and materiality—especially as it relates to the construction of gender roles—echoes a growing (and long overdue) trend within the field to consider how adaptation works as part of a sociological system within culture.

31. Krebs, "Ghosts We Have Seen Before: Trends in Adaptation in Contemporary Performance," 582. Hutcheon, *A Theory of Adaptation*, 7.

32. Genette, *Palimpsests*, ix. Quoted in Sanders, *Adaptation and Appropriation*, 12.

33. Sanders, *Adaptation and Appropriation*, 160.

34. Murray, *The Adaptation Industry*, 185.

35. The notion of adaptation as an industry is also taken up by Wood, "Gentlemen Prefer Adaptations."

36. Laera, ed. *Theatre and Adaptation*, 5.

37. Although Laera and Krebs both discuss dramaturgy, the use of the word in their books references the structure of a text, rather than the process and product of developing scripts and productions for audiences.

38. Murray, *The Adaptation Industry*, 10.

39. See Elleström, *Media Borders*; and Lavender, "Modal Transpositions."

40. For example, although Vincent Murphy approaches adaptation as a practitioner in his *Page to Stage: The Craft of Adaptation*, this book is not designed to engage with theory as much as it is a guidebook for how to make stage adaptations.

41. Edwards, "Adaptation: Two Theories," 372. Emphasis in original. The phrase "knowing audience" is quoted from Hutcheon, *A Theory of Adaptation*, 120.

42. Hutcheon, *A Theory of Adaptation*, 109. Quoted in Edwards, "Adaptation: Two Theories," 373.

43. Hutcheon, *A Theory of Adaptation*, 107 ("We need to know 'why'"). Quoted and expanded upon ("which is to say 'why now,' or 'why here, for this audience,'") in Edwards, "Adaptation: Two Theories," 373.

44. In translation studies, this kind of approach is often considered intersemiotic or a transmutation between two sign systems. See Jakobson, "On Linguistic Aspects of Translation." Quoted in Laera, *Theatre and Adaptation*, 6, n11.

45. See Lavender, "Modal Transpositions"; and Levin, *Performing Ground*.

46. For more on the consumer backlash following Hasbro's oversight of Rey (upon which one witty reader ["Kitty Fo"] commented, "Duh you guys it's right there in the name: HasBRO"), see Domonoske, "#WhereIsRey? She's On Her Way, Says Hasbro." The collection of Rey-themed items on Etsy range from hoodies ("Straight Outta Jakku") to paintings to menstrual cloth pads printed with Rey's image. See https://www.etsy.com/market/star_wars_rey. This demand for Rey products was eventually met by Hasbro's supply, with Rey figures appearing on shelves by January 2016.

47. For a useful basic illustration of how adaptations can change between media or cultures (or both), see Mark O'Thomas, "Turning Japanese: Translation, Adaptation, and the Ethics of Trans-National Exchange," in Albrecht-Crane and Cutchins, eds., *Adaptation Studies*, 49.

48. For further examples of how to consider intra- and intermodal changes in adaptation, see Laera, *Theatre and Adaptation*, 5–7.

49. For more on Lessing's contributions to the development of dramaturgy, see Lessing, *Hamburg Dramaturgy*.

50. Schupbach, "Laocoon and the Expression of Pain."

51. Lessing fragment, quoted in David E. Wellbery, *Lessing's Laocoon*, 103.

52. Schupbach, "Laocoon and the Expression of Pain."

53. Elleström, *Media Borders*, 39, n1; some historians question when the sculpture was created, suggesting that perhaps Virgil was the adapter rather than the sculptors, as Lessing assumed. For this view, see Boardman, *The Oxford History of Classical Art*, 199; in contrast, see Smith, *Hellenistic Sculpture*, 109.

54. These questions are frequently the first questions asked of intermedial adaptations, but by listing them here I do not mean to suggest that we stop our analysis at this level—dramaturgs should, as several scholars have suggested, trouble our Cartesian model of epistemology and consider a phenomenological or cognitive science approach as well.

55. Some might say that William Shakespeare's work outshines the sources from which it borrows, eclipsing the reader's ability to enjoy the adaptation aspects of his plays and poetry. For more on Shakespeare's sources and adaptations of his writing, see the *World Shakespeare Bibliography*, a robust online resource edited by Laura Estill.

56. I discuss one film and two stage adaptations that are not confined to the same boundaries as my principal ones.

57. Hutcheon, *A Theory of Adaptation*, 7. Her exact phrase is, "Adaptation is repetition, but repetition without replication."

58. Robert McCrum, "The 100 Best Novels: No. 17—*Moby-Dick* by Herman Melville." *The Guardian*. Web. 13 Jan. 2014. Accessed 29 Jan. 2016.

59. Abbott, *The Cambridge Introduction to Narrative*, 108. This cogent observation, partially cited in Hutcheon, *A Theory of Adaptation*, in its entirety reads, "Adaptation to the shorter, continuous forms of stage and screen is, then, a surgical art."

2. The Rise of American Dramaturgy

1. Romanska, *The Routledge Companion to Dramaturgy*, 2.

2. Wightman, "'Smash': 'The Dramaturg' recap." In her summary of the episode ("Smashed"), Wightman's first bullet reads, "'Dramaturg' is a funny word."

3. Rogers, "Smash: The Dramaturg."

4. Blickers and Quirt, "Ecologies of Dramaturgy," 251.

5. Hopkins, "A Note from the Editor," ix–x; x.

6. By "critical proximity" I reference both Shelley Orr's contribution to the aforementioned special issue of *Theatre Topics* as well as the reference upon which she bases this approach to dramaturgy (Jane Simon's "Critical Proximity" in *Cultural Studies Review* 16, no. 2 (2010): 4–23). See Orr, "Critical Proximity."

7. Chemers, *Ghost Light*, 10. There are numerous other books about dramaturgy, of course—an excellent compilation of these resources can be found in Appendix B of *Ghost Light*.

8. Another leader in the field is Mark Bly, the resident dramaturg of The Acting Company. Having published two volumes of *The Production Notebooks* (TCG 1995 and 2001), Bly has had a profoundly generative impact on the practice of dramaturgy in North America. As chair of the playwriting program at the Yale School of Drama (1992–2004), he mentored both emerging playwrights and dramaturgs.

9. My essay in the fifth section, "Literary Adaptation for the Stage: A Primer for Adaptation Dramaturgs," was the starting point for this book. It is the only chapter in *The Routledge Companion to Dramaturgy* that explicitly addresses adaptation dramaturgy, however.

10. Romanska, *Routledge Companion*, 5.

11. Ibid., 6.

12. Trencsényi and Cochrane, eds. *New Dramaturgy*, xi.

13. Ibid., xii.

14. Ibid., xiii.

15. Trencsényi, *Dramaturgy in the Making*, xxii.

16. See Leahey and Bruton, "The Goal of the Emancipated Spectator," 205–9.

17. The few times Trencsényi (2015) mentions adaptation are nevertheless instructive—she quotes G. E. Lessing (12) and Bertolt Brecht on the subject (119–20), but usually in the service of a larger discussion about the dramaturg's role overall.

18. Trencsényi, *Dramaturgy in the Making*, 263.

19. Ibid, 264.

20. Versényi, *Oxford Encyclopedia of Theatre and Performance*, 386. This definition was cited in the coauthored article by Michael Chemers and Versényi, "Kinesis

as Mimesis," which argues for a similar pairing between martial arts and dramaturgy that I suggest exists between adaptation and dramaturgy.

21. Chemers and Versényi, "Kinesis as Mimesis," 199.

22. With Ken Cerniglia as the president (2016–17), LMDA has made a commitment to take "the Hemispheric name change seriously" with plans to host a conference in Latin America by 2019, but as of this writing LMDA serves North America exclusively. Cerniglia, "Keynote" in "Livestreaming the 30th Annual Literary Managers and Dramaturgs of the Americas Conference."

23. LMDA website, "About Us." That LMDA made this connection encourages readers to ask how dramaturgs might be similar to personal computers, but that inquiry exceeds the limits of this project.

24. Trencsényi and Cochrane, *New Dramaturgy*, xviii.

25. Trencsényi and Cochrane, *New Dramaturgy*. 169.

26. Turner and Behrndt, *Dramaturgy and Performance*, 170.

27. Quoted in Trencsényi and Cochrane, *New Dramaturgy*, 102.

28. Jackie Smart, in Trencsényi and Cochrane, *New Dramaturgy*, 112.

29. The Yale School of Drama began its MFA program in dramaturgy and dramatic criticism in 1977. For more about dramaturgy graduate degrees in the United States, see "A Sampler of Graduate Dramaturgy Programs in the U.S.," a supplement to Lenora Inez Brown's "You Can't Tell a Dramaturg by Her Title," in the January 2001 issue of *American Theatre*.

30. While most practitioners and dramaturgically savvy academics in the United States use the terminology "new play" and "production" to distinguish between these two kinds of dramaturgy, they do not (to my knowledge) identify the spectrum of practice as a continuum between these two poles.

31. This observation is based on conversations with dramaturgs from Canada (versus their counterparts in the US) at LMDA conferences and on the listserv. Federal funding for play development in Canada likely exceeds the meager budget allotted for theatre in the United States.

32. See New Play Exchange, at http://newplayexchange.org. The New Play Exchange is a program of the National New Play Network, http://nnpn.org.

33. For more on gender parity in theatre, see The Kilroys, "a gang of playwrights and producers in LA who are done talking about gender parity and are taking action," http://thekilroys.org/about/, and Evans, "The Unsung Gender-Parity Warriors." HowlRound, "a knowledge commons by and for the theatre community," continues to be a resource for increasing diversity and inclusion within the theatre, with its Latina/o Theatre Commons section and articles about race and representation in American theatre. See Ingersoll and Selenow, "You Want a Diverse Theatre? Prove it."

34. Video archive of "Author Rights . . . the conversation continues" in "Livestreaming the 30th Annual Literary Managers and Dramaturgs of the Americas Conference."

35. Sevush, "The Guild and Dramaturgy," 70.

36. Ibid., 71.

3. The Power of Adapturgy

1. "Source" may become plural for some adapters, such as Mary Zimmerman and Scott Kaiser, among others, who are working from multiple sources.

2. Theatricality can be a complex notion—one that I unpack further in chapter 9 —but for now, suffice it to say that I see theatricality as a process that transforms subjects, action, and objects into something witnessed as both recognizable and displaced from reality.

3. John Gentile, personal interview (via phone), 25 January 2016. See appendix 1.

4. This observation that other members of the creative team necessarily perform dramaturgical research is often used to dismiss the importance of dramaturgs.

5. Edwards, "Adaptation: Two Theories," 369.

6. The genesis of this model stems from an illustration created by University of Kansas undergraduate student Jackson Byam, who was enrolled in Authors and Adaptation, a class Darren Canady and I created and cotaught. Byam later sent me digital renderings of his impromptu blackboard drawing; although his model differs substantially from mine, I am grateful for his generosity and creative thinking, which inspired my own.

7. See Margherita Laera, "Introduction: Return, Rewrite, Repeat: The Theatricality of Adaptation," in Laera, ed. *Theatre and Adaptation*, 1 19.

8. As mentioned in the first chapter, there are several essays and books that investigate the adaptation history of Baum's 1900 book and the 1939 film. See Newell, "'We're Off to See the Wizard' (Again)"; Swartz, *Oz before the Rainbow*; and Burger, *The Wizard of Oz as American Myth*.

9. Maguire insists that the musical is "not a retelling of 'The Wizard of Oz,'" but most critics and the publicity surrounding *Wicked* assume that it is. Handler, "Hey, Watch Who You're Calling Wicked."

10. Bial, "Performance Studies 3.0," 410.

11. Leitch, "Twelve Fallacies in Contemporary Adaptation Theory," 165.

12. See, for example, Morris, "In 'The Wiz Live!' on NBC, a Search for More in the Emerald City."

13. Kissell, "'The Wiz Live' Ratings Strong: NBC Musical Draws 11.5 Million Viewers." This review notes that the show "fared especially well in markets with large African-American populations," before citing the ratings.

14. Eric Deggans, quoted in Siegel, "NBC Raises Its Musical Game with 'The Wiz Live.'"

15. Venuti, *The Translator's Invisibility: A History of Translation*. Quoted in Laera, *Theatre and Adaptation*, 8.

16. The 1978 film *The Wiz* transplants Dorothy to Harlem, resulting in a "peculiar study of urban melancholy," but also capitalizing on Sidney Lumet's talent for

filming New York City street life. Morris, "In 'The Wiz Live!' on NBC, a Search for More in the Emerald City."

17. Elliott, *Rethinking the Novel/Film Debate*, 4.

18. For Lessing, the image (the province of "show" and not "tell") was sculpture, but in adaptation studies it is usually considered the territory of film.

19. van Kerkhoven, "Looking without Pencil in Hand," 142. Emphasis in original.

20. Ibid, 146.

21. I refer to Joseph Roach's theory of "surrogation," Peggy Phelan's emphasis on ephemerality, and Marvin Carlson's notion of ghosting. See Roach, *Cities of the Dead*; Phelan, *Unmarked*; and Carlson, *The Haunted Stage*.

22. The root of the word *theatre* is *theatron*, a Greek word meaning "seeing place"; *auditorium* is a Latin word meaning "hearing place."

23. Elliott, *Rethinking the Novel/Film Debate*, 139.

24. Ibid., 167.

25. Ibid., 229.

26. While it is impossible to prove or locate the origin of theatre, our earliest extant records (thus far) point to the Abydos passion play in Egypt and the City Dionysia in Ancient Greece.

27. Otto, *The Idea of the Holy*.

28. Eliade, *The Sacred and the Profane*, 11.

29. Barnette, "Staging the Numinous," 416.

30. Sources in the public domain are typically sought for creative and financial freedom and flexibility, as previously mentioned.

31. Freud, "The 'Uncanny," in *Collected Papers*, vol. 4, 404. Emphasis in original.

32. See Schechner, *Performance Theory*.

33. Freud, "The Uncanny," 369–70.

34. "Colombari Mini Documentary."

4. Palimpsestuous Pleasures

1. See Alexander, *The Poetic Achievement of Ezra Pound*, 144. Following his statement that "it is pointless to deny that Pound is a magician, the question is whether his magic works," Alexander's only reference to this term is that "it becomes clear that Pound has a faculty for what might be called palimpsestuous-ness, the literary romance of the past carried to new depths of verbal resonance. He also, by an act of neo-humanism, brings the past alive into the present."

2. Hutcheon, *A Theory of Adaptation*, 6. Genette, *Palimpsests*, 5.

3. Genette, *Palimpsests*, 5.

4. Ezra Pound's *The Cantos*, a long and unfinished poem, combines different languages and cultural/historical references in a seemingly unstructured order.

5. Alexander, *Poetic Achievement*, 144.

6. Chemers's *Ghost Light* uses the sequence of "Go deep!" "Go wide!" and "Go long!" to introduce educational exercises meant to facilitate the introductory practice of dramaturgy. In his preface he explains that to "go long!" is to place the information "in the context of a long conversation among theater practitioners, historians, and critics in changing social conditions through time," xiii.

7. Ermath, "Agency in the Discursive Condition," 47.

8. Ermath, "Agency in the Discursive Condition," 57.

9. On pleasure and spectatorship, see Ubersfeld, "The Pleasure of the Spectator." On pleasure and dramaturgy, see Koszyn, "The Dramaturg and the Irrational."

10. Proehl, "The Images before Us," 130.

11. Proehl, *Toward a Dramaturgical Sensibility*, 81.

12. For more on fanfiction, see Grossman, "How Harry Potter Became the Boy Who Lived Forever."

13. See, for example, Magelssen, *Simming*.

14. Lehmann, *Postdramatic Theatre*, 8.

15. Fusco, "Elevator Repair Service."

16. Bailes, *Performance Theatre and the Poetics of Failure*, 179.

17. Elevator Repair Service. "Shows: *Gatz*."

18. Elevator Repair Service. "Shows: *The Sound and the Fury*."

19. For an intriguing discussion of the way that ERS's *Room Tone* (2002) "managed to unsettle something fundamental in [his] definition of how space works and how it is even defined," see Petralia, "Reshaping Spatiality," 11.

20. Elevator Repair Service. "Shows: *The Sound and the Fury*."

21. Stoicheff, Muri, Deshaye, et al., eds., *The Sound and the Fury*: A Hypertext Edition.

22. Padgett, "William Faulkner Trivia."

23. Stoicheff, *The Sound and the Fury*: A Hypertext Edition. These passages are in "Sequential display of narrative time in Benjy's section" under "Visual Displays" on this website, contributed by Kathleen Murphy, a member of the hypertext team.

24. Sartre, "On *The Sound and the Fury*: Time in the Work of Faulkner." See Stoicheff, *The Sound and the Fury*.

25. Intriguingly, Stoicheff's scholarship, like Alexander's, is on Pound.

26. Shakespeare, *Macbeth*, act 5, scene 5, lines 19–28. The "idiot" in question here is not necessarily Benjy. As Joel Deshaye reminds readers: "All the Compson brothers are incapable of rational conduct at some point. . . . It is clear that Quentin, Jason, and Benjy all misrepresent the world in their minds. " See Deshaye, "A Brief Analysis."

27. Bailes, *Performance Theatre*, 149, emphasis in the original.

28. The role of Caddie was sometimes played by Maggie Hoffman, one of the newcomers to this production, and the role was originated by Kate Scelsa.

29. Elevator Repair Service, Program for *The Sound and the Fury*. 2015.

30. Personal interview with Vin Knight, New York City. 22 April 2015.

31. That said, the trend for contemporary theatre is away from such predetermined experiences, in what Andy Lavender has called "theatres of encounter," including immersive theatre events like those produced by Punchdrunk.

32. Personal interview, John Collins. New York City. 22 April 2015. See appendix 1.

33. Interest in this family has proliferated, apparently. There is now another documentary, *The Wild and Wonderful Whites of West Virginia* (Tribeca: 2010).

34. Personal interview, Ben Williams. New York City. 23 April 2015. See appendix 1.

35. Ibid.

36. According to Williams, as it turns out, several of his friends from Tennessee knew Stanley Hicks and reported that he had once made them a banjo out of opossum hide.

37. Williams interview.

38. Ibid.

39. Bailes, *Performance Theatre*, 149.

40. Collins interview, his emphasis.

41. Ibid.

42. Ibid.

43. Ibid.

44. For more on their approach to problem solving through ensemble theatre, see Bailes, *Performance Theatre*, as well as Ana Pais, "'A Way of Listening': Interview with John Collins" in Trencsenyi and Cochrane, *New Dramaturgy*, 115–24.

45. Collins interview, his emphasis.

46. Williams interview, his emphasis.

47. Collins interview.

48. For the remount, the new actors were: Daphne Gaines, Rosie Goldensohn, Maggie Hoffman, and Lucy Taylor. The previous actors were unavailable for the Public run. There were also three new technicians, two stage managers, and one costume assistant.

49. Williams interview.

50. Ibid.

51. According to Faulkner's first rendering of the fictional Yoknapatawpha County of Mississippi (circa 1936), within twenty-four hundred square miles, the population was made up of "Whites, 6298; Negroes, 9313." See "Mapping Yoknapatawpha."

52. Collins interview. Although Sokol is a woman, her portrayal of the (castrated) Benjy does not feel like a collision.

53. Collins interview.

54. We will return to this question of representation via casting as a tool of stage adaptation in greater detail in chapter 8.

55. I did not inspect earlier production programs for *The Sound and the Fury.*

56. Collins interview.

5. How to Do Things with Birds

1. Iñárritu, *Birdman* (screenplay), 81.

2. Taylor, "Watching the Skies," 2.

3. Ibid., 3.

4. Taylor, "Watching the Skies," 6. According to Taylor, the gates to Ianus Geminus (the shrine for Janus) stood open whenever Rome was at war, and closed in peace—this latter the rarest of events. According to tradition, over the course of the regal period and the republic the shrine was closed only twice: once under Numa Pompilius and again briefly by T. Manlius in 235 B.C. (Varro, *Ling* 5.165). Augustus closed the shrine three times during his principate, and later emperors occasionally followed suit.

5. Green, *Ovid, Fasti 1,* 75. He admits that this is an indirect and "extravagant etymology" but claims it is in keeping with Ovid's innovative work in *Fasti.*

6. Nagle, *Ovid's Fasti,* 40, lines 1.111, 113–14. All direct translations of *Fasti* are taken from Nagle's translation.

7. Nagle, *Ovid's Fasti,* 40, lines 1.105–10.

8. Nagle, *Ovid's Fasti,* 41, lines 1.143–44. Nagle translates this reference as Diana but others (e.g., Green) prefer Hecate for 1.141; this stems from a conflation of the two goddesses that dates back to the nineteenth century. For more on this, see Green, *Ovid, Fasti 1,* 85.

9. *Fasti* 1.39.

10. Green, *Ovid, Fasti 1,* 83.

11. Kaster, *Macrobius,* 93. *Sat* 1.9.4.

12. Taylor, "Watching the Skies," 12.

13. Ibid., 14.

14. Ibid., 12.

15. Ibid., 37 (*Fast.* 6.105–68).

16. Festus, 422, quoted in Taylor, "Watching the Skies," 26. See also note 108 on this page of Taylor for more about liminal gods.

17. Taylor, "Watching the Skies," 16–17.

18. Aronson, "Their Exits," 340.

19. Neill, "Hooked on Classics," 6.

20. Newlands, *Playing with Time,* 144.

21. Although Ovid names Janus's victim Carna or Cranaë in *Fasti,* it appears that he means to reference Cardea, since she is more typically associated with hawthorn (or whitethorn) wands and is the Roman goddess of hinges (a power that Ovid oddly suggests Janus gave her). Cranaë (or Carna) "held the keys of the Underworld" and was known as the "harsh or stony one," but had no known links

to Janus or doors or hinges outside of Ovid's fiction. Robert Graves, *The White Goddess*, 65. See *Fasti*, lines 6.101–30.

22. *Birdman* received four Academy Awards in 2015, for best picture, best director, and best original screenplay.

23. Although Simone Murray primarily focuses on literary adaptations in her groundbreaking book *The Adaptation Industry*, the Marvel Cinematic Universe (a media franchise responsible for producing the *Iron Man* movies and Norton's *The Incredible Hulk*, as well as summer 2017's *Spider-Man: Homecoming*) is an excellent example of the phenomenon she describes as "an intricate, hugely complex institutional and industrial system" (185). For more about the material process and consequences of adaptation as an industry, see Murray.

24. Emma Stone in *Birdman: All Access—A View from the Wings* (DVD Extra).

25. Harold Bloom, quoted in Clark, "Raymond Carver's Monologic Imagination," 240. *Askesis* stems from Ancient Greek and is connected to asceticism. It means the practice of intense self-discipline.

26. Carver, *What We Talk About*, 243.

27. Iñárritu, *Birdman* (screenplay), 45.

28. Carver, "Late Fragment," as quoted at the top of Iñárritu (film).

29. Ibid., 35.

30. Ibid., 33.

31. Ibid., 32. Carver, *What We Talk About*, 151.

32. Iñárritu, *Birdman* (screenplay), 31; Carver, *What We Talk About*, 146.

33. Carver, *What We Talk About*, 153.

34. Ibid., 154. These lines are also spoken in *Stuck in Love* (2013) with Greg Kinnear.

35. For more about the impact of "star power" on the adaptation industry, specifically with regard to celebrity-status literary adapters, see Murray, *The Adaptation Industry*, 147–51.

36. My use of the phrase "prominently obscure" is inspired by what Louise Adams Holland calls the "obscure prominence" of Janus in literature, as quoted in Taylor, "Watching the Skies," 2. See Holland, *Janus and the Bridge*.

37. *Birdman: All Access—A View from the Wings* (DVD Extra).

38. Iñárritu, *Birdman* (screenplay), 84–85.

39. Ibid., 53 and 85. Emphasis in original.

40. As David Bordwell points out, in an earlier scene featuring "Sam's tirade about Riggan's irrelevance," the drama is heightened by the camera's sole focus on Sam, disallowing any reaction shots of Riggan. "This scene's concealment of the reverse angle—what is Sam seeing?—anticipates the film's final image."

41. In the screenplay, there's also a short voiceover sequence between Birdman and an anonymous man, where Birdman says, "You won't be hearing from him anymore." The man asks, "Is he . . . ?" and Birdman answers, "He's gone." Although this voiceover exchange was ultimately scrapped for the aforementioned montage, it gives credence to seeing the onstage death as reality and the hospital finale as fantasy.

6. Geographies of Adaptation

1. The way Bentley phrases it differs a bit: "A impersonates B while C looks on." *The Life of the Drama*, 150.

2. Brook, *The Empty Space*, 9.

3. "This [spatial] configuration is suggested by the word 'theatre' itself—a place where one observes." Carlson, *Places of Performance*, 128.

4. Tompkins, "Space and the Geographies of Theatre: Introduction," 537.

5. Carlson unpacks these assumptions in *The Haunted Stage: The Theatre as Memory Machine*, 132–33.

6. This disagreement mostly stems from the difference between how Michel de Certeau defines place from Henri Lefebvre (among others). For more on this subject, see Merrifield, "Place and Space: A Lefebvrian Reconciliation."

7. Augé, *Non-Places*, 81. Quoted in Petralia, "Reshaping Spatiality,"19.

8. Quoted in Tompkins, *Unsettling Space*, 5.

9. Tompkins, *Unsettling Space*, 5.

10. Petralia, "Reshaping Spatiality," 19. Emphasis in original. See also de Certeau, *The Practice of Everyday Life*.

11. Indeed, this extension of the space and time of the theatrical event can include performances wherein a shared meal is planned for the intermission. SAÏAH produced some of these events at the Goat Farm in Atlanta. Another example of this can be seen in Theatre du Soleil, as mentioned by Carlson, *The Haunted Stage*, 161.

12. See, for example, McAuley, *Space in Performance;* Carlson, *Places of Performance;* Fuchs and Chaudhuri, *Land/Scape/Theater;* and Tompkins, *Unsettling Space.*

13. Chaudhuri, *Staging Place*, xii.

14. See, for example, Lavender, "Modal Transpositions"; Elleström, *Media Borders*; and Petralia, "Reshaping Spatiality." Also: Lakoff and Johnson, *Philosophy in the Flesh.*

15. See Merrifield, "Place and Space"; Lakoff and Johnson, *Philosophy in the Flesh;* and McConachie, *Evolution, Cognition, and Performance.*

16. We might recall, for example, Bentley's equation here, which favors sight ("looks on") and Brook's statement ("whilst someone else is watching him"). That said, the word auditorium recognizes the act of hearing for performances.

17. Linda Hutcheon's sections on showing and telling in *A Theory of Adaptation* are useful as an overview of the modal transformation between stage or screen and novel.

18. It is said that Melville initially wanted to write an encyclopedia entry about whales and whaling but Nathanial Hawthorne encouraged him to weave it into a story.

19. A year after it was produced at KSU, Gentile's *Moby-Dick* was performed in Morocco for the Twenty-First Annual Festival International de Théâtre Universitaire

de Casablanca (Casablanca Theatre Festival), where it won awards for both best performance and best actor (for Phillip Justman, who played the role of Captain Ahab). For this tour, Gentile abridged the script and made it trilingual (English, French, and Arabic).

20. As Carlson notes in *The Haunted Stage*, Richard Schechner has called for more scholarly attention to the thresholds surrounding theatre spaces: "Too little study has been made of the liminal approaches and leavings of performance, how the audiences get to and into the performance place, and how they go from that space" (156). See also: Schechner, *Performance Theory*.

21. My dramaturgical assistant for the 2008 production of *Moby-Dick* was Paula Bowen, who had worked with the workshop draft of Gentile's emerging adaptation and was a great resource to both Gentile and me.

22. Gentile, "The Pilgrim Soul," 410.

23. Notably, spectators for the SAÏAH production of *Moby-Dick* were required to sign a waiver (regarding possible harm and liability) before entering the space for the performance.

24. Hopkins, ed., *Performance and the City*, 240.

25. Justman, "Phillip Justman's Venture into the Whale."

26. For each performance, SAÏAH capped the event at sixty spectators.

27. Khalid, "SAÏAH Takes on the Whale."

28. The House Theatre's version took the most license with their production *Season on the Line*, a story about a troubled theatre company led by "an aging artistic director with a singular focus: the first-ever production of *Moby-Dick*" (http://www.thehousetheatre.com/playsandevents/seasonline). Tellingly, the company calls this version "based on" rather than an adaptation of Melville's novel.

29. Melville, *Moby-Dick*, 365.

30. Miller and Talaske, "The Isolation of Lookingglass Theatre."

31. Ibid.

32. Thomas, "In Defense of the Puppet Stage," n.p.

33. Thomas, "About the Artist." See appendix 1 for interview with Thomas as well.

34. There was no framing context for the video loop, and with the echoes of conversation in the lobby it was difficult to hear the interview, so it was not possible to determine with certainty whether the clips of performance were from earlier versions of *Moby Dick* or from this version. See: Thomas & Co.: *Moby Dick*, YouTube video.

35. Thomas, "About the Artist."

36. Turner, "Liminality and Communitas," 99. Emphasis in original.

37. In Lefebvre's words (*The Production of Space*), "Phallic erectility bestows a special status on the perpendicular, proclaiming phallocracy as the orientation of space, as the goal of the process—at once metaphoric and metonymic—which instigates this facet of spatial practice" (287).

38. The "mind palace" or "method of loci" has recently been popularized by the BBC's *Sherlock* television show—see: Zielinski, "The Secrets of Sherlock's Mind Palace."

39. Chicago Humanities Festival, "Blair Thomas: Melville's Moby Dick and Puppetry."

40. Ibid.

41. Khalid, "SAÏAH Takes on the Whale."

42. Personal interview, David Catlin, phone call, 16 September 2015. See appendix 1.

43. Melville, *Moby-Dick*, 7.

44. The whale also appeared in the marketing strategy for the Lookingglass production—on social media outlets, the company used pictures of a giant inflatable white whale "on location" at various sites throughout Chicago to publicize the production, using the hashtag #FindTheWhiteWhale.

45. Barnette, "Staging the Numinous," 416. The numinous is discussed in chapter 3 of this volume as well.

46. Slotkin, *Regeneration through Violence*, 544.

47. Gentile, *Moby-Dick, by Herman Melville: Adapted for the Stage by John Gentile*, 24.

48. It is worth noting that all the women who performed in both of these versions were Caucasian.

49. Slotkin, *Regeneration through Violence*, 546.

50. Indeed, in Blair Thomas and Company's adaptation, the blimp-as-whale reads as object without gender, and the choice to set the play in a monastery further solidifies the masculine (and chaste) focus.

51. In addition to gender, of course, we must recognize that "historically marginalized persons (non-white, lower class, queer, etc.) have been relegated to the background or have been made to stand in for the formal properties of space itself." Levin, *Performing Ground*, 17.

52. For a detailed gender analysis of Punchdrunk, see Levin, *Performing Ground*, 82–87.

7. Working with the Script (The Spirit of the Source)

1. A common critique of adaptations is that they serve material needs, rather than aesthetic ones. Both Hutcheon and Sanders address this concern in their books on adaptation. For a sociological analysis of the machinery behind book-to-film adaptations, see Murray, *The Adaptation Industry*.

2. Most Crane scholars agree that the likely setting for the events that occur (from the Union's perspective) in *The Red Badge of Courage* is the Battle of Chancellorsville, a surprising victory for the Confederacy that included the second bloodiest day of the Civil War (2 May 1863). While the Union outnumbered the Confederates by two to one, their leader (Joseph Hooker, a Union army major general) was not as decisive as General Robert E. Lee was. Among the wounded was Lt. Gen. Thomas "Stonewall" Jackson, who was accidentally hit by friendly fire and ultimately died of his wounds in this battle.

3. Mitchell, *New Essays on "The Red Badge of Courage,"* 20.

4. Quoted in Butler, "Richard Wright's 'Between the World and Me,'" 375.

5. Wood, "Crimson Blotches on the Pages of the Past," 50.

6. Crane, *Red Badge of Courage*, 5.

7. *Oxford English Dictionary*, s.v. "spirit," 1a.

8. See: Roach, *Cities of the Dead*; Phelan, *Unmarked*; and Carlson, *The Haunted Stage*.

9. Posner, "The Dramaturg(ies) of Puppetry and Visual Theatre," 337. Posner references Basil Jones, "Puppetry and Authorship," in Jane Taylor's *Handspring Puppet Company*, 255.

10. See, for example, the TYA adaptations by Kathryn Schultz Miller (1990) and Joe Sutton (2005). Both of these adaptations use narration (in Sutton's version it is an old man remembering his experience with war; Miller's take has an outright narrator character). A more recent TYA adaptation by Eric Schmiedl uses hip-hop lyrics rapped by "The Voice" to give life to Henry's conscience (2007, 2013), to mixed reviews. One exception to the young audience storytelling approach is Catherine Bush's take, which does not include a narrator; instead, her play uses flashbacks and dream sequences to move fluidly between the battlefield and Henry's memories of home (2011).

11. Haverty and Barnette, adapters, *Red Badge of Courage* (version 2), 2.

12. Ibid., 1. For the Auburn production, Fereshteh Rostampour (a professor in the Department of Theatre) was the lighting and set designer.

13. Ibid., emphasis in original.

14. Ibid., 11.

15. In the Auburn production, this sequence was different: instead of trees that appeared to be bullets, we used real tree branches, carried by actors who entered from either side of the projection screen.

16. Haverty and Barnette, adapters, *Red Badge of Courage* (version 6), 5. Catherine Bush's adaptation also uses memories of the circus as a flashback sequence in her stage adaptation.

17. Haverty and Barnette, adapters, *Red Badge of Courage* (version 6), 6.

18. These sections are taken verbatim from chapter 9 in Crane's novel, 60, with ellipses indicating words or phrases omitted.

19. For the Atlanta-area productions, Kristin Haverty was the animation designer.

20. The etymology of *psychedelic*, according to the *Oxford English Dictionary*, is "a borrowing from Greek, combined with an English element," wherein "psyche" means mind, soul, or spirit, and *del* comes from a Greek word that means "to make manifest, reveal."

21. Quoted in Posner, "The Dramaturg(ies) of Puppetry," 337.

22. Haverty and Barnette, adapters, *Red Badge of Courage* (version 6), 10.

23. Here I refer to the Auburn production, wherein the actors used real tree branches to signify their transformation into trees. As aforementioned, in the

Atlanta productions, the trees were large props, designed to look like bullets as they entered through the portal.

24. Haverty and Barnette, adapters, *Red Badge of Courage* (version 6), 11. See chapter 7 in Crane.

25. In the Atlanta version of this production, there were actually three puppets—the third was a worm puppet, designed to crawl out of the corpse's mouth when the Youth first encounters him.

26. Because this was my first encounter with Stephen Crane, I did not initially realize that the novel I read was so different from the one Michael knew and loved.

27. The blasphemy stems from the fact that in these excised passages, Henry proclaims his dominance over all things, as if he himself were a god.

28. Binder, "The 'Red Badge of Courage' Nobody Knows," 25.

29. Crane, quoted in Binder, "The 'Red Badge of Courage' Nobody Knows," 12.

30. Haverty and Barnette, adapters, *Red Badge of Courage* (version 6), 29.

31. In the Atlanta-based productions (at KSU and 7 Stages), Josh Brook played the Youth. Other cast members included: Bryan Mercer (Tall/Lieutenant/Tompkins), Devon Hales (Mama/Tattered), Laura Driskill (Loud), and Megan Jance (Sarcastic/General). In the Auburn production, David Tourtellotte played the role of the Youth, and in this scene he stood (waving a flag) atop a fallen tree trunk that was our primary scenic design object for the Auburn production. Other cast members included: Steven Hatcher (Tall/Lieutenant/Tompkins), Tara Folio (Mama/Tattered), Michael Sanders (Loud), and Alexander Horn (Sarcastic/General).

32. Crane, *Red Badge of Courage*, 138.

8. Working with the Production

1. Mira Rafalowicz contends that there are four stages of production dramaturgy that follow what she calls the "basic level" of meeting with the director to brainstorm ideas: (1) carving out the area to explore; (2) sharpening the focus on the material, identifying what will be communicated; (3) considering what the performance communicates and making necessary changes to align it with the conceptual goals; (4) reflecting on how well the production achieves the goals and how to keep it fresh each night. Rafalowicz's stages are used to organize "Product-Led Production Dramaturgy" in Trencsényi, *Dramaturgy in the Making*, 129–62. See Rafalowicz, et al, "Dramaturgs in America," 27–29, for further detail.

2. For reference, the other ten adaptations are: Ric Averill's *Midnight Visit to the Grave of Poe: A Grotesque Arabesque* at the Lawrence Arts Center; KSU's *Silence and Stillness: The Voice in Beckett, Red Hanrahan, The Cocteau Hour, Dark Forest, Splittin' the Raft, Redwing: Voices from 1888, Everything That Rises Must Converge*, and *Moby-Dick*, and the Georgia Shakespeare production of *The Odyssey: A Journey Home.*

3. The *Jesus in India* controversy at Clarion University came on the heels of publicity about a production of Katori Hall's *The Mountaintop* at Kent State University in late September and early October of 2015, in which the role of Dr. Martin Luther

King Jr. was played by a white actor for three nights and a black actor for the other three nights of the production's run. Michael Oatman, the African American creative director of the African Community Theatre at the university who directed this production, stated that he did so "to see how the words rang differently or indeed the same, coming from two different actors, with two different racial backgrounds." However, it appears that no black actors performed in this production after all. See Howard Sherman, "When a White Actor Goes to 'The Mountaintop.'"

4. Eyring, "Standing up for Playwrights and against 'Colorblind' Casting," 10.

5. For more on the intricacies and history of casting in the United States, see Brian Herrera's "The Best Actor for the Role," and "There is Power in Casting."

6. My use of "conscientious casting" is intentionally distinct from conversations in public scholarship about inclusive casting, color-conscious casting, or conceptual casting. It is more closely aligned with Patricia Ybarra's concept of "coalitional casting," insofar as conscientious casting is also committed to "the cause of telling a marginalized story." However, unlike Ybarra's coalitional casting, conscientious casting is not always about dedicating oneself to "the work it takes to get over one's trepidation over telling someone else's story," as much as it is about choosing actors for roles with dramaturgically informed rationales for how those choices resonate within the context of "Why This Play Now?" or, in the case of adapturgy, "Why This Source as Theatre Now?" See: Ybarra, "A Message from TAPS Chair."

7. There is also a passing reference to a "dark-haired girl" in the book, which some scholars have taken to suggest a young woman of color or mixed race.

8. Crane, *Red Badge of Courage*, 1.

9. See Mitchell, "Reading 'Race' and 'Gender' in Crane's *The Red Badge of Courage*"; Ellison, *Going to the Territory*; and Kaplan, "The Spectacle of War in Crane's Revision of History."

10. Schneider, *Performing Remains*, 55. Emphasis in original.

11. Crane, *Red Badge of Courage*, 55.

12. Personal interview, Kaneza Schaal. New York City. 23 April 2015. See appendix 1.

13. Ibid., her emphasis.

14. Long, "We're Not Ready for Huck Finn," 5.

15. The role of Jim/Douglass was played by John Stewart, who was "one of only four college actors in the nation recognized at the Kennedy Center for his 'Outstanding Performance in a Play'"—"CET Highlights: Theater Performance 'Splittin' the Raft.'" Kennesaw State University. Web document. Accessed 20 Jan. 2016.

16. Coates, "Between the World and Me: Letter to My Son."

17. Long, "We're Not Ready for Huck Finn," 5.

18. There are over two hundred utterances of the N-word in Twain's *Huck Finn*.

19. Long, "We're Not Ready for Huck Finn," 2.

20. Harvey, "Declarations of Identity," 2. The two actors Harvey mentions are Annie Power (Huck) and Shannon Sparks (ensemble).

21. "In Rehearsal with *Everything That Rises Must Converge.*"

22. O'Connor, like Twain, did not mince words in her depiction of racism: the N-word is prevalent throughout "Everything That Rises Must Converge."

23. Jimmy Bickerstaff, American College Theatre Festival Respondent Report for *Everything That Rises Must Converge*, Kennesaw State University. 2009.

24. In 2016, there were multiple instances of whitewashing casts that called for Latinx actors—including productions of *Evita* and *In the Heights* in Chicago and *West Side Story* in Atlanta, to name a few. See: Tran, "Whitewash 'In the Heights'? Chicago, You Can Do Better," which discusses all three of these controversial productions. (Latinx is a gender-neutral term for Latinos.)

25. Black Lives Matter, a movement to protest the physical and psychic violence against African Americans in the United States, was created in 2013 by Alicia Garza, Opal Tometi, and Patrisse Cullors. See blacklivesmatter.com/herstory.

26. For more on digital dramaturgy possibilities, see LaRonika Thomas, "Digital Dramaturgy and Digital Dramaturgs." A key omission in Thomas's essay is the importance of *private* wikis, as these can be used during the process of rehearsal and never shared with the public unless so desired.

27. Notably, for the Auburn University production one of the veterans who visited with the cast was a woman, but she did not take part in battle directly. She worked for the morgue, and shared those experiences with us.

28. Personal interview with James Maloof.

29. Ibid.

30. Cleage, "The Nigger Speech."

31. Long, "We're Not Ready for Huck Finn," 5.

32. These include sites for *Redwing*, *Dark Forest*, *Red Hanrahan*, and *Moby-Dick*, for example. Unfortunately, these sites are no longer accessible, even though they continue to be listed as part of the production history of TPS at KSU.

33. The scenic designer for *Red Hanrahan* was Ming Chen.

34. See Londré, *Words at Play*.

35. For more about the decorum expected between directors and dramaturgs, see Chemers, *Ghost Light*, especially 150–53.

36. Postshow discussions, or talkbacks, require skillful facilitation. For tips on how to manage them, see Chemers, *Ghost Light*, 169–73. For guidance on new play talkbacks, see Irelan, Fletcher, and Dubiner, *The Process of Dramaturgy*, 88–91.

37. See Martine Kei Green-Rogers, "Talkbacks for 'Sensitive Subject Matter' Productions: The Theory and Practice."

9. Postmortem Adapturgy

1. Arguably this is also true for premieres or other productions of new plays: in those cases, it would be wise (if feasible) to have the playwright/s in the room as well.

2. Edwards, "Staging Paradox," 233.

3. Hutcheon, *A Theory of Adaptation*, 8–9.

4. Féral, "Theatricality," 105.

5. Edwards, "Staging Paradox," 233.

6. It is also possible that the cross-gender casting dissuaded veteran attendance.

7. Digests like *The Week* are useful, especially for dramaturgs without database or electronic-journal access.

8. See Hutcheon, *A Theory of Adaptation* and Sanders, *Adaptation and Appropriation.*

9. There was original music composed for *Red Badge of Courage* (by Damon Young) and *Red Hanrahan* (by Henry Scott), for example. In *Red Hanrahan* this music was also performed live; for *Red Badge* it was prerecorded.

10. Murray, *The Adaptation Industry*, 157—the last word of her sentence is "cinemas," since Murray focuses almost exclusively on the book-film relationship in this study.

11. The fidelity expectation can arise for production and new play dramaturgs as well as those working with adaptation.

12. It is equally or even more vital elsewhere, perhaps, but this particular study has concentrated on US theatre making specifically.

13. "Livestreaming the 30th Annual Literary Managers and Dramaturgs of the Americas Conference."

14. Dawkins, *The Selfish Gene*, 193. Quoted in Hutcheon, *A Theory of Adaptation*, 176.

15. Romanska, *Routledge Companion to Dramaturgy*, 14.

BIBLIOGRAPHY

Abbott, H. Porter. *The Cambridge Introduction to Narrative.* Cambridge: Cambridge University Press, 2002.

Alexander, Michael. *The Poetic Achievement of Ezra Pound.* London: Faber, 1979.

Albrecht-Crane, Christa, and Dennis Cutchins. *Adaptation Studies: New Approaches.* Madison, NJ: Fairleigh Dickinson University Press, 2010.

Aronson, Arnold. "Their Exits and Their Entrances: Getting a Handle on Doors." *New Theatre Quarterly* 20, no. 4 (2004): 331–40.

Augé, Mark. *Non-Places: Introduction to an Anthropology of Supermodernity.* Translated by J. Howe. London: Verso, 1995.

Bachelard, Gaston. *The Poetics of Space.* Translated by Maria Jolas. Boston: Beacon, 1994. First published 1958 by Presses Universitaires de France.

Bacon, Wallace A. *The Art of Interpretation.* 3rd ed. New York: Holt, 1979.

———. "The Dangerous Shores—One Last Time." *Text and Performance Quarterly* 16 (1996): 356–58.

Bailes, Sara Jane. *Performance Theatre and the Poetics of Failure: Forced Entertainment, Goat Island, Elevator Repair Service.* London: Routledge, 2011.

Barnette, Jane. "Staging the Numinous," *Text and Performance Quarterly* 29, no. 4 (2009): 415–17.

Bateman, John A. *Multimodality and Genre: A Foundation for the Systematic Analysis of Multimodal Documents.* Houndmills, England: Palgrave, 2008.

Bell, Elizabeth. "Performance Studies as Women's Work: Historical Sights/Sites/Citations from the Margin." *Text and Performance Quarterly* 13 (1993): 350–74.

Bentley, Eric. *The Life of the Drama.* New York: Applause, 1964.

Bial, Henry. "Performance Studies 3.0." *The Performance Studies Reader.* 3rd ed. Edited by Henry Bial and Sara Brady, 402–12. London: Routledge, 2016.

———. *Playing God: The Bible on the Broadway Stage.* Ann Arbor: University of Michigan Press, 2015.

Bickerstaff, Jimmy. American College Theatre Festival Respondent Report for *Everything That Rises Must Converge,* Kennesaw State University, 2009.

Binder, Henry. "The 'Red Badge of Courage' Nobody Knows." *Studies in the Novel* 10, no. 1 (1978): 9–47.

Blickers, Beth, and Brian Quirt. "Ecologies of Dramaturgy." *Theatre Topics* 24, no. 3 (2014): 249–53.

Bloom, Harold, ed. *William Faulkner's* The Sound and the Fury. New York: Chelsea House, 1988.

Bluestone, George. *Novels into Film.* Baltimore: Johns Hopkins Press, 1957.

Boardman, John, ed. *The Oxford History of Classical Art.* Oxford: Oxford University Press, 1993.

Bolter, Jay David, and Richard Grusin. *Remediation: Understanding New Media.* Cambridge: MIT Press, 1999.

Bordwell, David. "*Birdman*: Following Riggan's orders." *Observations on Film Art* (blog). http://www.davidbordwell.net/blog/2015/02/23/birdman-following-riggans-orders/.

Bourdieu, Pierre. *The Field of Cultural Production: Essays on Art and Literature.* Edited by Randal Johnson. New York: Columbia University Press, 1993.

Bowman, Michael S. "'Novelizing' the Stage: Chamber Theatre after Breen and Bakhtin." *Text and Performance Quarterly* 15 (1995): 1–23.

Breen, Robert S. *Chamber Theatre.* Evanston, IL: Wm. Caxton, 1986.

Brook, Peter. *The Empty Space.* New York: Atheneum, 1968.

Brown, Lenora Inez. "You can't tell a dramaturg by her title." *American Theatre* 18, no. 1 (2001): 22–28, 95–102.

Burger, Alicia. The Wizard of Oz *as American Myth: A Critical Study of Six Versions of the Story, 1900–2007.* Jefferson, NC: McFarland, 2007.

Bush, Catherine. *The Red Badge of Courage, adapted from the novel by Stephen Crane.* Abingdon, VA: Barter Players, 2011.

Butler, Robert. "Richard Wright's 'Between the World and Me' and the Chapel Scene in Crane's *The Red Badge of Courage:* A Literary Relationship." *CLA Journal* 53, no. 4 (2010): 373–86.

Carlson, Marvin. *The Haunted Stage: The Theatre as Memory Machine.* Ann Arbor: University of Michigan Press, 2001.

———. *Places of Performance: The Semiotics of Theatre Architecture.* Ithaca, NY: Cornell University Press, 1989.

Carroll, Rachel, ed. *Adaptation in Contemporary Culture: Textual Infidelities.* London: Continuum, 2009.

Carver, Raymond. *What We Talk about When We Talk about Love.* New York: Vintage, 1989. First published in 1974 by Raymond Carver.

Catlin, David. "Curiouser and Curiouser: Reflections from Twenty Years in the Lookingglass (Theatre), or ~~Stealing~~ Borrowing from the Best." *Triquarterly* 134 (2009): 94–122.

Chaudhuri, Una. *Staging Place: The Geography of Modern Drama.* Ann Arbor: University of Michigan Press, 1997.

Chemers, Michael Mark. *Ghost Light: An Introductory Handbook for Dramaturgy.* Carbondale: Southern Illinois University Press, 2010.

Chemers, Michael, and Adam Versényi, "Kinesis as Mimesis: On the Application of Martial Arts to Dramaturgical Practice." *Theatre Topics* 24, no. 3 (2014): 199–204.

Chicago Humanities Festival. "Blair Thomas: Melville's Moby Dick and Puppetry." YouTube video, 12 November 2013. https://youtu.be/xIMLEgl4urc.

Clark, Miriam Marty. "Raymond Carver's Monologic Imagination." *MFS Modern Fiction Studies* 37, no. 2 (1991): 240–47.

Cleage, Pearl. "The Nigger Speech." Keynote Address at SETC 62nd Annual Convention, 3 March 2011. *Southern Theatre* 52, no. 3 (2011): 9–16.

Coates, Ta-Nehisi. "Between the World and Me: Letter to My Son." *The Atlantic.* 4 July 2015.

"Colombari Mini Documentary." Accessed 29 December 2016. http://www.colombari.org/blank-c1ldw.

"A Conversation with Frank Galati." *Stay Thirsty Magazine.* Accessed 30 January 2016. http://www.staythirstymedia.com/201404-084/html/201404-thirsty-galati.html.

Crane, Stephen. *The Red Badge of Courage and Four Stories.* 1960. Edited by R. W. Stallman. New York: Signet Classics, 2011.

Dawkins, Richard. *The Selfish Gene.* 2nd ed. Oxford: Oxford University Press, 1989.

de Certeau, Michel. *The Practice of Everyday Life.* Translated by S. Rendall. Berkeley: University of California Press, 1984.

Deshaye, Joel. "A Brief Analysis of *The Sound and the Fury*'s Namesake." *The Sound and the Fury*: A Hypertext Edition. Edited by Stoicheff, Muri, Deshaye, et al. Updated Feb. 2011. University of Saskatchewan. Accessed 5 June 2017. http://www.usask.ca/english/faulkner.

Dieckmann, Lara E. "Toward a Feminist Chamber Theatre Method." *Text and Performance Quarterly* 19 (1999): 39–56.

Dillon, Janette. *Theatre, Court and City, 1595–1610: Drama and Social Space in London.* Cambridge: Cambridge University Press, 2000.

Domonoske, Camila. "#WhereIsRey? She's on Her Way, Says Hasbro." *The Two-Way: NPR.* 6 January 2016. Accessed 30 January 2016. http://www.npr.org/sections/thetwo-way/2016/01/06/462144156/-whereisrey-shes-on-her-way-says-hasbro.

Duncan, Nancy, ed. *Bodyspace: Destabilizing Geographies of Gender and Sexuality.* London: Routledge, 1996.

Edinger, Edward. *Melville's Moby-Dick: An American Nekyia.* Toronto: Inner City, 1995.

Edwards, Paul. "Adaptation: Two Theories." *Text and Performance Quarterly* 27, no. 4 (2007): 369–77.

———. "Staging Paradox: The Local Art of Adaptation." *Sage Handbook of Performance Studies.* Edited by D. Soyini Madison and Judith Hamera, 227–53. Thousand Oaks, CA: Sage, 2006.

Eliade, Mircea. *The Sacred and the Profane: The Nature of Religion.* Translated by Willard R. Trask. Orlando: Harcourt, 1987. First published 1957 by Rowohlt Taschenbuch Verlag GmbH.

Elleström, Lars, ed. *Media Borders, Multimodality and Intermediality.* Houndmills, England: Palgrave, 2010.

Elliott, Kamilla. *Rethinking the Novel/Film Debate.* Cambridge: Cambridge University Press, 2003.

Ellison, Ralph. *Going to the Territory.* New York: Vintage, 1987.

Ermath, Elizabeth Deeds. "Agency in the Discursive Condition." *History and Theory* 40, no. 4 (2001): 34–58.

Estill, Laura, ed. *World Shakespeare Bibliography.* Johns Hopkins University Press /Folger Shakespeare Library. www.worldshakesbib.org/.

Evans, Suzy. "The Unsung Gender-Parity Warriors." *American Theatre.* 21 Sept. 2015.

Eyring, Teresa. "Standing up for Playwrights and against 'Colorblind' Casting," *American Theatre* 7 Jan. 2016: 10.

Faulkner, William. *The Sound and the Fury.* 1929. 2nd ed. Edited by David Minter. Norton Critical Edition. New York: Norton, 1994.

Féral, Josette. "Theatricality: The Specificity of Theatrical Language." Translated by Ronald P. Bermingham. *SubStance* 31, nos. 2 and 3 (2002): 94–108. doi: 10.1353/sub.2002.0026.

Festus, Sextus Pompeius, 2nd century. *De verborum significatu.* Translated by W. M. Lindsay. Leipzig, Germany: B. G. Teubneri, 1913.

Freud, Sigmund. "The Uncanny." *Collected Papers.* Vol 4. Translated by Alix Stratchey. New York: Basic, 1959.

Frus, Phyllis, and Christy Williams, eds. *Beyond Adaptation: Essays on Radical Transformations of Original Works.* Jefferson, NC: McFarland, 2010.

Fuchs, Elinor, and Una Chaudhuri, eds. *Land/Scape/Theater.* Ann Arbor: University of Michigan Press, 2000.

Fusco, Coco. "Elevator Repair Service." *Bomb* 67 (Artists in Conversation issue) Spring 1999. http://bombmagazine.org/article/2231/elevator-repair-service.

Galati, Frank. "Adapting *Kafka on the Shore.*" *TriQuarterly* 134 (2009): 29–52.

———. *John Steinbeck's The Grapes of Wrath.* New York: Dramatists, 1991.

"Gatz." *Elevator Repair Service:* Shows. Accessed 5 January 2016. https://www.elevator.org/shows/gatz/.

Genette, Gérard. *Palimpsests: Literature in the Second Degree.* Translated by Channa Newman and Claude Doubinsky. Lincoln: University of Nebraska Press, 1997.

Gentile, John. Moby-Dick, *by Herman Melville: Adapted for the Stage by John Gentile.* SAIAH Version, March 2013.

———. "The Pilgrim Soul: Herman Melville's *Moby-Dick* as Pilgrimage." *Text and Performance Quarterly* 29, no. 4 (2009): 403–14.

Graves, Robert. *The White Goddess: A Historical Grammar of Poetic Myth.* Edited by Grevel Lindop. Manchester: Carcanet, 1997.

Green-Rogers, Martine Kei. "Talkbacks for 'Sensitive Subject Matter' Productions: The Theory and Practice." In *The Routledge Companion to Dramaturgy,* edited by Magda Romanska, 490–94. London: Routledge, 2015.

Green, Steven J. *Ovid, Fasti 1: A Commentary.* Leiden: Brill, 2004.

Grossman, Lev. "How Harry Potter Became the Boy Who Lived Forever." *Time Magazine Online.* 7 July 2011.

Handler, Daniel. "Hey, Watch Who You're Calling Wicked." *NYTimes.com.* 29 June 2003.

Harvey, Melissa. "Declarations of Identity." Program Notes for *Splittin' the Raft,* Kennesaw State University, Department of Theatre and Performance Studies.

Haverty, Michael, and Jane Barnette, adapters. *Red Badge of Courage.* Atlanta: 7 Stages, 2014.

Herrera, Brian. "The Best Actor for the Role, or the Mythos of Casting in American Popular Performance." *The Journal of American Drama and Theatre* 27, no. 2 (April 2015) http://jadtjournal.org/2015/04/24/the-best-actor-for-the-role-or-the-mythos-of-casting-in-american-popular-performance/.

———. "There Is Power in Casting." *Youth Theatre Journal* 29, no. 2 (October 2015): 146–51.

Holland, Louise Adams. *Janus and the Bridge,* Rome: American Academy, 1961.

Hopkins, D. J. "A Note from the Editor." *Theatre Topics* 24, no. 3 (2014): ix–x.

Hopkins, D. J., et al., eds. *Performance and the City.* London: Palgrave, 2009.

The House Theatre of Chicago. "Season on the Line." Updated 2014. Accessed 5 June 2017. http://www.thehousetheatre.com/playsandevents/seasonline/.

Hutcheon, Linda, with Siobhan O'Flynn. *A Theory of Adaptation.* 2nd ed. London: Routledge, 2006.

Hutchins, Zachary. "*Moby-Dick* as Third Testament: A Novel 'Not Come to Destroy but to Fulfill' the Bible." *Leviathan* 13, no. 2 (2011): 18–37.

Iñárritu, Alejandro G. *Birdman: All Access—A View from the Wings* (DVD Extra). Fox Searchlight, 2014.

Iñárritu, Alejandro G., and others. *Birdman or (The Unexpected Virtue of Ignorance),* screenplay. Century City, CA: Fox Searchlight Pictures, 2014.

Ingersoll, Karena Fiorenza, and Deena Selenow. "You Want a Diverse Theatre? Prove It." *HowlRound.* 18 Aug. 2015. http://howlround.com/you-want-a-diverse-theatre-prove-it.

Inglis, David, and John Hughson, eds. *The Sociology of Art: Ways of Seeing.* London: Palgrave, 2005.

"In Rehearsal with *Everything That Rises Must Converge.*" StageBuddyTV, YouTube video, 3:05, posted by "StageBuddyTV," 14 Apr. 2014, https://youtu.be/SvG16JMSbUY.

Irelan, Scott R., Anne Fletcher, and Julie Felise Dubiner. *The Process of Dramaturgy: A Handbook.* Newburyport, MA: Focus, 2010.

Jakobson, Roman. "On Linguistic Aspects of Translation." In *The Translation Studies Reader*, edited by Lawrence Venuti, 138–43. 2nd ed. London: Routledge, 2004.

Johnston, David. "Theatre Pragmatics." In *Stages of Translation: Translators on Translating for the Stage,* edited by David Johnston, 57–66. Bath, England: Absolute Classics, 1996.

Justman, Phillip. "Phillip Justman's Venture into the Whale." Interview with Bang! Arts. 18 April 2013. http://www.bangarts.com/questions-and-answers/phillip-justmans-venture-into-the-whale.

Kaplan, Amy. "The Spectacle of War in Crane's Revision of History." In *New Essays on* The Red Badge of Courage, edited by Lee Clark Mitchell, 77–108. Cambridge: Cambridge University Press, 1996.

Kaster, Robert A., ed. *Macrobius Saturnalia*. Translated by R. A. Kaster. Cambridge: Harvard University Press, 2011.

Kaufman, Charlie, and Donald Kaufman. *Adaptation: The Shooting Script*. New York: Newmarket, 2012. Film produced 2002 by Columbia Pictures Industries.

Khalid, Marium. "SAÏAH Takes on the Whale." Interview. *Busking at the Seams*. Accessed 30 January 2016. https://buskingseams.com/2013/04/08/saiah-takes-on-the-whale/.

The Kilroys. Accessed 29 December 2016. http://thekilroys.org/about/.

Kissell, Rick. "'The Wiz Live' Ratings Strong: NBC Musical Draws 11.5 Million Viewers." *Variety,* 4 December 2015. http://variety.com/2015/tv/news/the-wiz-live-ratings-nbc-musical-1201653402/.

Knight, Vin. Personal interview. New York City. 22 April 2015.

Koszyn, Jayme. "The Dramaturg and the Irrational." In *Dramaturgy in American Theater,* edited by Susan Jonas et al., 83–87. New York: Wadsworth, 1996.

Krebs, Katja. "Ghosts We Have Seen Before: Trends in Adaptation in Contemporary Performance." *Theatre Journal* 66, no. 4 (December 2014): 581–90.

———, ed. *Translation and Adaptation in Theatre and Film*. London: Routledge, 2014.

Laera, Margherita, ed. *Theatre and Adaptation: Return, Rewrite, Repeat*. London: Bloomsbury, 2014.

Lakoff, George, and Mark Johnson. *Philosophy in the Flesh: The Embodied Mind and Its Challenge to Western Thought*. New York: Basic, 1999.

Lavender, Andy. "Modal Transpositions toward Theatres of Encounter, or, in Praise of 'Media Intermultimodality.'" *Theatre Journal* 66 (2014): 499–518.

Leahey, Kristin, and Ilana Bruton. "The Goal of the Emancipated Spectator: A Dramaturg and a Museum Educator's Facilitation of a Theatre and Museum Collaboration." *Theatre Topics* 24, no. 3 (2014): 205–9.

Lefebvre, Henri. *The Production of Space*. Translated by Donald Nicholson-Smith. Oxford: Blackwell Publishers, 1991.

Lehmann, Hans-Thies. *Postdramatic Theatre*. Translated by Karen Jürs-Munby. London: Routledge, 2006.

Leitch, Thomas. *Film Adaptations and Its Discontents: From* Gone with the Wind *to* The Passion of the Christ. Baltimore: Johns Hopkins University Press, 2007.

———. "Twelve Fallacies in Contemporary Adaptation Theory." *Criticism* 45, no. 2 (2003): 149–71.

Lessing, Gotthold Ephraim. *Hamburg Dramaturgy: A New and Complete Translation.* Translated by Wendy Arons and Sara Figal. Edited by Natalya Baldyga. Media Commons Press (2012). http://mcpress.media-commons.org/hamburg/.

Levin, Laura. *Performing Ground: Space, Camouflage, and the Art of Blending In.* London: Palgrave, 2014.

"Livestreaming the 30th Annual Literary Managers and Dramaturgs of the Americas Conference." *HowlRound.* New York City. http://howlround.com/livestreaming-the-30th-annual-literary-managers-dramaturgs-of-the-americas-conference-new-york-city.

LMDA website, "About Us." Accessed 12 July 2015. http://www.lmda.org/about.

Londré, Felicia Hardison. *Words at Play: Creative Writing and Dramaturgy.* Carbondale: Southern Illinois University Press, 2005.

Long, Harrison. "We're Not Ready for Huck Finn: An Important Story Struggles to Be Told." *Faculty Publications.* Paper 3353 (2014). http://digitalcommons.kennesaw.edu/facpubs/3353.

Luckhurst, Mary. *Dramaturgy: A Revolution in Theatre.* Cambridge: Cambridge University Press, 2006.

Magelssen, Scott. *Simming: Participatory Performance and the Making of Meaning.* Ann Arbor: University of Michigan Press: 2014.

Maloof, James. Personal interview. Kennesaw, GA. 25 March 2009.

"Mapping Yoknapatawpha." University of Virginia. Accessed 29 December 2016. http://people.virginia.edu/~sfr/FAULKNER/09mapsf.html.

McAuley, Gay. *Space in Performance: Making Meaning in the Theatre.* Ann Arbor: University of Michigan Press, 1999.

McConachie, Bruce. *Evolution, Cognition, and Performance.* Cambridge: Cambridge University Press, 2015.

McCrum, Robert. "The 100 Best Novels: No. 17—*Moby-Dick* by Herman Melville." *The Guardian.* 13 January 2014. Accessed 29 January 2016. http://www.theguardian.com/books/2014/jan/13/100-best-novels-observer-moby-dick.

Melville, Herman. *Moby-Dick, or The White Whale.* New York: New American, 1961.

Merrifield, Andrew. "Place and Space: A Lefebvrian Reconciliation." *Transactions of the Institute of British Geographers* 18, no. 4 (1993): 516–31.

Miller, Gregory, and Richard Talaske. "The Isolation of Lookingglass Theatre, or How An Active Water Pumping Station in Chicago Became the Site for an Award-Winning Successful Playhouse." *166th Acoustical Society of America Meeting.* http://acoustics.org/pressroom/httpdocs/166th/3aAAa3-Miller.html.

Miller, Kathryn Schultz. *The Red Badge of Courage: A Play Based on the Novel by Stephen Crane.* Woodstock, IL: Family Plays, 1990.

Mitchell, Lee Clark, ed. *New Essays on* The Red Badge of Courage. Cambridge: Cambridge University Press, 1986.

Mitchell, Verner D. "Reading 'Race' and 'Gender' in Crane's *The Red Badge of Courage*," *CLA Journal* 40, no. 1 (1996): 60–71.

Morris, Wesley. "In 'The Wiz Live!' on NBC, a Search for More in the Emerald City," *New York Times*, 4 December 2015. Accessed 30 January 2016. http://nyti.ms/1NvaHA1.

Murphy, Vincent. *Page to Stage: The Craft of Adaptation*. Ann Arbor: University of Michigan Press, 2013.

Murray, Simone. *The Adaptation Industry: The Cultural Economy of Contemporary Literary Adaptation*. London: Routledge, 2012.

Nagle, Betty Rose. *Ovid's Fasti: Roman Holidays*. Translated by B. R. Nagle. Bloomington: Indiana University Press, 1995.

Neill, Rosemary. "Theatre Directors Are Hooked on Classics as the Adaptation Takes Over." *Australian*. 25 May 2013. Accessed 3 June 2017. http://www.theaustralian.com.au/arts/review/hooked-on-classicsnews-story/3ce0411ae01ebe6c6faa32f721eb04aa.

Newell, Kate. "'We're Off to See the Wizard' (Again): *Oz* Adaptations and the Matter of Fidelity." In *Adaptation Studies: New Approaches*, edited by Christa Albrecht-Crane and Dennis Cutchins. Madison, NJ: Fairleigh Dickinson University Press, 2010.

Newlands, Carole E. *Playing with Time: Ovid and the Fasti*, Ithaca, NY: Cornell University Press, 1995.

New Play Exchange. Accessed 29 December 2016. http://newplayexchange.org.

Orr, Shelley. "Critical Proximity: A Case for Using the First Person as a Production Dramaturg." *Theatre Topics* 24, no. 3 (2014): 239–45.

Otto, Rudolf. *The Idea of the Holy*. Translated by John W. Harvey. Oxford: Oxford University Press, 1968.

Padgett, John B. "William Faulkner Trivia." *William Faulkner on the Web*. University of Mississippi. Modified 9 October 2000. Accessed 5 January 2016. http://www.mcsr.olemiss.edu/%7Eegjbp/faulkner/trivia.html#w13.

Paulson, Michael. "A Black Actor in Virginia Woolf? Not Happening, Albee Estate Says." *New York Times*. 21 May 2017. Accessed 21 May 2017. https://nyti.ms/2rH3R4v/.

Pavis, Patrice. *Dictionary of the Theatre: Terms, Concepts, and Analysis*. Translated by Christine Shantz. Toronto: University of Toronto Press, 1998.

Persley, Nicole Hodges. "Hip-hop Theater and Performance." In *The Cambridge Companion to Hip-Hop*, edited by Justin A. Williams, 85–98. Cambridge: Cambridge University Press, 2015.

Petralia, Peter S. "Reshaping Spatiality: Cognitive Perception and the Fracturing of Theatrical Space." Thesis. Lancaster University. September 2010.

Phelan, Peggy. *Unmarked: The Politics of Performance*. London: Routledge, 1993.

"Play on! Further Reading." *Oregon Shakespeare Festival.* Accessed 30 January 2016. https://www.osfashland.org/en/experience-osf/upcoming/play-on/play-on-faq.aspx.

Pollack-Pelzner, Daniel. "Why We (Mostly) Stopped Messing with Shakespeare's Language." *New Yorker.* 6 Oct. 2015.

Posner, Dassia N. "The Dramaturg(ies) of Puppetry and Visual Theatre." In *The Routledge Companion to Dramaturgy,* edited by M. Romanska, 335–41. London: Routledge, 2015.

Proehl, Geoffrey S. "The Images before Us: Metaphors for the Role of the Dramaturg in American Theatre." In *Dramaturgy in American Theater: A Source Book,* edited by Susan Jonas, Geoff Proehl, and Michael Lupu, 124–36. Fort Worth, TX: Harcourt Brace, 1997.

———. *Toward a Dramaturgical Sensibility: Landscape and Journey.* 2008. Madison, NJ: Fairleigh Dickinson University Press, 2012.

Rafalowicz, Mira, et al. "Dramaturgs in America: Eleven Statements." *Theater* 10, no. 1 (1978): 15–30.

Roach, Joseph. *Cities of the Dead: Circum-Atlantic Performance.* New York: Columbia University Press, 1996.

Rogers, Nathanial. "Smash: The Dramaturg." *The Film Experience.* 20 February 2013, accessed 14 July 2016. http://thefilmexperience.net/blog/2013/2/20/smash-the-dramaturg.html.

Romanska, Magda, ed. *The Routledge Companion to Dramaturgy.* London: Routledge, 2015.

Sanders, Julie. *Adaptation and Appropriation.* London: Routledge, 2006.

Schechner, Richard. *Performance Theory.* Revised and Expanded. London: Routledge, 2003. First Published 1977 as *Essays on Performance Theory* by Ralph Pine.

Schmiedl, Eric, adapter. *The Red Badge of Courage.* By Stephen Crane. 2007.

Schneider, Rebecca. *Performing Remains: Art and War in Times of Theatrical Reenactment.* London: Routledge, 2011.

Schupbach, William. "Laocoon and the Expression of Pain." *The Wellcome Trust.* http://www.wellcome.ac.uk/en/pain/microsite/culture3.html.

Seeger, Mike. *Talking Feet: Buck, Flatfoot and Tap—Solo Southern Dance of the Appalachian, Piedmont and Blue Ridge Mountain Regions.* Berkeley: North Atlantic, 1992.

Sevush, Ralph. "The Guild and Dramaturgy." *The Dramatist,* September–October 2014, 70–72.

Sherman, Howard. "When a White Actor Goes to 'The Mountaintop.'" *Howard Sherman.* 29 Oct. 2015. http://www.hesherman.com/.

Siegel, Robert, host. "NBC Raises Its Musical Game with 'The Wiz Live.'" *Monkey See, NPR,* 4 December 2015. Transcript.

Simon, Jane. "Critical Proximity." *Cultural Studies Review* 16, no. 2 (2010): 4–23.

Slotkin, Richard. *Regeneration through Violence: The Mythology of the American Frontier, 1600–1860.* Middletown, CT: Wesleyan University Press, 1973.

Smith, R. R. R. *Hellenistic Sculpture: A Handbook*. London: Thames and Hudson, 1991.

"The Sound and the Fury." *Elevator Repair Service:* Shows. Accessed 5 January 2016. https://www.elevator.org/shows/the-sound-and-the-fury/.

Stam, Robert, and Alessandra Raengo, eds. *Literature and Film: A Guide to the Theory and Practice of Adaptation*. Malden, MA: Blackwell, 2005.

Stoicheff, Muri, Deshaye, et al., eds. *The Sound and the Fury:* A Hypertext Edition. Updated February 2011. University of Saskatchewan. Accessed 5 June 2017. http://drc.usask.ca/projects/faulkner/.

Sullivan, Garrett A., Jr. *The Drama of Landscape: Land, Property, and Social Relations on the Early Modern Stage*. Stanford: Stanford University Press, 1998.

Sutton, Joe, adapter. *The Red Badge of Courage*, by Stephen Crane. Seattle: Seattle Children's Theatre, 2005.

Swartz, Mark Evan. *Oz before the Rainbow: L. Frank Baum's* The Wonderful Wizard of Oz *on Stage and Screen to 1939*. Baltimore: Johns Hopkins University Press, 2000.

Taylor, Jane, ed. *Handspring Puppet Company*. New York: Krut, 2009.

Taylor, Rabun. "Watching the Skies: Janus, Auspication, and the Shrine in the Roman Forum." *Memoirs of the American Academy in Rome* 45 (2000): 1–40.

Thomas, Blair. "About the Artist." In the program for *Moby Dick, or the Brotherhood of the Monastic Order of Ancient Mariners Purges the Ills of Society through a Reading of the Tales of Moby-Dick*. Blair Thomas and Company. MCA Stage. 1 April 2016.

———. "In Defense of the Puppet Stage." In *Stages of Enchantment: The Puppet Theatres of Blair Thomas and Company*. Mansfield, CT: Ballard Institute and Museum of Puppetry, 2015.

Thomas, Blair, and Company. *Moby Dick*, YouTube video, 5:02, posted by Museum of Contemporary Art Chicago. 16 March 2016. https://youtu.be/bg9LHor0vGA.

Thomas, LaRonika. "Digital Dramaturgy and Digital Dramaturgs." In *The Routledge Companion to Dramaturgy*, edited by Magda Romanska, 506–11. London: Routledge, 2015.

Tompkins, Joanne. "Space and the Geographies of Theatre: Introduction." *Modern Drama* 46, no. 4 (2003): 537–41.

———. *Unsettling Space: Contestations in Contemporary Australian Theatre*. London: Palgrave, 2006.

Tran, Diep. "When a Writer's Rights Aren't Right: The 'Virginia Woolf' Casting Fight." *American Theatre*. 22 May 2017. http://www.americantheatre.org/2017/05/22/when-a-writers-rights-arent-right-the-virginia-woolf-casting-fight/.

———. "Whitewash 'In the Heights'? Chicago, You Can Do Better." *American Theatre*. 27 July 2016. http://www.americantheatre.org/2016/07/27/whitewash-in-the-heights-chicago-you-can-do-better.

Trencsényi, Katalin. *Dramaturgy in the Making: A User's Guide for Theatre Practitioners*. London: Bloomsbury, 2015.

Trencsényi, Katalin, and Bernadette Cochrane, eds. *New Dramaturgy: International Perspectives on Theory and Practice.* London: Bloomsbury, 2014.

Tuan, Yi-Fu. *Space and Place: The Perspective of Experience.* Minneapolis: University of Minnesota Press, 1977.

Turner, Cathy, and Synne K. Behrndt. *Dramaturgy and Performance.* London: Palgrave, 2008.

Turner, Victor. "Liminality and Communitas." In *The Performance Studies Reader,* 3rd ed., edited by Henry Bial and Sara Brady, 97–104. London: Routledge, 2016.

Ubersfeld, Anne. "The Pleasure of the Spectator." Translated by Pierre Bouillaguet and Charles Jose. *Modern Drama* 25, no. 1 (1982): 127–39.

van Kerkhoven, Marianne. "Looking without Pencil in Hand." *Theaterschrift* 5–6 (1994): 140–49.

Venuti, Lawrence. *The Translator's Invisibility: A History of Translation.* London: Routledge, 1995.

Wellbery, David E. *Lessing's Laocoon: Semiotics and Aesthetics in the Age of Reason.* Cambridge: Cambridge University Press, 1984.

Wightman, Catriona. "'Smash': 'The Dramaturg' recap." *DigitalSpy,* 20 February 2013. Accessed 14 July 2016. http://www.digitalspy.com/tv/smash/review/a460179/smash-the-dramaturg-recap/.

Wolf, Stacy. *A Problem like Maria: Gender and Sexuality in the American Musical.* Ann Arbor: University of Michigan Press, 2002.

Wood, Adam. "'Crimson Blotches on the Pages of the Past': Histories of Violence in Stephen Crane's *The Red Badge of Courage.*" *War, Literature and the Arts* 21 (2009): 38–57.

Wood, Bethany. "Gentlemen Prefer Adaptations. Addressing Industry and Gender in Adaptation Studies." *Theatre Journal* 66 (2014): 559–80.

Ybarra, Patricia. "A Message from TAPS Chair, Dr. Patricia Ybarra." Theatre Arts and Performance Studies, Brown University. 3 December 2015. https://www.brown.edu/academics/theatre-arts-performance-studies/news/2015-12/message-taps-chair-dr-patricia-ybarra.

Young, Jacob. *Dancing Outlaw.* DVD. MovieFish, 2005.

Zeder, Suzan, with Jim Hancock. *Spaces of Creation: The Creative Process of Playwriting.* Portsmouth, NH: Heinemann, 2005.

Zielinski, Sarah. "The Secrets of Sherlock's Mind Palace." 3 February 2014. *Smithsonian.com.*

INDEX

Page numbers in italics indicate illustrations.

Jane Barnette is an assistant professor of theatre at the University of Kansas, where she teaches dramaturgy, adaptation for the stage, theatre history and theory, and script analysis. Her articles and reviews have appeared in *Theatre Topics*, the *Journal of Adaptation in Film and Performance*, and *Theatre Symposium*. She is a freelance dramaturg specializing in adapturgy.

Theater in the Americas

The goal of the series is to publish a wide range of scholarship on theater and performance, defining theater in its broadest terms and including subjects that encompass all of the Americas.

The series focuses on the performance and production of theater and theater artists and practitioners but welcomes studies of dramatic literature as well. Meant to be inclusive, the series invites studies of traditional, experimental, and ethnic forms of theater; celebrations, festivals, and rituals that perform culture; and acts of civil disobedience that are performative in nature. We publish studies of theater and performance activities of all cultural groups within the Americas, including biographies of individuals, histories of theater companies, studies of cultural traditions, and collections of plays.

Queries and Submissions
Scott Magelssen, Editor
magelss@uw.edu

Founder and Editor, Robert A. Schanke, 2000–2014